Writing the
JOURNEY JOURNAL

Copyright 1998 by Susan Laubach
All rights reserved.

No part of this book may be reproduced in any form or by any electronic means, including information storage and retrieval systems, without permission in writing from the publisher, except by a reviewer, who may quote passages in a review.

Published by Bancroft Press
P.O. Box 65360, Baltimore, MD 21209
(800) 637-7377(for general queries)
(888) 40-READS (for orders)
www.bancroftpress.com

Library of Congress Catalog Card Number
ISBN 1-890862-00-2
Printed in the United States of America

First Edition

1 3 5 7 9 10 8 6 4 2

Distributed to the trade by National Book Network, Lanham, MD

Writing the JOURNEY JOURNAL

Your Travels for Fun, Family & Posterity

Susan Laubach

bancroft press

BALTIMORE, MARYLAND

[CONTENTS]

PART I—WRITING THE JOURNEY JOURNAL

Chapter 1 . . . . *3*
Why write a Journey Journal?
    Personal reasons: Avoiding the innocuous postcard
    See what you are looking at: two-step journey-journaling
    Getting your money's worth: Take your trip over and over
    Building the family archives
    Developing a travel bookshelf: resource for other trips and other travelers
    Adding photos for illustrations: A picture book for the children
    Using the Journey Journal for talks, travelogues, volunteer work
    This isn't for everyone
    How to use this book

Chapter 2 . . . . *17*
Pre-trip preparation
    It starts with a list
    Materials for your Journey Journal
    Group-travel tip: The personal trip-tik
    The guide: "All present and accounted for..."
    Notes, facts, and what happened?
    Notes
    Word-finding exercise
    Facts
    What happened?
    Another model
    Supplies for your Journey Journal

Chapter 3 . . . . *27*

The Trip Segments
    1. Departure transition: Getting from here to there
        Write to relieve anxiety
        Write to relieve boredom
        Get an early start
        Pre-journey ignorance
        Transition-writing exercise
    2. Arrival
    3. Group travel: Meeting fellow travelers
    4. At your destination: What happened? And, what happened next?
        First impressions: how could you tell you were there?
Scenes:
        a. Encounters and interaction
        b. Events
        c. Observations
        d. Sights, sounds, tastes
    5. Return transition: Getting from there—back to here
    6. Reflections: The real souvenirs

PART II—THE JOURNEY JOURNAL

Chapter 4 . . . . *49*
    Two long Journey Journals: Australia/New Zealand and Russia by Riverboat

Chapter 5 . . . . *169*
    Comparing styles: The Best of Eastern Europe as written by neophyte Bob and experienced Susan

Chapter 6 . . . . *221*
    A short Journey Journal: Treasures of Vietnam

Chapter 7 . . . . *251*
    An even shorter (and domestic) Journey Journal:
    A Chautauqua Reunion

Chapter 8 . . . . *259*
    Troubleshooting: Possible problems and likely solutions

Chapter 9 . . . . *261*
    Reflections: What lasts? Did you gain anything but weight?

[PREFACE]

For several years, I taught a writing course for adults at a local college. Most of my students didn't lust after writing careers—in fact, they didn't much care if their works were ever published or not. Their simple goal was to write down important experiences from their lives, or the lives of relatives, primarily for the sake of posterity.

Some didn't think they were up to the task.

"But I don't know where to start," said a woman seated in the front row the first night of class.

"I don't know *how* to start," said the man beside her that semester.

"I don't know how to *stop*," laughed the lady on the other side of the room. "I've written about 600 pages and I'm afraid it's not, well..." she paused and started again. "...I'm afraid it's dull. How do I cut it down?"

"I'm like her. I write too much," a guy in the back called out. "How do I make it more interesting?"

To address these problems, I asked each student to carry a notebook at all times during the semester and to record their observations of encounters, experiences, overheard conversations, anything funny, anything poignant, anything sad that they saw during the week between classes. I asked them to note, as briefly as possible, all the sounds, colors, smells, and/or tastes that would evoke the original experience.

Not everyone was thrilled with this idea. I got a lot of "I keep forgetting my notebook" and "I tried to remember when I got home but I couldn't..." But those who carried paper and pencils and wrote down their observations kept up a steady witness to the exercise's value.

"Writing things down is easy now. I'm getting used to it."

"I'm looking at things more closely now."

"I'm getting better at finding the words to describe things."

"I find I don't forget as much."

When I was asked to give a travel journal workshop at Chautauqua Institution's Writers Center, I'd been teaching writing and doing my own Journey Journals for years. "The people in your new workshop are sophisticated," the director told me. "They travel a lot. Can you show them how to write about their travels so that other people will want to read what they've written?"

I thought back to my former writing students at the local college, and quickly realized that journey-journaling is really just a matter of closely observing the world around you. If a traveler were to take his or her observations from any given day on the road, and expand them in a journal, using thick and accurate description and appealing to as many of the five senses as possible, who could resist such a good read?

The workshop was a success, as were the ones that followed. I offered the same ideas on-board a cruise ship recently and fellow passengers responded enthusiastically to the idea of journey-journaling. I heard the same comments I had heard from my earlier students. "I'm looking at things more closely." "I'm getting better at remembering things."

Well, that's how and why this book was conceived and, finally, born. I hope you'll join us and begin (or continue) to write down your on-the-road observations so that your journeys will live forever in the pages of your Journey Journals. The road might be taking you to the Malacca Strait or the Poconos—to Eastern Europe or Eastern Pennsylvania. But be assured that if you follow this book's guidelines, you and others will find your experiences read-worthy.

In fact, unless you have won the Nobel Prize or some comparable award, you may just see journey-journaling as your best stab at immortality.

Writing the Journey Journal

[PART ONE]

[CHAPTER ONE]

Why write a journey journal?

As I turned the fat book over and over, feeling its heft in my hands and admiring its pink, blue, and green tapestry cover, my son Trevor informed me, "We got it at a craft fair."

"You can send for refills," Laura, his wife, quickly added.

I fanned the gilt-edged pages with my thumb. There were hundreds of them, all empty. I tried to imagine my writing enough to need refills.

It was Christmas 1992, and in three weeks time, I was to embark on a journey fulfilling a long-held dream to live in France. Amended for reality, this meant staying in France longer than the one-week vacations my husband and I had taken in Paris and the Dordogne. It was my foolish belief that an extended visit would give fluency to my halting and fractured French.

My husband Bob didn't share this ambition, but encouraged me to go for it. We decided that January was the best month to be away. Nothing much happens in Baltimore in January and Bob would be too busy at work to miss me much. It was also the best time for temporarily shelving my work as a teacher and writer on investing.

After much poring over travel literature, I finally arranged through a Connecticut organization called "Language Partners International" to live with two families in southern France for three weeks each—one in the village of Tourves near Aix-en-Provence, the other in Montpellier. The idea was to live in the homes of non-English speaking people and learn to converse with them in their language.

In the elegantly-covered book of empty pages, I was to describe the experience of each day. I had warned my parents, my sister, and all five of my children: Don't expect postcards. I hate to buy them. I hate to buy postage for them. Most of all, I hate to write on them. What of importance can be said on a postcard? "Food good. Trip great. Having a wonderful time."

Postcard-speak. Mindless drivel. Speed-writing meant to give the impression of dash—"I'm on my way somewhere wonderful and I'm late. No time for complete sentences."

Actually, it isn't time that's lacking for writing postcards. It's the energy to write the same message over and over. I have just enough energy to put pen to paper once—whether it be to write "having a wonderful time" or something more meaningful.

So the Christmas gift from my son and daughter-in-law was meant to record the whole experience once. Upon return, the plan was to type it up and copy it seven times for family members, so all could share in my high adventure. The challenge was to translate the experience into words that would bring it all to life for my husband, my children, my sister, and my parents. This was the first of my Journey Journals.

Its original intention was the simple avoidance of postcards, and a detailed actual explanation of what "having a wonderful time" entailed. But that first Journey Journal did much more. It linked me daily to the family I missed. It forced me to notice things, to concentrate on everything more deeply, so I could write it all down accurately and with color. After all, I didn't want people to find it dull. I looked for humor, for drama, for *le diference*.

I wrote in Kennedy Airport, waiting to leave, and in Schiphol, Amsterdam's airport, waiting for connections, and in Marseille's airport, waiting for the arrival of my hosts. I wrote early every morning in my cold little room behind the garage. I wrote sitting in cafés and on park benches. The journal was my best friend, my constant companion, my word-camera, recording the sights, the sounds, the stories that bombarded me daily.

I wasn't recording many inner-most thoughts—the personal growth stuff of which most journals are made. This was un-confidential material, meant to be read by others. I wasn't writing a guidebook, either. My Journey Journal wasn't to be a substitute for a Michelin or Let's Go guide, but a recap of *my* journey. This was about the France that *I* was seeing and experiencing while living with strangers for six weeks in the winter of 1992. I wanted to get it so right that the whole thing could be experienced by other people.

Well, it worked. It was so successful that I wouldn't consider going on a trip of any duration without an empty journal and pens. The Journey Journal is the best souvenir a trip can offer—so much better than a shelf full of tchochkes or a closetful of local costumes, if the purpose for souvenir-buying is to remember the experience.

I've journey-journaled around the world and back again. By doing so, I have deepened my pleasure of travel, and that of my husband, my children, my parents, my friends. May it do the same for you.

See what you are looking at

If you have never written much of anything on paper, other than the occasional postcard or office memo, the thought of writing the Journey Journal may be daunting. For that reason, we start in Chapter 2 with the smallest and simplest of efforts. I recommend this two-step journey-journaling method

STEP ONE: *Notes*

Begin your Journey Journal by taking the most minimal of notes. You'll find that there is value in translating the picture you see with your eyes into a couple of words scrawled quickly in a small spiral notebook (which can also be used for recording expenses).

The simple act of taking notes is worthwhile on its own. Just forcing yourself to put on paper a word or two of what's happening will cement the experience in your mind and help you retrieve it more easily later. The difference between worthwhile and worth*less* is in what you choose to note.

On a bouncing bus speeding across Central Asia, I observed a man named Howard sitting across the aisle from Bob and me, jotting notes on a small pad that he occasionally pulled from his shirt pocket.

"What do you do with your notes when you get home?" I asked.

"Nothing," he laughed. "I put them in the guidebook usually and forget about them. But writing things down helps me to remember them better. I know I can always refer to the notes later if I forget something that happened."

But Howard may not find this to be so, should he ever read his notes. He handed me the little notebook and I read his entries. "Konya—123,000 pop. 236000 square meters" and the like. He had recorded the longitude and latitude and major industry for each of the cities we'd visited. And that was all. There was not a word about what he saw, what he experienced. Of the people and their habits and culture, not a jot.

"It helps me remember better," he had said. Remember *what*? Well, Howard was a retired engineer, so his memories of the romantic and mystical Konya as a place of 236,000 square meters and 123,000 people may well suffice for him. But one of the purposes of this book is to find more of life to note—to truly see a place and its people, and to attend your own trip with all your senses. To be there and, through your Journey Journal, to be there again whenever you want.

Here is the first easy rule to follow. If it's in the guidebook, don't write it down. This is your trip, seen through your eyes. This Journey Journal will sit next to the guidebooks on your bookshelf. Anyone can flip through the guidebooks if they want to, finding longitude, latitude, major industry, and points of interest. Your readers will find the human stuff in your Journey Journal: the people stories, the interesting encounters, and the odd ways people do things all over the world.

Here's a daring suggestion: While on your journey, carefully remove the relevant pages of your guidebook with nail scissors. Scotch-tape the guidebook's information to the page opposite your reflections. You may draw the line at desecrating books, but remember, this guidebook is for the current year and will no doubt be revised before you need it again. Also, the remaining pages are on the places you have not visited. So what you would visit on the next trip—what you have not already seen—is still intact. If you agree that the guidebook pages will enhance your Journey Journal and are more useful there than in its original state, remember to include scotch tape on your list of things to pack.

The challenge for a Journey Journaler is to expand observational skills in order to find the heart and humanity in the places one visits. With very little effort, just about anybody can do this. Seeing what you are looking at is one of the most important benefits of writing the Journey Journal.

STEP TWO: *Journal entries*

Write at least ten minutes a day in your Journey Journal. Keep your Journal with your overnight bag, accessible to you quickly, in the room where you spend the night. *When* to write depends on the activities of the day and your ability to concentrate. You will need to commit yourself to a brief period of quiet-time daily.

What to write will be covered in detail throughout this book.

My friend Bruce once told me that he loves to talk with his father when his parents get home from a trip. "Dad's always very insightful and has lots of wonderful stories to tell," he said. "So we have a kind of debriefing session. I ask him questions and he comes up with these terrific anecdotes. I almost feel like I've been on the trip with them."

I'll bet that Bruce's father, aware of his interest, anticipates those "debriefing sessions" and keeps his antennae up throughout the trips for stories and scenes that he will be able to tell his son. He sees what he is looking at, in order to be ready for Bruce's questions. Both the seeing and the questioning give additional value to travel experiences. (*You can arm yourself with Bruce's questions. They are in the section entitled "Pre-trip preparation."*)

Getting your money's worth: Take the trip over and over
Travel is expensive. No matter how many times you substitute baguettes and apples for a sit-down restaurant lunch, no matter how often you spurn four-star lodging in favor of the shared-bathroom variety, it still costs plenty. Always, always, it's over too soon. And, sadly, memories fade before the Visa bill arrives—before the photos are sorted and mounted in albums.

"Great Scott, Ethel. What did we buy in Phuket for this many baht?" you cry, thrusting the bill under your spouse's nose.

"Do you remember this cathedral? Or this marketplace? Or this quaintly ramshackle cottage?" she asks you, holding out a fistful of photos.

Aside from the convenience of being able to refer back to your Journey Journal for answers to all these questions, there is the serendipitous pleasure of reading and re-reading each day's adventure after it's over. This extends the length and life of your travel experience for as long as the paper holds up and the print can be seen. When you can take the trip two, twelve, or twenty times without additional cost, you are getting your money's worth, increasing the value of your travel dollars.

A month after returning from France, the details of an evening visit to a centuries-old former monastery and winery, owned by friends of my hosts, had faded in memory, crowded out by so many other experiences. (Actually, the details faded while they were happening, thanks to multiple dips into barrels of vintage wines by the vintner and me.) But I had written down all that I could recall as soon as we got back to the house in Tourves. And there it was, the evening intact on the pages of my Journey Journal.

I laughed to recall how super-fluent I had become as the tasting went from sips to full glasses—and how astonished Colette and Gerard, my French family hosts, were at the lively conversation in French their previously tongue-tied, mostly silent guest was carrying on with the vintner.

Holding the Journey Journal in my hands, I was no longer sitting on a sofa in a house in Baltimore, but transported back to Provence, France, to a crumbling stone building, a hulk against the moon, into which we stepped carefully with flashlights until the cord for the one swaying electric light bulb could be located and pulled. It was all there, that memorable scene, which I had nearly forgotten because so many other memorable scenes followed it.

If you amortize your trip over all its repetitions through re-reading, the cost goes down to, what? Pennies per day? The Journey Journal is a gift to yourself that keeps on giving.

Family Archives

My grandparents left their native land of Norway and took a boat to the United States, settling in Chicago in the early part of the twentieth century. We don't know what their journey was like or even why they transplanted themselves so far away from home and family. Did they travel steerage or in comfort? What did they take with them from "the old country" to the new? Did they meet people on the journey who became friends? What did they eat? What did they talk about? We'll never know. If only they had written down what was happening in their lives. When energy flags during travel and I'd rather take a nap than jot down notes, I think of my grandparents' unwritten Journey Journals and press on.

My parents traveled extensively in Europe for pleasure. We know nothing about their experiences except for the occasional comment thrown into conversation. Usually it was something like "we loved that trip to Spain" or "we met the nicest people in Ireland." And once, "I was surprised that the Hermitage was so dirty."

Traveling for pleasure was my father's great joy. For years, he worked hard in order to afford the trips my parents took. At the cost of a few minutes a day, we might now have a record of the day-to-day travel experiences of the Indiana farm boy who grew up to travel the world. We would have my father's first impressions and insights; his dry humor would continue to amuse long after his death.

Keeping a Journey Journal is a sure way for your children and grandchildren to know who you are as a person, not a parent. It transforms you into an individual through whose eyes your family can see what *you* saw and feel what *you* felt, coping with the joys and challenges of places that are not home.

Imagine your Journey Journals sitting on the bookshelf of some future generation. A great- or great-great- grandchild pulls it down, flips through its yellowing pages, and says, "This is wonderful stuff! I feel like she (he) is talking to me!"

Weighed against the very minimal "costs" of preparing your Journey Journal, things don't get much more beneficial than that.

Building a travel bookshelf:
A resource for other trips and other travelers
"Didn't you go to Singapore a few years ago?" my friend Annie asked me recently. When I told her yes, she said, "We'll be there for a few days next month. What do you recommend that we do?"

All sorts of ideas bubbled up, but the names of streets and restaurants eluded me. Fortunately, my Journey Journal was close at hand for consultation. I thumbed through it, telling her about Boughee Street and the best museum and a surprisingly inexpensive restaurant along with directions on how to find it.

Annie started to write all this down. Then she asked, "May I borrow your book for a day or two? I'll be very careful. But I'd love to read about your trip."

"Of course you can. That's what it's for," I told her, thrusting the Journey Journal into her hands.

Later, Annie told me that she and her husband were the only people on the trip who went to the Empress Museum or rode the public bus system because she'd read about both in my Journey Journal.

"And thank heavens I knew how hot it was going to be," she said. "None of the guidebooks stressed the heat and dreadful humidity. It was only because we read your Journey Journal that we were ready for it with the right clothes and, well, I guess you'd say, mental attitude."

Add photos for illustration: A picture book for adults and children
Gloria, a grandmother several times over, has found a most practical use for both her Journey Journals and the photographs that her husband shoots on their trips. During travel, she writes in one of those "wireless notebooks" measuring 10 1/2" by 8".

When they return home, Gloria simply rips out the pages of her Journey Journal and slides each day's entries into one side of a three-ring glassine protector—the kind sold for photo albums. Then she chooses photos to mount opposite the page. She puts both into a three-ring notebook-style photo album (any three-ring notebook will suffice).

The result is a library of wonderful picture books: illustrated Journey Journals for people of all ages. Fortunately, her handwriting is large and legible. She prints instead of scrawls so even young children can read about her adventures.

These picture books are equally interesting to adults. Have you ever watched your guests' eyes droop while you turn the pages of a photo album and try to explain each picture? "Here's the prettiest church you ever saw. It was in, uh, somewhere outside of the city."

Or, "this was the most fantastic place in Anatolya." Or, "We were so impressed with this place. It was...simply gorgeous."

Somehow, the words of simple evaluation just don't convey your experience. Even *you* get bored with your narrative. Gloria never explains her photos. Neither she nor her husband launches into long windy re-hashes of their travels. They just walk over to their bookshelf and pull out their latest picture book of photographs integrated neatly with interesting and informative Journey Journal entries, made fresh, on the spot.

And, according to Gloria, there's a side benefit: Both she and her photographer-husband have become more selective in choosing what pictures to shoot. "We've been known to substitute a really good picture-postcard if the light of the day isn't bright enough for our own shots," she says.

For talks and travel letters

Not everyone is fortunate enough to be able to travel. It's costly, time consuming, and requires energy and physical health. Well, aren't you the lucky one? Hospitals and retirement homes where residents are unable to see the world as you have will welcome your contribution as a volunteer, sharing your travels with a slide show "travelogue." You can schedule your travelogue through the social activities (or programming) directors working for the facilities you want to visit.

You can also extend your good fortune and re-live your adventure by putting together a talk (whether or not there are accompanying slides) for church groups, associations and clubs to which you belong, or study groups (physicians and dentists frequently form these and welcome speakers on subjects of interest.)

In order to make your program interesting to other people, focus on a theme such as "Survival eating in China" or "Faces of children in Africa" or "Folk crafts of Eastern Europe." So much the better if you have a special interest and knowledge on a subject, such as public health or folk singing or Peter the Great. We met a woman once who gave a fascinating *and* hilarious slide show on signage in foreign countries.

Proficiency as a public speaker is not required for this kind of assignment, but accuracy is. The Journey Journal becomes a necessity. Correct details, such as place names and routes taken, are important—you won't be able to fluff and bumble with vague descriptions ("I'm not sure of the name of the place, but the ruins were in great shape!") or ambiguous directions ("We got to the restaurant by following the guide").

Our close friends, Carol and Russell Hicks, write a kind of travel newsletter, using their computer skills to brighten up the pages with graphics and fancy type. For illustration, Russell scans in his professional-quality photographs, then sends the final copies to their wide circle of friends, including those they have met on their most recent travels. Their Journey Journals are the sources for these fine travel letters.

Marie Crocetti, an artist from Boston, sketches quickly in an 11"x13" sketchpad—buildings, skylines, people, landscapes. Under each day's heading, she writes in an inserts explanations for the sights she has drawn. Of course, Marie has the requisite talent to do this kind of Journey Journal. But she assures me that anyone can learn how to block a memorable sight and draw its outlines—to give it perspective.

For people with artistic interest, Marie says, some pre-departure sketching lessons at the local adult school can help you produce just such a souvenir. Not only do you end your trip with a wonderful chronicle of its events, but you have forced yourself to really look at what you are seeing, to pay it focused attention.

The Journey Journal isn't for everyone

OBJECTION # 1: *"Too exhausting..."*

"I think I take trips to keep from doing housework," mused Barbara. She and her husband were sitting behind us during a long bus-trek across Turkey and the subject of why we traveled came up.

"When we go home, Tom hauls out the lawnmower and I get the vacuum cleaner and we begin to work. Then it's just work, work, work, until we leave on the next trip. Travel's the only thing that makes us stop working."

"Frankly, we travel so much that I can't keep all the trips straight," Tom said. But neither kept a Journey Journal, or wanted to. "Too exhausting," Barbara said.

"Too much like lawnmowing and vacuuming—just another chore."

Until their trips stop substituting for long naps, Barbara and Tom will continue to escape into a kind of upscale oblivion, hurling around the globe without capturing any of it for posterity.

OBJECTION #2 : *"I hate to write."*
"I hate to write," Karen said. "I wouldn't mind speaking into one of those little tape recorders, though. Would that work?"

Sadly, no. At least, not for me. Talking to a tape recorder is either too much or too little work in order to achieve the goal of capturing travel experiences for posterity.

I tried it once, slipping one of those tiny recorders into my travel vest, feeling like an agent for the CIA. During the trip, I was self-conscious murmuring into my shirt pocket or whispering into the palm of my hand. And upon our return home, transcribing the tapes seemed like much more of a chore than the quick capture of each day's stories in my early-morning write-and-drink-coffee sessions.

Now when we arrive back in Baltimore, I have a notebook filled with the trip in written words. I can type them up or not, but there they are, ready to be read. With tape recorders, the words are held captive until you release them onto the page at some point in the future. Unfortunately, upon return, most people's energies flag, their interest in their most recent travel experience begins to fade and fade rapidly.

That is not to say that using a tape recorder wouldn't work for you. But remember that the object of journey-journaling is the written record of your experience. Don't let the untranscribed tapes gather dust and be forgotten, along with all those fine recorded thoughts and perceptions.

OBJECTION #3: *"I start out...and then...lose interest."*
"I start out taking notes like crazy and then I just lose interest," Sam told me. "You can tell how long we've been traveling by how many notes I'm taking,"

he laughed, holding up a nearly-blank page during a day in Queenstown, New Zealand.

As you'll see in Chapter 3 ("The Trip"), note-taking during the travel day is best kept to a bare minimum. After all, you're there to observe, to enjoy, to experience this new place. Notes, when taken at all, should be so spare that they can be written on the back of a sales receipt. (Or on the cuff of your shirt, as I saw one man do on a recent trip. "It washes out," he explained. "I once misplaced my notebook and never fully recovered.")

What Sam needed was to take Step #2. He lacked a reason to turn his notes into daily stories, an activity which can be completed in very few minutes a day. The challenge is to find both the commitment and the minutes.

Hint: Find a Journal Journal buddy to share with or read to. (Spouses make good Journey Journal buddies.)

OBJECTION #4: *"There isn't enough time..."*
I have found that the most convenient time to write in my Journey Journal is early in the morning, while my husband sleeps. I boil water in the electric pot that we carry everywhere, measure coffee into the filter paper which sits in its plastic cone atop our small thermos.

While pouring the water over the coffee grounds, I contemplate the previous day's activity. Then, when the coffee is ready to be poured, I sit at whatever space I can find (it's often the bathroom counter to keep the light from waking Bob) and quickly writing down the day's most memorable moments in my Journey Journal, referring to any notes I may have taken.

I write for ten to thirty minutes, depending on how good the coffee tastes and how soon we're leaving for the day's activities. Add a few extra minutes for the water to boil and I've taken a minimum of twenty minutes, and a maximum of forty minutes, out of my day.

Early a.m. may not be your best time for writing You may prefer that brief downtime before dinner. If so, dress a little faster and write.

Or just before bed may be your prime writing time. Undress a bit faster and write then.

If your travel schedule includes hour-long mealtimes, you may find your choicest time during the last ten minutes of breakfast or lunch. Find a chair in a private place and write.

Be assured, there are ten minutes somewhere in the day during which you could concentrate on writing in your Journey Journal. The effort is so small compared to its eventual rewards.

Of course, whenever you write, you'll need to have your Journey Journal handy. I recommend storing it in a backpack or totebag, where it will fit nicely.

OBJECTION #5: *"I can't write..."*

Yes, you can. Writing a Journey Journal isn't like writing for publication or for the Pulitzer Prize. If you can talk, you can write. The more it sounds like your own voice, the better for posterity. By using a few simple techniques, you will capture your experience more than adequately.

For example, jot down exact quotes in your little on-the-road notebook. Then you don't have to worry about describing what someone said. You just quote him or her saying it.

If you want to write about an encounter, get the setting of the scene and the sequence of events straight in your mind. Then write down what happened, step-by-step. At first, it may seem tedious to go back over a scene and re-visit it this way. But by doing this, details such as color, size and shape, and facial expressions will pop back into your mind. Just set those words on paper, one after the other. Imagine that you are talking to someone about the scene, telling it as a story to the folks back home.

"Then this big guy came into the room," you might say. "He looked really mad. Scared us all just looking at him."

But instead of talking, you are writing, word after word, until you get the big guy in the middle of the room and the other people reacting. Soon the contretemps that made the whole scene memorable is on paper, just as you saw it.

When it comes to description, I find similes to be effective. A simile is a description that, for explanation, uses something similar from a different context. For example, if the big guy is so big he reminds you of a tree, we get a good picture of his size when you write, "The big guy, legs like redwood trees, came into the room."

If someone reacted to him with fear, you might write, "she was shaking like a leaf." But, frankly, that's just an ordinary cliché which, when you think about it, isn't descriptive at all. Clichés are so over-used that the reader doesn't get the true sense of what you mean. How many leaves have you seen shake?

Try to avoid worn-out cliches. It's fun to close your eyes and imagine something else with the same characteristics. Instead of "...like a leaf," think of a more accurate simile to bring shakiness to mind. For instance, you could write, "she quivered like jello."

But there is no requirement for similes or metaphors or analogies or anything fancy in your Journey Journal. Just plain words will do the job well. "The big guy came into the room. We were scared. She was scared, too."

OBJECTION #6: *"...Nobody wants to know about my trips."*
Ah, but you are wrong. People may not want to know that there are 236,764 people living in the city of Czenchin or that the Carpathian Mountains reach a height of 3000 meters, but there are many who care about your impressions of the local food, the opportunities to hear local music, the value of the sightseeing trips to local high spots. Don't underestimate yourself.

OBJECTION #7: *"...Writing the Journey Journal is not for me"*
If you are still not convinced that this is worth doing—if you have neither the energy nor the inclination to put words on paper during your travel—then this book isn't for you. Please pass it on to someone more interesting. *Just* kidding. I meant, someone more interest*ed*.

How to use this book

I've organized this book to encourage you to use it on the road. It is small enough to tuck into your purse or pocket for easy access and reference. However, parts of the book (including this introduction) are specifically to get you into the mood to write a Journey Journal.

In Chapter Two, I offer ideas on pre-trip tasks that include tips unrelated to the actual Journey Journal, but ones I've found useful for making travel easier and for subtracting on-the-road anxiety. These have been gathered from other travelers and from personal experience.

Also included in Chapter Two is a model for the journey-journaling method. Reading about it will enable you to progress from brief notes made while traveling, to stories, to personal reflections. When you put the key in your door at journey's end and cross the threshold into your home once again, you will have a completed Journey Journal. Your experiences will have been captured, like so many wild horses. You will have corralled your stampeding thoughts and impressions and tamed them into words.

You can put your Journey Journal, as is, on the shelf or coffee table as a finished product. Or, you can take ten or fifteen minutes out of each subsequent day, typing the entries into your computer, until you've worked your way through your own handwriting. This results in a more legible Journey Journal. Of course, typed pages are more suitable for copying, too.

But, be assured, if this kind of polishing is not in your interest, you need not proceed to this final step. The work is finished and you should be proud of yourself for your accomplishment.

In Chapter Three ("The Trip"), a journey's segments are separately presented as potential opportunities for note-taking and storytelling. I use examples from several Journey Journals—all mine, rather than those wonderful, awe-inspiring works-of-art written by the great travel writers. The idea here is to inspire your own observations and, most of all, to motivate you to convert your own un-retouched, unedited first impressions into a polished Journey Journal.

In Part II ("The Journey Journal"), you will find five complete Journey Journal I produced during trips both long and short. In them, I point out the reasoning and efforts behind the writing as well as the unwritten—those things that were not included and why. One of the Journey Journals—to Eastern Europe—includes the entries of my husband Bob. Like you, he had never done a Journey Journal before. In fact, he hates to write anything. But he took part in the experiment, and, in the end, acquitted himself more than nicely.

The all-important section on "Reflections" is also included in Part II. Without reflection, your travel experiences slide away like raindrops on oilskins and you are left with dry words that lack meaning and long-term value. I've said it before and I say it here again: Your reflections are your real souvenirs.

So, Journey-Journalers, let's get on with it.

[CHAPTER TWO]

PRE-TRIP PREPARATION

For me, a trip really begins when I start making lists for it. My husband has a master list for travel, a kind of generic set of stuff to do, buy, and bring which serves him well and to which he refers in the hours before departure.

My lists, on the other hand, are trip-specific and are begun early, sometimes months in advance of travel. Making this list starts me mentally preparing for a trip. It requires me to envision us on-the-road and to anticipate the needs that might arise in another, vastly different setting. I begin to travel in my head, pondering potential problems caused by weather, health, and transportation. I don't make my list to raise anxiety levels or to create excess worry, but to enable us to include in our suitcases whatever might be medically palliative, like prescriptions, mineral oil, and Pepto-Bismol, and, in case of cold weather in normally temperate zones, those little bitty stretchy gloves for hands and a cotton scarf for head or neck.

I carefully choose at least seven paperback books and two blank Journey Journals, and place them in the outer pocket of my roll-aboard carry-on bag. This is done in recollection of the nine nightmarish hours spent waiting out bad weather in a midwest airport with no book to read. The book kiosk sold only unacceptable pink paperbacks with heaving bosoms adorning their covers. And I had no Journey Journal with me to record the comings and goings of the milling crowd. Since that day, I've never never been without an excess of both. I hear of people waiting in airports for days.

The key to a list's effectiveness is using it. Riding in to London from Heathrow Airport on a business trip, I tried to recall what shoes I had included for the fancy dress I'd brought for formal dinners. None came to mind. In horror, I realized that I had packed all kinds of complicated combinations of tops, skirts, and jewelry, but no shoes. While others slept off their jet lag, Bob and I shopped Marks & Spencer for a pair of all-purpose black pumps, size 10. Sure, sure, shoes were on the trip list. I just hadn't checked it carefully enough. That's the problem with all lists—writing something down does not actualize it. Now I always remember: list first, then do.

Your personal table-of-contents

Years ago, Bob and I acquired travel vests with so many pockets that they nearly obviate the need for suitcases. There are six pockets inside and eight outside, plus a long, webbed pocket in the back. Along with this generous vest storage space, I also wear a thing around my waist for emergency stuff like makeup and sunglasses. A folding canvas wallet hangs from my neck and holds my passport, money, and credit cards. On my back is a pack, and from my shoulder swings a purse.

Fully loaded, I can haul enough on my person to keep us going for a week. The trick is to find something I've brought without always patting myself down or, like someone suspected of smuggling, emptying everything out. You can keep track of all you haul with a table of your contents—a little list kept somewhere accessible that states in big print what is where.

After a few trips through security archways which sing out the secrets of your storage space, you will learn, as I have, to slip rapidly out of the backpack, slide off the travel vest, and lay the waist bag and shoulder purse on top. Then place the neckpurse in the little plastic dish along with keys and change and dash through the arch to collect everything quickly. A confession: If the neckpurse is inside a sweater, out of sight, it rarely makes the alarm go off. (Don't tell.)

Materials for your Journey Journal

GROUP TOURING TIP: *The Personal Trip-tik*

Beverly, a fellow traveler on a trip to Israel, knew every day's agenda and all routes to be taken before her tour bus left the hotel. She carried with her at all times a spiral stenographer's notebook, the kind that's bound at the top. She had cut out and taped each day's journey to the top right-side of the page and portions of the country's map, xeroxed from an atlas, to the left.

Thus, Beverly created a kind of trip-tik similar to those issued to AAA members. Her addition to the AAA model was to leave the lower page blank, ready for her notes on her travel experiences. Brilliant! It was dazzling in its simplicity and in its utility for those of us whose trip information lay in the bottom of the suitcase in the hotel or in the bowels of the tour bus. She had to keep passing it around the bus for people to finger and admire and read.

The personal trip-tik isn't difficult to duplicate for yourself. If you know each day's itinerary or the general region in which you will be traveling, you can construct one easily with or without an atlas. For domestic travel, maps are readily available through AAA or through Rand McNally. For foreign travel, detailed maps are sold at travel bookstores for nearly all destinations. Most libraries have copy machines. For about twenty-five cents a page, you can reproduce and slice up the result for the pages of your Journey Journal, leaving the original intact for your spouse to fold and refer to each day.

When you don't know where you're going each day, refer to a guidebook for the area's noteworthy sights and list them to the right of the map.

The Guide: Notes, facts, and happenings

If journey-journaling is new to you, you'll find it easier to follow a guide than to create one yourself. This one is simple and allows for the inclusion of a wide variety of observations. It has three components and six segments (*see Chapter 3*).

1. notes

2. facts

3. happenings

The components are meant to be fairly exhaustive, enabling you, the Journal-er, to say to yourself of the day's occurrences, "All present and accounted for..."

Remember, this is meant to be a guide only, not a set of rules or a formula. Some days, you won't need to write any notes. Some trips may not present new facts to record.

But it's safe to say that something worthy of writing happens every day. Otherwise, why did you go? A lot of the fun in journey-journaling comes from recognizing memorable stories and scenes.

Let's explore the components of a Journey Journal.

1. Notes

When on the road and sightseeing, the temptation is to either write no notes, on the assumption that you'll never forget such a sight, or to write something ambiguous, like "gorgeous" or "beautiful," and capture nothing of the scene—not image or thought.

"Gorgeous," "beautiful," "wonderful," and the like taste like tissue paper. They are vacuous words of no value. They represent the junk-food of vocabulary: empty calories. With such words, you give fat, not fiber, to the content of your notes, wasting both space and energy.

If these anonymous descriptors are followed by accurate ones, okay. But why waste time on them at all? Get used to finding specific, exact, appropriate words, worthy of your note-taking efforts. Consider those words as diamonds in a pile of cubic zirconia, as live blooms among artificial flowers, as the real things among the faux. Mine your vocabulary for authentic words, and avoid the imitations.

Notes are to be made quickly, capturing the fleeting image or flash of perception from the windows of a bouncing bus or in a crowded waiting room or anywhere that travel is taking place. In note-taking, the crucial step is making sure that your notes, though spare, conjure up images or recollections quickly and accurately. Therefore, choosing the appropriate word or words is essential.

Here's a real-travel situation that I once encountered: Seated in the early evening on a wooden bench overlooking the Indian Ocean on the south shore of Bali, we watched the sun make a spectacular descent behind a small island offshore. Unwilling to look away even for an instant, I groped for my notebook in the backpack. On its pages, I scrawled, still not looking down, "Back-lit, peach, ripe cantaloupes, smears of blood, lined with liquid gold. Noisy drinking crowd silenced, reverent," knowing that bowing to temptation and writing, "spectacular, awesome sunset. We all watch in silence," might or might not reconstruct the scene adequately.

The key to finding better words is to actively search for something similar in color, texture, or nature. They translate into word-pictures so much more easily and are well-worth the effort to find them. Think of this as pinpointing what you are seeing (color, texture, nature of it) rather than conveying its emotional impact ("beautiful, spectacular, awesome").

Here's how I found the words to describe the Bali sunset:

"Back-lit" reminded me of my little IBM notebook computer with its screen visible in a dark room because it is back-lit.

"Peach, ripe cantaloupes, smears of blood" was meant to bring back the precise colors of the cloud striations.

But the sight required more. It took me a minute to realize that the cloud's dazzle was enhanced by the gold lining. "Lined with liquid gold."

And then there was that sudden hush and I added:

"Noisy drinking crowd, silenced, reverent."

Jotting these words down enabled me to recall not only the spectacle of the sunset, but our arrival at Tanalot and the fifteen minutes or so before we found our seats and sat to watch. They returned me mentally to the scene. The next morning, I was able to turn those few notes into the following scene:

"Leaving the rented car and driver in the grassy field crowded with buses and cars, we followed Kandy Man (our guide's name was Kandeh, but Tim dubbed him "Kandy Man") over a rise and down a wide dirt path to the rocky shoreline. Crowds milled ahead of us. We hurried along in the fading light.

At the base of the path, people were picking their way through the puddles and rocks, moving to the left, up a path to a group of shops. But Kandy Man turned right. We followed as he lightly jumped from rock to rock, not looking back but rushing ahead, up a stone path, higher and higher to the top of a cliff. Only then did he turn to us, as we puffed and hauled ourselves up behind him.

"See?" He waved his arm to the view. Waves crashed and spewed spray high into the air. The shoreline, dotted with small rock islands, stretched for miles. Bob and Tim aimed their cameras. Bob snapped, Tim video'd. Helen and I posed. Then Kandy Man took both camera and video and shot us all posing in the rapidly fading light. It was a race against time—to catch the wonder of Tanalot before the sun reached the horizon and sank from view.

"Come. Come." Kandy Man was off again, back down the rocky slope, calling, "Be careful! Slippery! Slippery!"

This time, he walked around the puddles and rocks to the path the crowds were taking up the hill to the shops. He hurried ahead. At the top of the path, waiters with trays of glasses moved among the people now seated on benches, folding chairs, and rocks, all facing the sea. Noisy, laughing, shouting at each other, calling to children and dogs, it was cacophony.

Kandy Man found an empty bench and turned to us. "Here you sit!" he said triumphantly.

Helen and I sat, while Bob flagged a waiter and ordered us all something to drink. Kandy Man faded away to find other guide-pals and shoot the breeze while we sat to watch the sunset at Tanalot. It was one of those sure-fire hypnotic things, like putting little children in front of a Barney video. He knew we'd be rooted to the spot and wouldn't need his services for a while.

"Your faces are reflected in the sunset," said Tim from behind his running video camera. "They are as red as Susan's hair."

The sky. Oh, the sky. It was changing from pale blue to peach, smeared with the colors of ripe cantaloupe and blood. It looked lined with gold, back-lit like a computer screen. A patch of rocky island lay just off the coast, topped with a small temple silhouetted and black against the sky.

The crowd noises stopped. In the presence of this awesome gift of nature—the sunset, the rocky cliffs, the spewing crashing waves, the outline of the little temple—voices were suddenly hushed.

People could only whisper to each other. "Look."

Finding accurate words quickly requires focus and imagination. But accepting the challenge to describe with exactitude is worthwhile. Later you will be able to recall, with your own words, nearly all of the scene surrounding the sight you captured. Of course, this comes more easily with practice.

You will not always take notes. Some travel days contain no difficult place names, you have no flashes of insight, no remarkable first impressions. But when you do need to take notes, in order to remember details for later journey-journaling, you will probably have to do it quickly. Note-taking on the road is usually an exercise in speed-writing. Therefore, I offer this pre-trip exercise to sharpen your skills.

Word-finding exercise

Look around you. How would you describe the setting in which you are reading this book? Pretend that you are being charged $100 per word or that you have only a sales receipt or the back of a business card on which to write. And you have only 30 seconds in which to put it all down. Start with the details and add ambience, if time permits. Reject the easiest and dig for the most accurate words in your vocabulary.

Details: What is the predominant color of walls, furniture, other decor? Are the ceilings high, low? Is there any smell in the air? What else does this place remind you of? A funeral parlor? A doctor's waiting room? A dorm room? A library? Who else is in the room? Why? Could whatever is happening in the room be interpreted incorrectly?

Ambience: Is the atmosphere of the room comfortable? Noisy? Sleep inducing? Are you relaxed in these surroundings? Nervous? Contented? Anxious? Why?

2. *Facts*

Place names—cities, restaurants and hotels—and routes taken are essential to the authenticity of your Journey Journal. But these things are so easy to forget, especially if the names are long and complicated, like Petrogavordsk or Anatolya or Yojakarta. To remember them with accuracy, you can either mark a map or collect a brochure or simply ask for the correct spelling and write it into your notes while on the road. But these "facts" are important.

They are the difference between:

"Yesterday, we drove between a large city and this small village where we spent the night. We ate in a charming little restaurant near the center of town. Our hotel is quiet and well-located."

and:

"Yesterday we drove between Marseilles, huge and crowded, and Tourves, a rural crossroads about 40 km to the east. We ate at Les Moules on the main square of town, one of those red-checked tablecloth, stone fireplace, family-run restaurants so typical of Provence. It was next door to our hotel, the Auberge Gaspar."

I wrote the latter with the aid of a one-page brochure from the hotel, now stashed in an envelope taped to the back inside cover of my Journey Journal for France. It also lists the hotel's rack rates. Who knows? We may want to return to the Auberge Gaspar someday for a longer visit.

3. *What happened?*

Okay, this is where it gets to be fun. Authentic words captured in notes, facts collected with brochures—these are good things, but only enhancements to the major part of your Journey Journal. If you don't write a single on-the-road note or pick up any brochures (knowing that all facts are in your guidebook), you can be certain that your memories of the day will be clear if you set aside just a few minutes each day or evening to capture the most memorable experiences on paper.

Earlier, in the word-finding exercise, you wrote quickly in order to record the place in which you now sit. Given only 30 seconds, you recorded the most outstanding descriptors: color of walls and furniture, size of room, those things that struck you as memorable.

Use your few daily journey-journaling minutes (while your husband is shaving or your wife is watching CNN) to repeat this rapid response method and put on paper the first thing that comes to your mind about the day's activities. Was it the food at lunch, the long bus ride, the visit to a museum?

And why was it memorable? Did you eat mud frogs? Did the bus driver get lost? Did you move like a herd of cows through the museum? What was it about this experience that you would tell someone back home, that makes it different from your everyday life?

You may not have time to write down the second thing that comes to mind or the third. Given the brevity of available journey-journaling time, this may be all you can write each day. But be assured that you've captured the heart of your journey, making your Journey Journal compelling reading after you return.

In those few minutes a day, you can tell us the important stuff: what actually happened on this trip? In years to come, your words and facts will illuminate and revitalize your experience, but it is the experience itself that makes the trip yours. What people did you see? What encounters did you witness? What surprised you, depressed you, delighted you, amused you?

Watch for these things. Be alert to them. Don't miss anything. It is your witness to the world you are visiting that gives value to your Journey Journal.

Another guide

Remember Bruce's father? He's the inveterate traveler who answers his son's post-trip questions and thus, with words, reconstructs the essence of his experiences, tailored for his son's interests. The questions, known in advance after so many iterations, form the guide he will use to reflect on the trip.

Because neither questions nor answers are written down, his insights and observations are lost to posterity. Too bad! With just a little additional effort, his trip would last much longer, be of more value, and give joy to many more people than can be reached in one verbal debriefing session.

But enough of this hectoring. Bruce's debriefing-session model is still a useful one and can guide the Journey-Journaler to record those things that are of the greatest interest to others. If you respond well to the Q&A method, here are his questions for which you might find answers on your next trip. Just remember to take the next step and write the answers down in your Journey Journal.

1. What was the chronology of the trip? (*Arrival date, itinerary, departure date*)

2. What were its daily events (walking/bus tours)? And what were the destinations?

3. What is your starkest memory of each event? (*Because Bruce is a former journalist, he probes each highlighted event for details, asking "who," "what," "when," "where," and "how" questions, until, he says, "I feel, in a few minutes, that I'm there with him."*)

4. How do you rate the overall enjoyability of the trip and what are your conclusions about the destination? Friendly? Comfortable? Affordable? Worth a return visit?

To use these questions yourself, refer to them at the close of each day, or in the early morning of the next. Write the answers in your Journal Journal as if each day's itinerary were the complete trip.

Supplies for your Journey Journal

1. A spiral notebook, small enough to fit into your shirt or travel vest pocket for on-the-road notes.

2. A "wireless" notebook, 3-ring size (8 1/2" X 10"). This is your Journey Journal, kept at your hotel or in your overnight bag. It is into this notebook that you transfer notes, stash brochures with "facts," and write "what happened" during your ten-minute (minimum) Journey Journal session.

3. Pens—I prefer "Pilot Explorers" and "Uni-ball Vision" for Journey Journal writing and any medium-point ballpoint for note-taking. Find the pen which writes most easily under the pressure of your hand and buy several. On the road, pens tend to disappear, like socks in the clothes dryer. Pencil leads break too easily. We've not included any pens, but we have packaged this book with matching, Journey Journal spiral and wireless notebooks. They're the size and style we think you'll like, and, with this book, they make for a great gift for the travelers in your life.

Now let's go through the segments of a journey to help you find the story you want to remember and write it in your Journey Journal.

[CHAPTER THREE]

THE TRIP SEGMENTS

When does your trip begin? When does it end? As I said earlier, for me, the trip begins with the lists I put together, sometimes months before departure. It ends when I record my reflections and choose photos to include in my Journey Journal. The time devoted to preparing for the trip, plus the time spent traveling *to* your destination, plus return-trip travel and wrap-up, can be at least as long as the time spent at your destination.

I have found that including all of these segments in a Journey Journal adds immeasurably to its later enjoyment and worth as a record of your trip. The segments are:

1. Departure-transition—Getting from here to there

2. Arrival

3. Group travel—Meeting fellow travelers

4. At your destination—What happened?

5. Return-transition—Getting from there to here

6. Reflections

1. Departure-transition: Getting from here to there

Often the least enjoyable, most physically-taxing portion of a trip is its transition time, the travel from home to destination. As to transportation from here to there, the best that can be said about it is, "It was eventless." The excitement and anticipation have been for the place you're visiting. Getting there is something to get through as quickly and painlessly as possible. But there are good reasons to record this transition in your Journey Journal.

Write to relieve anxiety

For me, an invaluable use of the Journey Journal has been to relieve pre-flight anxiety by focusing on something other than the knots in my stomach. They are especially prevalent if weather is bad, or the waiting area is overcrowded. I welcome the distraction of the writing. It gives me something to do other than fret.

For my aforementioned solo trip to France in the winter of 1993, I arrived at the airport, hours before my flight was scheduled to leave. Not being able to concentrate on reading a book, I wrote the following in my Journey Journal. From its tone, I can still recall the slight edge of creeping hysteria, kept at bay by writing:

Kennedy Airport, January 6, 1993

My adventure has begun. I checked the large suitcase and big duffel but still look plenty packed. The oversized fanny-pack is strapped to my middle, bulky with overnight essentials. The heavy black passport/money carrier hangs around my neck. The strap of my new green purse, which is loaded with phrase books and magazines, runs across my back and over my shoulder. In my coat pocket is a list of which bag holds what: a table of my contents.

Wearing sensible lace-up shoes, blue kneehose, and a shapeless wool cardigan, I feel like Miss Marple. With all this hanging gear, I could also be mistaken for a fully loaded packhorse or one of those huge garment bags I've seen business people dragging onto planes. Maybe they'll try to hang me in the forward cabin closet.

Thanks to the tranquilizer pill from Dr. S, I glided through the train trip from Baltimore and the Gray Line bus ride from the Penta Hotel across from Penn Station in Manhattan. Now I am at Kennedy waiting for the flight to Amsterdam to be announced. From Amsterdam I will fly to Marseilles, France.

I sit wedged into a plastic chair next to the vending machine, drinking its $2 coffee and watching small knots of veiled, gowned people as they study the departure board, murmuring in exotic languages to each other. The board lists Madrid, Morocco, Haifa, Vienna, Berlin, and Jakharta.

I have called Bob twice on his 800 number. It's like I left my arm or my leg behind. Six weeks away. It's beginning to hit me.

(And later, on the connecting flight, I was too excited to read or sleep, so I wrote.)

January 7

The NYC flight to Amsterdam was without incident. Miraculously, I was assigned seat 1B in business class with plenty of leg room. Probably this was because I had shown up so early, the first person to check in. KLM delivered the special vegetarian meal I ordered and I slid into the semi-sleep of air travel. If there was a movie shown, I didn't see it.

I am now on the plane to Marseilles, fuzzy-headed and pasty-faced. Why, when I'm tired, does rouge stand out like traffic lights on my face? It is 3 a.m. Baltimore time, 9 a.m. in France.

The attendant just announced that "In za case of emergency evacuation, za lights weel be eliminated." Seems an odd safety measure.

This flight is KLM's "city hopper." Few passengers and plenty of handsome Dutch men and women are in attendance. They gave me yogurt for breakfast with fruit. It's a two-hour flight to Marseilles.

The blue knee hose are now anklets. I should have worn slacks. Not even Miss Marple looks this rumpled.

Write to relieve boredom

Not all trips include hours in the airport prior to leaving or pre-trip anxiety-knots. But flights can be l-o-n-g, very long, and the boredom can become overwhelming. The time passes more quickly if you spend it by writing in your Journey Journal. I wrote the following on a seemingly-endless flight to Singapore.

"I'm not sure how this happened, but we have gone through two nights with one very short day in between, all aloft. We boarded the Singapore Airlines flight at 9 p.m. last night, slept intermittently, stopping over briefly to refuel in Amsterdam at 4 a.m."our" time (10 a.m., theirs) before taking off an hour later. In a very short time, it was night again, sometime before "our" noon.

We had a meal of real food last night. This morning, breakfast was fruit and a biscuit, then an odd bouncy fish-smelling roll of something gray with veins. Not even Bob would eat it.

I ate a cracker, the biscuit, and the grapefruit slices. Since then, we've been served only a couple of dainty tea sandwiches. But the next meal we get, the attendant told us, will be breakfast again. "In one hours and a hahf."

What happened to lunch and dinner? It's early afternoon for us, evening for Euros who joined us in Amsterdam. Which of us is due for breakfast? Not us. Not them. Go figure.

We've seen three movies, but they were all pretty dumb so we read and tried to sleep. The last movie ended with eight hours left in the flight. The cabin is dark so it's somebody's night. Can't be ours, unless it is 2 a.m. and not 2 p.m. for us. Anyway, we'll arrive in Singapore's morning. I think."

Use your Journey Journal to capture your mental state during flight, to make note of fellow passengers, to remember the names of the movies you saw and the food you ate. This part of the trip is simply too long to be ignored.

Get an early start
Need another reason for beginning your Journey Journal with your departure from home and your travel to the destination? Doing so gets your journalistic juices flowing, gets *you* going, and even starts your mind working. Force yourself to pull out your notebook and begin to write words. Whether it's a quick 30-second word-jot in the airport or the ten-plus minutes of writing about the transition as it unfolds in order to stave off anxiety or boredom, you'll have the equivalent of wet feet at the water's edge.

I have found that it's much easier to add to my Journey Journal upon arrival than to start it after the adventure has begun. I'm not sure why this is so, except that it seems there is so much to write about then that the idea of trying to catch up is often daunting.

Remember, there is no wrong way to write a Journey Journal, except not to write one at all. There is simply no downside and lots of upside potential in capturing the moments of your travel experience. Aside from the sheer joy of reading it in future years, you are increasing your observational skills and using your brain while you write. Finding the right words requires concentration, an often neglected, and frequently limited skill, but one which increases with use.

(If nothing else convinces me to begin writing when I feel more like reading, sleeping, or doing anything else, I remember the research that suggests exercising the brain is as beneficial to well-being as exercising the body, and may be instrumental in staving off Alzheimer's disease.)

Pre-journey ignorance

Finally, the Journey Journals have been valuable evidence that I understand more about a destination when the trip is over than when it began. In a kind of "pre-/post-test" evaluation (*see"Reflections"*), I look back on Bob and me as a couple of Innocents Abroad, or as a Couple About to Go Abroad, sitting in the waiting room of some mode of transport, clutching our bags and consulting our watches. And I think, "We didn't know anything about (fill in the region/country/city) back then."

I ponder the change in us, Bob and me, (or just me, if I'm traveling alone) between our waiting to leave, before the adventure and our return, after it happens. How differently we think about a place when we know more: what it looks like, its people, its food, its politics. Reading about departure and the first impressions upon arrival, I can quickly recall my pre-trip ignorance and reflect on how much more interested we will now be to hear the country's name on the evening news, or read of its elections or wars or celebrations in the newspapers.

Transition-writing exercise

Have you ever had the experience of driving an oft-traveled route and suddenly wondering, "where am I?" Your foot has been on the gas and brake pedals, your hands have steered the wheels, but your mind has been somewhere else. You haven't been paying attention. Paying attention is what this book is all about. To start the process before you travel somewhere more exotic than to the grocery store or the office, try this simple exercise.

Place a pad of paper on the passenger seat with a pen that requires only slight pressure for its ink to flow. And the next time you drive somewhere—anywhere—practice paying attention. At each stop light or traffic jam, note on the pad something interesting: the rock music in the car next to you which rattles your windows, the people waiting at the corner bus stop, the bumper stickers on the car ahead.

Maybe you notice the color of the leaves or the well-tended flower beds at a gas station. Maybe you see children waiting for the school bus, jostling and joking with each other. Pretend that you are traveling this road for the first time and that you will have to describe your trip, however brief, to someone when you arrive. Try to find a story in this little commute.

One word or two will evoke the memory for you, so there's no need to do more than simple jots. After all, you are driving. Don't try to make the words neat and legible. The point is to see what you are looking at and to find something of interest in this oft-made, probably boring trip.

2. Arrival

Ah, at last you are there. Stumbling out of the plane, dizzy with jet lag, pleats in your face and not in your slacks, you clutch your passport and customs form. Instinct alone enables you to follow the surge of fellow passengers through passageways, down and up staircases, until you finally reach the Customs Hall. It is teeming with other irritable, sleep-deprived tourists and citizens.

Arrival is, for me, the nadir of the travel experience. It is simply something to be borne. Those first few minutes out of the plane and into the arrival area are difficult even in the most civilized, modern, and user-friendly airports. My only consolations are that this part of the trip is over soon, and if I concentrate, I can find good material to log later into my Journey Journal.

I found this note to myself in a Journey Journal, written while standing in a long line at Passport Control in Tel Aviv.

A warning: This is not your finest hour. Avoid anything that reflects your image. You are not a pretty picture. And your breath smells. Because the line on the plane for the only working toilet was twenty-four deep, you are in serious need of a bathroom. If anyone crosses you now, particularly your spouse, you will react fiercely. Stay calm. In these moments, silence is golden. Snap at that sullen cow fingering your passport and your journey might be to the local jail.

First impressions of a new place will usually be your sharpest and most vivid.

The way people are dressed, the language of the signs, the technology in the restrooms—all stark reminders that you are not back home. It often takes much longer to realize you are there at your destination, in Sidney or Singapore or Paris. But this first landing, the initial phase of a trip, can convince you at least that you are no longer in Baltimore or Tulsa or Detroit, wherever here is.

Later, when you are more accustomed to your surroundings, your impressions may be dulled. So take the first opportunity to jot a note or two—no more—about what you see.

Notes jotted during this arrival interlude, between plane landing and hotel, will jog your memory later when you emerge from jet-lag into your journey.

Istanbul, Turkey
woman in ladies room gleaming porcelain toilets sparkle sour passport man

Later, these few words brought back the memory starkly enough to record the following:

11/11/96—Istanbul
Yesterday is lost to history and nearly to memory. I took brief notes and now must try to resurrect meaning from them. "Woman in ladies room"—that would be the astonished woman from New Something, Kansas, who stood outside the door to the stall and squealed, "It's in the floor! It's a hole in the floor!"

Indeed it was—one of those toilets sunken in the floor and actually called "Turkish toilets." There are porcelain treads embedded on either side so you don't slip into the hole itself. It was noon Istanbul time, 5 a.m. ours. The corridor and bathroom were empty of Turks who might otherwise have been offended by this woman when she flounced out, horrified to the very toes of her Reeboks.

"I'm not going in a HOLE," she announced to the line of waiting women, who stood in stony silence, gray faced, clutching kleenex from their fanny packs and purses, in case there was no toilet paper. "Wait'll you see THAT," she thundered, gesturing at the stalls and stalking out.

The airport was strange only in its cleanliness, its Sunday quiet, the general courtesy of its employees, and the spotless porcelain of its bathrooms. Oh, Turkish-style to be sure, but those are not strange in Turkey.

Our bags arrived when we did and we were out of the customs enclosure in minutes. Bob tried to coax a smile from the no-nonsense clerk checking passports but even his infectious grin couldn't distract the man from the serious nature of his job

Traveling to new places can create anxiety. Sometimes the only way to unburden yourself is to jot down some notes for your Journey Journal, as it was with me when I wrote the following upon arrival in Marseilles:

Marseilles airport
Sitting in area set aside for arriving passengers to meet people. No sign of hosts DeVignes. In bathroom, forced duffel and suitcase into stall with me then couldn't close door. Didn't care. That kind of mood. Where the hell are they? What to do? Is there another airport in Marseilles? If they're not here by noon, I'll go to Travelers Aid.

The DeVignes appeared shortly after writing this, twittering with apologies. They thought my plane landed an hour later. By the next day, I had nearly forgotten my arrival anxiety. By then, it seemed unimportant to the travel story. The sole purpose of the writing had been to maintain my composure, and it worked.

3. Group Travel—Meeting your fellow travelers
When you travel with a group, your initial impressions introduce this cast of characters to your Journey Journal and add interest to your narrative. You don't yet know who, if anyone, you'll get to know better, or who will become more important to your story. Rather than searching your memory for names of fellow travelers every time you meet, jot them down in your notes as soon as possible. Add a brief physical description and a word or two nailing down a character's most prominent features and characteristics.

My airport notes in Istanbul:
net plump 55 blue polyester "my sun shines." "call me net" charles radio voice edward not ed red-blonde these are BIG happy people

These words became:

Fending off dark men in mustaches who wanted very much to carry our luggage (baggage carts are free), we rolled out to our guide who stood just outside customs, holding a sign "Educational Opportunities." He is a fiftyish man with a big voice. "Ah, you are here! My sun shines!" he boomed. "Call me Net. Welcome you to Eeestanbool!"

Net wore a powder blue polyester suit with contrasting navy blue trim and straining seams. He has a gentle, open face, kind eyes and a sweet smile. Turning to his right, he pointed out the money changer's booth and sent Bob and me off to exchange currency (97150 lira per U.S. $).

We returned to our tour group, a knot of groggy people standing alongside their bags, trying to be as alert as possible at 5 a.m. after a sleepless night. Although we are all traveling with Educational Opportunities ("World Travel with a Purpose"), we are a collection of several smaller groups, each with a separate "tour host"—someone who is getting the trip free for our bookings.

The entire bunch is overseen by a large pear-shaped man with an Indiana School of Broadcasting radio voice. The woman standing next to me nodded at his waving arms as he beckoned us, his flock, to follow him and Net. "That's our leader," she said reverently. "His name is Charles. He's a televangelist." Oh, good news.

The other hosts, (who seem to be assistants to Charles, each responsible for his little group), are Edward ("Not Ed," he requested)—tall, pale, with lank, reddish-blonde hair, and ours, John. John and his wife Betty are friends from our trip to Israel. Both are jolly, good-natured, and look a little like Mr. and Mrs. Santa Claus, without the white hair and beard.

Looking around, I saw lots of other Claus-type tummies. Nearly all these people are—well—large. Big substantial bodies. Most have been on several previous EO trips. Travel, it seems, is broadening.

It is a merry group, friendly in spite of the sleepless night. Betty (John's wife) is almost terminally cheerful. And her good cheer is contagious. There are about forty of us, ranging in age from fairly young for this kind of off-season tour (Edward and his wife look to be in their late thirties) to elderly. Two hobbling ancients were pointed out as Charles' parents. They must be at least in their late eighties, the only ones not smiling. The poor souls looked baffled, eyes fixed on Charles and not moving from his side.

Think of your unfolding journey as a play with scenes and characters. The stage and scenery of a play are important, of course. But the play is about characters. Characters move the plot along and make it interesting. A Journey Journal without people is pretty dull stuff. Your traveling companions (if you travel with a group) will often be as interesting as some of your destinations, so why not write about them? The interplay and group dynamics are part of the journey's plot and will add color to your story.

Introduce the characters in your travel adventure as you meet them. Introductions can be spare. Snippets of conversations and physical descriptions, along with names, when you learn them, will be sufficient to build word pictures of your fellow travelers—and other human beings you encounter on your journey. The point (for you and for your Journey Journal readers) is to learn who they are as soon as possible.

4. At your destination—What happened? And what happened next?

How can you tell you're there? Is it the street signs? I remember our first trip requiring a passport. It was to London. What a thrill to read "Car Park" on a billboard next to a Heathrow Airport parking lot. The "Please Give Way" signs at traffic circles ("roundabouts") seemed such an extraordinarily courteous way to ask drivers to yield.

But the ultimate British civility in written communication was found in the public restrooms of Windsor, England. I noticed that the toilet paper sheets there were patterned with what appeared to be lines of writing, but I couldn't make out what they said in the darkened stall. So I carefully tore off a sample length, stepped outside into the light, and squinted at the tiny blue words. They read,

"Now wash your hands, please. Now wash your hands, please. Now wash your hands, please...."

You won't find that in Baltimore.

First impressions
What is it about your destination that gets your attention first? As soon as possible, and in spite of jet lag, be alert to your surroundings. Try to be aware of what you are noticing about them. First impressions—those initial moments of clashing cultures (yours meeting theirs) or, if travel is domestic, of similarities—in temperature, clothing, friendliness, whatever—are the foundations of your Journey Journal.

In a small pocket notebook, on the paper sleeve of your airline ticket, or on your shirt sleeve, for heaven's sake, record those thoughts. Your first little memos that you are not at home will recreate your arrival state of mind when you sit down to write in your Journey Journal later.

Okay, okay, I can hear you saying, "But I'm practically sound asleep after an all-night flight. There is no way I can start writing notes as soon as we arrive." All I can say in reply is, "Try." You'd be surprised at the clarity of your thoughts, the things that you notice first, and how quickly you forget those things if you don't jot them down.

Remember that recording your initial impressions is an act of awareness, evidence that you are attending your own vacation. From these first impression foundations, you will build the story of your trip, adding—with each entry—to your wonder or your pleasure or your intellectual growth.

What happened next: Encounters and interactions
Each day you will take part in or witness encounters and interactions. People meeting people, talking to each other, working together, arguing, hugging, sharing, stealing. Encounters and interactions develop the scenes in your day's drama.

If time permits, I usually follow a day's chronology, writing about events as they happened, one after the other. Many trips, however, don't allow for that luxury and afford little time to expand on more than one or two of a day's highlights. When a travel schedule is tight, I suggest listing "what happened" and "what happened next" and writing only about the happening with the biggest impact. Like this encounter at a museum in Antioch, Turkey:

"After wandering the high-ceilinged rooms—Greco-Roman mosaics on walls and floors, glass cases of broken jars and jewelry—a bloodless kind of place, clean and modern and boring, I waited for Bob alone in a hall near the entrance. Two young girls in green wool jumpers and green neckties approached me tentatively. Holding notebooks and schoolbooks to their chests, both wore wide, deeply dimpled, nervous smiles. They had very white teeth and big dark eyes. "May we esk you qveschun?" said one.

"Of course," I replied. We began a long conversation. The girls wanted to know my age, my religion, how many children I had. They wanted to know what we were going to see and where we came from and why. They wanted to know about my "hoosbahnd."

They told me that they are sixteen years old, go to boarding school in town, and are studying English and computers. In my small notebook, they wrote their names: Aysel Gungar and Neslihan Sarcah.

Both girls want to teach. Each day, they come to the museum and try to engage English-speakers in conversation. Boy, were they cute! Outgoing and smart. Bob showed up and was equally charmed. We took photos, videos.

Too soon it was time to leave them and board the bus. Neslihan said, haltingly, "I...lahv...you..um..um..very much" and kissed me on both cheeks. Aysel said, "Yes...yes" and did the same. We waved to each other until the bus turned the corner and they were out of sight. A lovely encounter.

Events

Events on your travel schedule, such as museum visits, or palace and cathedral tours, can be fascinating or deadly dull. Your guidebook will have the necessary facts about the place. To give color to your Journey Journal, enliven the events with detailed description.

Istanbul, Turkey

According to Net, the Hamom Baths are the best and oldest in Istanbul. But remember, that's Net talking. He led his little band of six women and eight men down the main street named Cadesi, to a cobblestoned side street, and pointed to a red neon sign with an arrow pointing down the dark road. "Hamon." He turned into it and we trooped along behind him. Some of us carried plastic bags of underwear and lotion. One lady clutched a small overnight bag with the strap of some garment hanging from its closure like a long noodle.

Net left us women waiting in the dark while he escorted the men into a brightly lit entrance. Then he hurried back to us and beckoned us follow around the corner to another yellow lighted doorway. Up the wooden stairs our little band climbed. It led into a dark reception hall where an ancient toothless crone in black scarf and sweeping skirts stood with a younger woman, still pretty old but not bent.

Net hurried forth and talked rapidly to the pair. The elder of the two stared at us impassively while the other stepped behind a wooden counter on which there sat a penciled, cardboard sign. She leaned down and retrieved a large journal-like book into which she wrote something.

Net wandered to the counter with calculated casualness and quickly palmed the sign, but not before I saw that it was a price list. We had paid him $20 for an $11 "bath and massage." He hung around until we were all dispersed into individual glass booths and handed small pieces of cloth "towels" in which to drape ourselves.

I shared a booth with Betty. We giggled self-consciously as we peeled off our clothes and wrapped up in the towels. We then joined the others—chattering nervously—and padded to a doorway where a young woman of extremely generous proportions stood. She beckoned us into the dimly-lit "bath room," a large space with a marble slab in its center, looking for all the world like a huge butcher's block. Lining the walls—about ten to twelve feet apart from one another—were long marble benches. In front of them were marble basins.

Two women sat leaning against the wall, eyes closed, mouths open, hands at their sides. We stole furtive glances as we passed them. They were naked and with their enormous breasts, they looked like two mountain ranges, with high peaks and deep dark crevices. I longed to throw my towel over them for aesthetic reasons, if nothing else. Not a pretty picture.

Three more spreading women, large and rippling and covered only with black bikini panties nearly lost in the ripples of their bodies, soaped each of us in turn, rubbed us with a kind of sandpaper glove, turned us over like dead tunas on a dock, and rubbed our backs. Our hair was quickly shampooed and rinsed and with grunts and hand gestures, we were dismissed. We huddled together, gripping our towels and hurried back into the reception hall and to our glass dressing rooms. The whole thing took no more than twenty minutes.

We could see Net sitting in his green trenchcoat in an outer room, sipping tea from a tiny cup. We dressed quickly and joined him. It was one of those "glad I did it but not sure why" experiences. We all felt vaguely ripped-off, suspecting that we coulda done it at the hotel, cheaper and better. But then, that would have been purely for tourists. I think the Hamom Baths are, if nothing else, authentic.

Observations

Have you ever been baffled by the way things work in other countries? How to make phone calls, buy produce in a supermarket, ride public transportation—all these mundane activities can be great mysteries to the foreign visitor.

Your observations on these subjects add value to your Journey Journal. By observing the local citizenry going about its business, one learns how things are done and how things work. Such observations are crucial for the solo traveler. When traveling with a group, the need to learn a lot about how things work and are done is obviated by the knowledge of the tour guide. You can just ask what is going on.

Observation can also include your assumptions and personal analyses of actions and events. Often, group travelers resort to guessing among themselves and can be hilariously off the mark. Outside of Mexico City:

We approached the pyramids from behind, bumping along a dusty street and looking up from the dirty windows of the mini-bus. "Look!" said the woman seating in front of me. "Look at that man! Is he a priest, do you suppose?"

I pressed my face to the glass and peered up at the figure of a person silhouetted against the sun, arms stretched up to the sun. He seemed to be raising and lowering his arms to a rhythm, up two-three, down two-three. The guide was too busy directing the driver to a favorable parking spot in the shade to ask, so I offered, "Maybe there's a ceremony going on."

We hurried through the crowds to the pyramids, priest momentarily forgotten as we looked with awe on the broad avenue of ancient peaks. There wasn't just one but many.

At the base of the largest, Bob said, "I'm going to climb it. Take a picture of me at the top." He turned and started up the narrow steps. A woman stood next to me shading her eyes with her right hand, holding a camera in her left. She squinted into the sun.

I looked up to the top of the pyramid and there...there he was. Our priest. Only he wore a tennis shirt and khakis. He was waving rhythmically, but we could now hear his words, "Mabel! Mabel! Up here! I'm up here!"

Your observations will be useful to your Journal readers. The following was helpful to my children when the same bathroom technology came to New York City a few years later.

From my France Journey Journal:
There are several public toilets scattered around Marseilles. These are small white buildings made of metal and are sort of lozenge-shaped. On the outside wall is a coin slot marked "2f." Today I decided to try one of these things and followed the directions over the coin slot to the letter. As soon as I dropped 2 francs into it, the door slid open.

I entered and the door automatically slid closed. I unhooked the belt to my slacks and squatted over the metal bowl. As I did, I swayed slightly and accidentally knocked the door handle with my hand. Thrown off balance, I tipped back and fell onto the toilet seat and...omigod. The door slid open again, wide and just out of reach. I could see the fishmongers and tour boats...and they could see me. Desperately, I lurched forward (slacks around socks) and with super-human strength, wrestled the door closed. I felt like one of those people who lift automobiles off trapped children.

As I did this, a curious bystander watched impassively from just outside the door. I think he was next in line. I should mention that this little w.c. building sits right on the Marseilles waterfront, hub of activity, centre of le centre ville.

As I said, helpful to my children. On their way toward using one of these contraptions a few years later in New York City, my son told his wife, "Remember. DON'T touch the door handle!"

Sights, sounds, tastes, textures, odor
Appealing to the senses is an effective way to enliven your Journey Journal. What you see when you look out of the hotel or the tour bus window will be different from what you'd see at home. Why?

And what sounds do you hear? Is that a shofar blowing? Is someone chanting from a minaret?

Did the multi-hued lumps in gravy that you ate for lunch have any taste? Can you describe the gelati you buy every night after dinner in Florence?

Were the rocks on the beach smooth? The wild roses prickly?

And, for heaven's sake, what is that smell?

Find the simplest, most accurate word or words to link your surroundings to the five senses and your description comes alive.

5. Return-transition: Getting from there to here
And now for returning home. This transition can take place over days, not hours. There are the arrangements to check out of the hotel and get to the place of departure (airport, train station, or bus station). There is the checking-in and boarding process, if you are flying or traveling by train. There is the anticlimactic flight (or train or bus or car-ride). There are the farewells to travel com-

panions. There is the necessary mental preparation for re-entry to real life.

Each one of these processes can be fraught with anxiety. "Phooey," said Betty on our return flight from Turkey. "I always forget to put my toothbrush in my carry-on."

"Not me," said her husband John, with chagrin. "But I forget to get out the car keys so I'll have them when we get to Dulles. Now I'll have to unpack the suitcase."

Every time we travel, we learn ways to decrease the stress of the return transition. But remembering what we've learned can be a problem, if I don't write it down in my small spiral notebook. These are the notes I will refer to in my final at-home Journal entry, when I recap the return trip with all its glitches and hints on how-we-coped. I call it, "To remember next time..."

When planning your next trip, it's also useful to include a list of "Most Valuable Things." Again, from the Journey Journal I wrote on the trip to Turkey:

Most Valuable Things
1. Coffee, water-boiler, thermos
2. Canteen
3. Travel clock/Sound machine and eye mask
4. Backpack with security pocket
5. Neck wallet
6. Lonely Planets guidebook (my personal favorite)
7. Face cream and Vaseline
8. Depends/Pepto-Bismol (for Turkey Trots)
9. Kleenex packs
10. Corkscrew
11. Bedtime/airplane books

Note: There is nothing in this list about clothes. In fact, my suitcase sometimes seems so loaded with small appliances that it almost clanks. Carrying a wide variety of clothes is not necessary on most trips, unless you are traveling for business purposes. For destinations with moderate climates, taking a pantsuit with skirt, washable blouses and comfortable shoes, works well for me. Bob takes a blue blazer, lots of tennis shirts, and two pairs of khakis, plus comfortable shoes. Sometimes, he stashes a cotton shirt and tie. We both take sweaters and large anorak-style windbreakers that fit over several layers, should it turn cold.

Now I know this seems spare. But after you've dragged your closetful of clothes through an airport because the wheels of your suitcase fell off, or the handle broke in flight, you'll see the wisdom in packing light. You can almost always buy something to wear on the trip, if you find that you require it.

6. *Reflections*

You are home again. You unpack, check in with family and friends, do the wash, catch up on your sleep, take the film to be developed. Yes, you are home again.

"How was your trip?" you are asked over and over.

"Wonderful." "Fine." "Great." "Glad to be home." "Over too soon." are among your repertoire of responses.

So how *was* your trip? I mean, really? Because you made the effort to write a Journey Journal, you didn't just float through time and space unchanged. You have had experiences. Just what do you make of it all?

Complete your Journey Journal with your reflections, best gathered when the clothes are washed and put away, the souvenirs and gifts have been distributed, and the film developed. Sit down with your Journal and think about the person you are now compared to the person you were before your journey.

Reflections can be minimal:

It was a tour of Russian history. From such a history can these people ever emerge free and independent?

Reflections can be comparative:

Why are sidewalk cafes so appropriate and successful in Paris and so ludicrous in Baltimore? Is it the heat? The pollution? The smell of the traffic? Paris has all of that, even the heat at times. And still people sit, facing the streets, drinking their coffees and aperitifs, and watching the world go by.

I guess that's it. The world doesn't go by in Baltimore. There is nothing and no one to look at here, other than the homeless guy standing on the corner with his sign "Will work for food" and the woman rushing toward her car to put a quarter in the meter before the meter maid shows up.

Reflections can be philosophical:
Looking back on our trip to China, I am struck by what a debt of gratitude the western world owes Mao Tse Tung. Without the ravages of his Cultural Revolution, the industrious intelligent Chinese would clearly be running the world by now.

The Journey Journal

[PART TWO]

[CHAPTER FOUR]

Two Long Journals: Australia/New Zealand and Russia by Riverboat

Australia/New Zealand

The first thing that surprised me: Australia's tropics.

Cairns, Queensland, Australia

It is Sunday, 5:15 a.m. April 13. Our first morning in Australia and we are in Cairns (pronounced "cans") Queensland on the tropical northeast shore. I was unprepared for the "white buildings, lots of palms and bougainvillaea," but only because I hadn't read our Frommer's before landing. I've always pictured Australia as dry and dusty. Not so.

Departure/Transition: This one was unpleasantly memorable.

We flew through an international night: dark from LA to Sydney from 10:30 Thursday to 8 a.m. Saturday with time changes. A 15 hour flight over the international date line. It was awful.

The Quantas 747-400 was so packed that we felt shrink-wrapped, trussed-up for Fed-Ex. The rows were arranged so close together that I couldn't wedge my arm down to retrieve anything from the bag stowed under the seat in front. I could smell the hair of the woman in front of me and when my seat back was released, I lay on the lap of the person behind, wondering if she could smell my hair.

The male flight attendants were the hands-off variety, sailing by lit-up call lights, eyes intent on some distant goal, while passengers flicked at malfunctioning *reading lights and silent headsets. Luckily, both our lights and headsets worked. So we watched two movies and I read through an Elizabeth George mystery. Quantas apparently has only ONE low fat meal in its repertoire: I got it for all five meals served from LA to Sydney. A bouncing ball of smelly steamed fish flanked by smaller balls of mushrooms, all gray. For dinner, breakfast, lunch, lunch, and dinner.*

Quantas, need I mention, was recently privatized. But the flight from Sydney to Cairns was a glimpse of the old pre-deregulated days—a 747-337 (63 fewer seats), clean, new-looking, with cheerful and attentive attendants. We passed the time between flights in a large, quiet transit lounge with complimentary coffee, tea, sodas, and cookies, not to mention television sets and big white bathrooms. This attention to detail improved our surly sleep-deprived moods immeasurably.

Meeting fellow travelers. What are initial impressions? Quick physical descriptions and the act of writing down their names will help me to remember them in the days to come.

About our group: friendly, gray-haired, good-humored couples, one eccentric elderly gentleman named Buddy, whose nose drips and who says unpredictable and peculiar things, and a single black lady, a former nurse named Vendetta (I must get the story behind that name).

These first impressions of a place and people are important to document.

We rode from the airport through mangrove trees growing out of salt water swamps in a shiny new bus driven by "Captain John" and accompanied by our guide, Kathy Samuels Devine. Kathy is a 20-plus year veteran of tour guiding for Grand Circle. She is an American, lives in Hawaii and has been with GC since its inception as a travel agency for AARP. (I didn't know—'til now—that AARP had been started by three women.) Kathy trained as an art historian and had been fired, she told us, from the Pasadena (now Norton Simon) Art Museum for mounting an Andy Warhol Show, just before she was hired by GC.

I suspect we're in for a treat with Kathy. She's funny, friendly, knowledgeable about big and little stuff, and has been in these parts for the past two decades. Another outstanding Grand Circle guide.

A few facts here. With my impressions added.

Back to Cairns. Kathy and Captain John gave us a quick tour of the downtown area. It lies on Trinity Bay (which is part of the Coral Sea and the larger South Pacific Ocean), so named by Captain Cook himself, and retains a small town atmosphere in spite of its having over 100,000 inhabitants.

Cairns is a resort town and many barefoot backpacking teens and twenties and aging wanderers drift around and line up at the banks of public phones. This town is considered "lovely" in guidebook literature. But the center is emblazoned with oversized store signs nearly as big as the stores themselves, multiple t-shirt shops, and souvenir stands. It seems just a mite tacky to me.

So far, Australia is cheerful. Everyone from the customs officer whose black lab leaped happily over our lined-up carry-on baggage searching for drugs, to the rangy redheaded fellow who declared our prunes to be "perfectly fane" for carrying into the country, to the currency exchange lady who called me "dear" (at least, it sounded like "dear") to the bus driver, introduced respectfully by Kathy as "the good Captain John."

There are good-natured smiles all around. In a shop where Bob bought a canvas Aussie hat, the salesman declared, "No tax!" and added, "No tipping either, anywhere in Australia," and everyone in the store grinned and nodded vigorously in agreement.

Weather conditions will interest future readers, including myself.

Cairns is near the rainforest, wet, blue-green and overcast. A light rain was blowing, almost horizontally, in the breeze. It's warm, too. We shed coats and sweaters in our rooms in the Tradewinds Esplanade Hotel, which is located (where else?) on the esplanade which lines the shore in town.

And the rooms are lovely. Dusty rose walls with soft teal blue carpet, off-white painted chairs, desk, bureau, and pink/rose/green flowered drapes and upholstery. The entryway is cool tile and there are plenty of tea and coffee packets, cups, saucers and an electric teakettle on top of a mini-fridge in the closet. Oh, joy. The bathtub is as deep as a coffin and I was in it by 8 p.m., asleep in bed soon after.

More facts. But these are part of the reason Australia is so interesting.

But before ending our first day in Australia, we walked through the town, picking up snacks, beer, wine, and the Aussie hat for Bob. Then to a brief orientation meeting with Kathy. She told us:

- Sydney is at the 45th parallel, below the equator and halfway to Antarctica.
- Cairns was General MacArthur's WWII headquarters.
- More Aussies died in WWII as a percentage of population than any other country's citizens.
- Australia is the world's largest sugar exporter.
- Wool is its #1 export.
- Australia is as large as the U.S. but with only 18 million inhabitants to our 275 million.
- Much of the country is arid; this wet area represents only 1% of the total.
- In the Outback, ranches can encompass more than a million acres but it takes fifty acres to feed a cow.

I found all of this fascinating. Somewhere in the dim recesses of my mind, I had categorized Australia as a kind of Southern Hemisphere America, almost exactly like home. It isn't anything like home.

After our talk, we walked down the street from the hotel to the Returned Service League Club to which Kathy had told us we could buy a one day membership merely by showing our passports. War service people are truly honored here. At 6 p.m., a voice from a loudspeaker asked us to stand and pause for taps. A brief poem was recited (I tried unsuccessfully to get a copy) which concluded with "lest we forget."

Food prices seem reasonable. Bob's fish, my soup and salad cost $16A, about $12 US.

A friendly couple—apple growers from Whitby Island, Washington—went with us, Bill (a retired engineer) and his wife Lael. Very nice pair, good at *conversation. We enjoyed ourselves immensely in spite of jet lag, and the nearly heroic efforts required to keep our eyes open.*

This morning it is raining, the soft gentle rain of yesterday. We are to go to the Great Barrier Reef today. This is a span of 2200 miles of coral reef where we can dive, snorkel or just lay around reading and sunbathing. We've been warned by Kathy and the Grand Circle literature about the strong sun. Even in yesterday's overcast weather, I got a slight red tinge on my face.

Monday, April 14 Cairns, Australia

I wanted to convey the atmosphere of the "Cat." Even its teenaged passengers. surprised us. They were plump, not small and slim, as most Japanese are.

Yesterday, we hopped aboard a "Fast Cat," a speedy bouncy boat which bangs against the waves in a dash to its destination, Green Island on the Great Barrier Reef.

Whoops. Is it kilometers or miles? Big difference.

The 16 (kms or miles?) journey took 45 minutes. Forty-five l-o-n-g stomach heaving minutes. Roving attendants snapped lots of paper vomit bags smartly out of their pockets. They ministered the bags and small cups of ice, placing both firmly in the palest people's shaking hands. Bob and I sat on the deck outside, eyes fixed on the horizon and managed to keep the nausea at bay.

Teenage girls in groups tend to scream everywhere in the world, I guess. And the Japanese teenagers (all girls) on-board were no exception. At first, they howled in delight at the high rolling waves. Then in a yippy kind of anxiety. Then they huddled in miserable silence and white-faced fear, with ministrations from the attendants and those discreet little bags and cups of ice.

These girls are of the age to be plagued with acne. It looked like an epidemic of measles on every fat cheek. They weren't thin, but ranged from lumpy to fat and they seem outfitted for a different day—high-heeled sandals and short skirts and dresses. Those few girls unafflicted with seasickness smiled at us and one asked Bob and me to pose with her friend for a photo. I felt sorry for their rapid descent from their initial whooping joy to misery.

Again, I start with the things I noticed first.

The Great Barrier Reef stretches from Australia up to Indonesia. The underwater coral ridge makes the waves break a quarter to a half mile off the shore of Green Island, a delicate white necklace of foam in the distance. Upon arrival, we walked around the island on a sandy beach, stepping into and out of the clear turquoise blue water with its patches of dark coral.

Going through the day, one step at a time.

Later in the morning we rode out toward the reef in a glass-bottomed boat and peered through its floor. A recent cyclone had stirred the waters and it was cloudy down there, but we could see spaghetti coral waving like hair; brain coral, looking like, well, brains; and coral clumps looking like marbles and bushy coral. The sea was an underground tropical garden of exotic foliage, all coral—white, purple, green. We didn't see any coral coral, strangely.

Our boat attracted a school of terum, along for the feed we were encouraged to throw. The huge fish leaped over each other in and out of the water in their frenzy to get next to us.

Hmmm. I should have written down the names of the fish with white faces and those of the "large fat guys," too.

Back at the pier, we visited the underwater observatory and saw in intimate closeup the exotic angel fish, red bass (whose meat is poisonous here), fish with strange white mask-like faces, and a species of large fat guys with discernible chins, overbites and sharply-snaggled teeth whose faces looked downright familiar. Tiny luminous purple and yellow angel fish darted in and out of their path. The fish floated by in groups of two, three, four. Never a red bass with a terum or a purple angel fish with a yellow one, but only with their own. Like people.

We were mesmerized by this scene and stood watching the sea world go by for at least an hour. Finally we climbed up and out of the little tube-like observatory. It was sunny and warmer now—about 75 degrees, I'd guess. So we changed into our bathing suits and walked down to the beach. Bob swam in the Coral Sea *and I stood watching in the shallow cool water.*

Lunch was outside and buffet-style. The most delicious-looking chicken, fish, beef, rice, salads, and fruit lay in stainless steel pans as we shuffled up, trays in hand. We scooped up spoonsful of each and sat at a table with a couple from Rutland, Vermont and the black woman, Vendetta.

Everything except the fruit tasted like kleenex. Awful. Only the egrets liked it. They stood watch on the top of table-umbrellas, swooping down and scarfing food from unattended plates, while folks were off looking for salt or soy or ketchup or anything to perk up the piles of imitation food.

I write about fellow travelers because they are so much a part of the whole experience. And we were happy to find them so congenial.

The couple from Vermont, Ted and Pat, are friendly and interesting. Ted, whose round open face smiles easily, is a judge back home and Pat is retired Navy. She is tall and slim with a hearty New England look, attractively seamed and tan. Vendetta is from Westchester, NY, traveling alone, also friendly. What a difference from the group on the "Russia by Riverboat" trip!

The couple in the hotel room next to ours is from Odessa, Texas—Ruby and Tom. Ruby is a snappy dresser, suited up today in a red outfit that was downright exuberant. She's cheerful and outgoing and as exuberant as her suit. Already I think of her as a dear lady. Her tall, silent husband lets Ruby do all the talking.

Another eye-catching couple is Faye and Charles. Each widowed, they only recently married and from the looks of things, it's not going well. Ted and Pat, who were on the pre-trip extension to the Outback with the couple, tell us that Charles and Faye don't sit together or even speak because they are feuding. Both are gray-haired, square-jawed and handsome. And tall, each well over six feet. Faye is a retired cop and exudes authority and strength. She's one of those people accustomed to giving service, quick to lend a hand when someone stumbles or looks ill or in need. You get the feeling that she's the one to wave to should you need CPR or the Heimlich Maneuver.

Charles, on the other hand, sits in injured silence, looking out of windows or doors or, at this buffet lunch, at his plate, saying not much to anyone. In the one brief conversation that I had with him, he wanted me to know that he is rich, has a "large portfolio of investments at Smith Barney" and that he has already "had enough of aborigines." I think my sympathies are with Faye here.

A few more words about the surroundings here.

After lunch, we took the guided nature walk on a raised wooden path through the dense foliage and banyan trees. It was offered by the Green Island Resort, which is the private company that manages the pool and restaurant, charging— we see by the posted menu—$10 a hot dog and God knows what for the tasteless buffet food. Thankfully, it was included in the day's tour for us.

The guide pointed out ebony trees, Pandennes palms, other fauna of interest. A recent cyclone (we call them hurricanes) has done lots of damage. Its debris is still being cleared.

We returned to the pier and caught the 4:15 p.m. "Cat" back to Cairns. It was a much quieter ride with the teenagers gone (they had left on the 2:15).

Back in our room, Bob and I had our beer, wine and snacks on the balcony, feet up and marveling at the sight of rain sheeting down on one side of the street and sunny dry sidewalks on the other. We marveled, too, at our continuing good fortune. Looking out at the sea and the sunset under gray and peach-colored clouds, the air warm and moist but breezy, we repeated to ourselves our mantra, "Aren't we the luckiest people on earth?"

Later, we walked the few blocks to Cairns' center and sat at one of the outdoor kebab stands, eating large messy wraps of gyros. Bob's was beef, mine felafel with sauce, tabouli, onion, and tomatoes. It was juicy, tart with hot chili sauce and gone too quickly, in spite of its size. This little dinner cost about $7 US for us both. Still a little off-time, we went to bed by nine o'clock.

Today we ride a train to the Kurando Rainforest in the mountains. According to our itinerary, we will descend in the Skyrail and visit the Tjapukai Aboriginal culture center.

We were impressed by the sponsoring tour company, so I made note here of why.

A word about Grand Circle here. This outstanding trip, with nearly everything included (airfare, hotels, meals, most tours, outstanding guide Kathy, bus trips, and lots of et ceteras) was incredibly reasonable for its high quality. We are amazed at the first class accommodations and wonder, how is this possible for the money? A truly good deal. I love it when that happens.

The survival skills ordinarily required for independent travel are not called upon on a trip like this. There is no need to concern ourselves with bus or train schedules, how or where to buy tickets, what we'll eat and where we'll eat it. Someone else has taken care of those things. So our concentration is limited to getting up on time, and getting breakfast-ed and bathroom-ed before meeting the group in the lobby at 8 a.m.

This is a beginning on "reflections," brief insights which should be noted as they come to mind.

What is my initial impression of Australia? The people we've seen here in Cairns are mostly young, enthusiastic, happy to be Australians. This country is young, settled by European convicts and their keepers shortly after the American Revolution (England could no longer send its prison population to America). The guide at Green Island pointed to a tree and pronounced it "very old" at eighty-five. If there are old people living here, they're staying inside.

There are wide smiles for us everywhere. In speech, a long "a" becomes long "i," and short "e" becomes short "i" as in "You've pied for that alridy" at a shop yesterday.

The all-around good cheer and easy informal courtesy make for a welcoming, warm atmosphere. The tourist is at ease, although the black tourist (I'll have to check this with Vendetta when we know her better) might not be. There are no native black people in sight (a curfew?) and no doubt the local attitude is well-known to African Americans. But white people are given a "you're one of us" feeling unlike anywhere else we've been in Southeast Asia.

Even the souvenirs are unusual.

What is the predominant item sold in tourist shops? A peculiar wooden cylinder—from three to eight feet long. Often heavily carved or decorated, it's called a "didgeridoo" and it's an Aboriginal musical instrument, which makes an odd hol-

low tuneless sound, weirdly catching, almost like a musical foghorn. Lessons are offered everywhere.

I think this is some kind of New Age delight among the backpackers. But how do they pack one of those things? Didgeridoos are costly, too, up to several hundred dollars each.

April 15 Cairns, Australia

These days are so full of activity that I just wrote them, step-by-step, trying to recapture the most memorable moments.

Yesterday was one of those chock-full of doings days. We rode the narrow-gauge railroad, called "vintage" here, to the Kuranda Rain Forest. This trip included a few moments of terror as the train inched forward, swaying slightly and lurching side to side, over 1/4 mile of skinny little trestle high in the sky, spanning the Barron Gorge which looked to be thousands of feet deep.

Kuranda is a tantalizing village of tasteful and pricey shops selling artwork and clothing. We visited a small, well-maintained butterfly farm where we were guided by a young woman scientist from Cairns with limp blonde hair and eyeglasses which kept fogging in the humid air.

More surprising facts. I found this information on butterflies to be fascinating.

The scientist explained the stages of the butterfly's life from egg to caterpillar to pupa to butterfly. This process can take from two weeks to two years and the ensuing life span ranges from three weeks to nine months.

The Ulysses butterfly, with deep iridescent blue-lined black wings, is the area's emblem. Another, called The Orange Cruiser butterfly, was covered with powder, a sign of its youth, said our guide. The butterfly's wings must flap to dry the protective powder, and eventually its wings can't flap anymore. Then it falls from the sky to its death. The Ulysses flaps too much and therefore dies early—its life span a mere three weeks.

The butterflies are attracted to the color red, so most of us tried to find something red in our wardrobes to wear. I struck out, though, having nothing but colorless neutrals at hand. Ruby, resplendent in her two-piece red outfit, was a major hit and was nearly encrusted with butterflies.

We returned from Kuranda on the Sky Rail gondola which skirts over the top of the Rain Forest canopy and was not nearly as terrifying a ride as I expected it to be.

Direct quotes enliven the narrative.

"Sit in the center," counseled Bob.

"Don't look out if it bothers you," said the young man who guided me by elbow into the little car. But, of course, I had to look out, over the expanse of deep-green mountains, and down through the thick forest. We were able to see the vegetation and even the butterflies floating below us.

The gondola made a few stops on the way down from Kuranda so that passengers could get off and walk around in the Rain Forest. At one such stop, we watched a huge python adjusting his bulk around a tree trunk and then we walked on the path to view the Barron Gorge from an overlook. Across the gorge, a waterfall spilling into the valley thousands of feet below looked like a fraying white rope against the rocks.

We stopped at an impressive little museum—its displays explaining the complicated eco system of the Rain Forest—then we re-boarded to ride to the base.

I included this paragraph because it showed what a pleasant guy Milt is and it also made me think about the benefits of traveling light.

On the final leg of the gondola ride, we sat with Milt and his wife, Eleanor. Milt has been wearing the same white t-shirt and khaki pants every day, because his suitcases were lost in transit. He's an even-tempered doctor from California and seems not at all bothered by this loss. "They'll be on our doorstep when we get home, I'll bet," he told us. "And I like not having a lot of stuff with me."

Again, just one event after the other, written down in order. But I could have made this more vivid by noting colors, sounds, etc. And where are the details on lunch? As I recall, it was a huge display of colorful dishes took up most of the dining room.

For lunch, we ate at the Tjapukai Aboriginal Culture Center where we spent the remainder of the day. Now there was an experience—from the Dance Theatre to the demonstration of bush medicine to the short recital of didgeridoo music (an acquired taste which I am acquiring—I bought a CD), to the boomerang and spear throwing opportunities (Bob did both rather well, I thought—all on the video), to the last event which was the viewing of a sad documentary about the near-extinction of the complicated Aboriginal culture by...us or, at least, by white Europeans.

Aborigines were long hunted by white men for sport (as "snipes"), enslaved, addicted, starved, and cheated. Only in recent times are they being acknowledged as an endangered species of people worthy of respect for their art, music, language, and ability to preserve the environment and to survive and flourish in the Outback—a most uncommodious spot.

The Aborigines' existence has been documented to be at least 40,000 years old. I am reading Songlines by Bruce Chatwin and am intrigued by this unique, peculiar, adaptive culture. Lots to learn here.

No last names for Jan, Noel, or George?

Last night we were bussed to Riverwalk, a sugar plantation outside of town, for a splendid fat-laden dinner prepared by a hearty pair of handsome, tanned Aussies named Jan and Noel. On a long buffet table set on their verandah, Jan and her neighbors set out trays of every kind of roast meat, with gravy, chutney, fresh local broccoli, carrots, beans, salads and at least fifteen different homemade cakes and homemade cinnamon ice cream.

We sat at round tables, each with a neighbor or family member to tell us about his/her life in Australia and to ask us about our lives. Isn't that a wonderful feature of the Grand Circle itinerary? Our local dinner partner was George, a retired planter who has moved with his wife to "the city," by which he meant Cairns. He talked about politics ("We have a pretty good thing going here.."), farming ("Too tough, bad weather, glad to be out of it"), the economy ("Not so good right now"). It was a memorable evening.

"What do you worry about?" I asked George.

"Government and taxes," he laughed. Then he added, "Well, not really. We don't worry about much here. We're very lucky."

Indeed they are. But I couldn't help thinking about the documentary we'd seen earlier, the unlucky Tjapukai people struggling to find their place in the late 20th Century. And I remembered the didgeridoo concert. For its finale, in a rather pathetic effort to be with it and appeal to the tourist trade, the four musicians set up two microphones and gathered around them, singing something that reprised each verse with,

"We're proud to be-e-e
Ab-o-ri-gin-eee..."

Instead of remaining unique, exotic, compelling and strange, they morph'd into the ordinary. With this little ditty, they were changed from a first rate Them into a second rate Us.

April 16 Cairns, Australia

More facts. The puzzling and complex philosophy of the Aborigines fascinated me. *Did I say that this country is young? The "Abos" have been here for as many as 100,000 years, living at one with nature, walking on padded feet as animals do, so as not to harm the earth, tilling the land by "fire culture," invisible to strangers, not leaving marks.*

Their music and poetry blend with the rocks, brush, and trees. The land, they say, is covered with "songlines," a topography of tracks legible only to Aborigines. Tribes communicated and co-existed with one another by the markings on their bodies and by understanding the boundaries of their songlines.

Each tribe was ruled by its most respected elders. Children were all taught the same, and treated the same, and each took a place in the society.

Then the Europeans arrived. Too ignorant to read the bodies or to sense the order that existed, the interlopers declared the vast land "terra nulla" and called it their own. The downward spiral in the native inhabitants' culture mirrored that of our own Native Americans. Because they're susceptible to alcohol and drugs and looked upon as inherently inferior ("the missing link" between apes and man) theirs is a sorry lot.

We learned all this from Colin Jones, a riveting Aboriginal speaker, who lectures throughout the world on this nearly-extinct culture. Although he is light-skinned with high cheekbones, narrow nose and lips, he brought with him a young woman with skin the color of coal, and the widely-spaced eyes, broad flat nose and lips common in the "purer" native. She is his relative—niece, I think. He explained his own features by saying that Aborigine can be "bred out" in three generations. His mission is to save his culture and his people from being "bred out."

As a youngster, Mr. Jones was removed from school for having "the potential to learn" and, in his words, for "being cheeky." He learned anyway and, far from being "cheeky," he is pleasant, humorous, articulate, and without anger. A gifted speaker, he is much in demand for his knowledge of Aboriginal culture and history. Kathy told us, "We won't be able to afford him for these talks much longer, I'm afraid."

Fortunately, Aboriginal art and music have become hot items here, both selling for soaring prices. People like Colin Jones are interpreting the complex Aborigine culture and philosophy and finding increased respect. It is a compelling idea—that the huge wasteland called the Outback is not nondescript sand and rock, but can be described and delineated by song. Its inhabitants know every inch of their own space by its poetry. I'd like to learn more about this.

On our last day in Cairns, we were on our own and it turned out to be special. We bought two "day" tickets each on the reliable local bus service (it runs regularly and on time) and took our first trip to the Botanic Gardens. The day was warm and humid under a cloudless, deep-blue sky. The gardens are a tangle of trees, vines, and palms, so intertwined that they looked like scaffolding.

It was difficult to capture this place accurately with words.

The most awesome sight in the Gardens is the Paper Bark Forest, which we entered on a raised wooden path (above damp and often watery forest floor). This is a towering collection of eucalyptus trees, each loosely wrapped with soft papery sheets of bark, which flaps and flakes and occasionally floats to the swampy ground. Bark color ranges from white to pink to clay to deep red. Mangroves and other fauna share the swampy expanse with the Paper Barks. One huge specimen *was hugged so tightly by a "strangler fig" vine that its was nearly unrecognizable as a tree.*

We left the Forest and returned to Cairns Center by public bus. There we hopped onto another bus destined for Palm Grove, north of the city. Bus drivers show great patience here, offering advice on ticket choices, how to reach one's destination, where and when to debark.

Again, initial impressions of a place: What did I notice first?

After a ride of about 45 minutes, the driver called to Bob, "it's 'ere, mate," and we stepped out of the bus and into a little settlement of wooden, pastel-colored buildings on the shores of the Coral Sea. The humid air was cooled by a gentle breeze and spicy-scented from the huge, pink, paper bark eucalyptus trees which shade the houses and main road across from the beach.

Towering palms stood like sentries along the shore side of the narrow road, and beyond them we saw the clean white sand which stretched north and south along the water's edge. The surf floated in without urgency, just a few dainty whitecaps here and there, no crashing around in this south sea haven. No marinas here. No people noises, no car noises, just the wind and those laid-back waves.

We sat at the water's edge, walked along the beach, poked into and out of the one small grocery store. Where is everybody in Palm Grove? This ideal spot for resort-ing was empty of tourists, except for us and a small family of Indians.

The Indian father, dressed in a dark business suit with white shirt and tie, sat stiffly on a bench watching his sari-d wife and small boy (the only one suited up to swim) arranging themselves on a blanket in the sand. They murmured to each other in voices inaudible to us a few feet away. The hush of the town is peaceful, relaxing. I suppose it hops in the season or maybe at night but yesterday Palm Grove was as quiet as a library.

Even the bus slid silently into town. We boarded it an hour or so later and were greeted with an upbeat "Hoi, goys!" from the freckle-faced driver. The return trip took us through lots of little seaside settlements in a southward weave from the highway to shore. Dress is casual in these parts; several passengers boarded barefoot, one in a bathing suit and t-shirt.

We leave Cairns today for Sydney. I'll remember its blue-green water and the Esplanade—the walkway along the town's shore lined with flower gardens, the bright sun and brief showers, the thick foliage on the mountains which stick up in the distance like mossy teeth.

4/17 Sydney, Australia

Found this first comment in a note jotted at the airport. Unimportant except that it does say something about the ambience of the place.

Yesterday at the airport, a thirty-ish blonde woman with two children bid farewell to her parents, the only ones in the party wearing shoes.

Before our flight, we walked on the Esplanade and caught sight of a giant black and white pelican. According to Kathy, Australian pelicans are the largest in the world. This one stood about six feet tall with its bill extended upward and looked like a man in a pelican suit.

The inclusion of a direct quote makes the narrative less dull, I think.

On the way to the airport, Capt. John drove the bus first to the Royal Flying Doctors Service (RFDS) station where we heard a talk and watched a video. This is a most moving and wonderful Australian treasure, a service which flies small planes into the huge desert Outback, to bring back the sick and injured, responding to calls and delivering health care within two hours. The planes are equipped to carry two lying and four sitting patients plus the doctor and nurse.

"See a doc sooner here than back in Sydney," said one fellow on the video we were shown.

Distance learning is also their mission. All this was the brainchild of a Presbyterian minister named Flynn, who wanted to combine the miracle of aerodynamics with medicine and technology. At first, the Service used radio and morse code for citizens to call for and receive help. Communication is now by computer and modem.

The RFDS is credited with the development of the Outback. "No one could live there without this benefit of health care and education," said our guide.

The dispensing of medicine by the RFDS was a challenge to describe, but important to the understanding of the Service.

The Service dispenses to each family a large deep chest of medicine with a lid like a Whitman's (candy) Sampler, a map of its contents. Included is a notebook to account for the medicine's use, two diagrams of the body (front and back), marked off with numbered and lettered squares. The sick or injured person gives the number or letter of "where it hurts" and is directed to the right medicine by its identification number on the lid of the chest.

The RFDS station in Queensland alone receives three emergency calls a day and holds clinics four times every week at different Outback locations. It is supported partly by the government and private corporations; the remainder comes from donations, including proceeds from the little shop attached to the station.

This was all the excuse we needed to swarm through its aisles and buy t-shirts, hats, patches, placemats—all marked with its emblem "RFDS."

The flight to Sydney was a relatively brief three hours. I was served the same low fat meal of boiled fish—less gray and not smelly but still stomach-churning. Well, this is really fine with me. I made do with Bob's roll. We have too many opportunities to overeat on this trip.

Physical description of first impressions.

Sydney. We are staying in the Southern Cross Hotel in a neighborhood of casinos and snooker shops, interspersed with "coffee shops," which are large open rooms full of pool tables and a coffee urn on a stand in the corner. We're a block south of the vast Hyde Park and three blocks east of George Street, which runs through the shopping area and north to "Circular Quay," and The Rocks, the first settlement of the convict population in the late 18th Century.

Just west of Hyde Park is a city block of construction for the new World Center, due for completion by the year 2000, in time for the Olympics.

We walked to the Sydney Returned Service League, which is a six-story building with its own casinos, bistros, night club and restaurant, as well as reasonably priced meals (at $6 for the "special," Monday through Thursday—one might say cheap).

A bakery, Delifrance, with a wallful of homemade breads on display, is on the corner a few blocks west of the hotel, and Chinatown, another block west of that, offers many choices for eating strange cuisine.

The hotel's neighborhood also has its share of adult bookstores, but we felt safe walking around at night. No surly street people muttered at us or anything. The Southern Cross, in spite of its location, is fine; we have a large clean room, double bed, and a little bar area with coffee pot and fixings on a tray next to a toaster. A hairdryer hangs on the bathroom wall and a closet unit divides the bathroom and bar area from the bed, sofa, desk and television set. No view, but who wants to look out on adult bookstores and snooker shops?

Oh, for heaven's sake. Again, no last name? And no name of Gary's shop? This is important information because others might want to visit his store or seek his counsel. Omission was just laziness on my part.

In the evening, we had a lecture from Gary (last name?), a former opal miner and current president of the Opal Miners Association who is an old friend of our guide Kathy. He owns several shops and instructed us on how to choose a stone, to determine its quality, and to assess the reliability of the retailer. I showed him the earring which I had toted all the way from Baltimore. (About thirty years ago, my in-laws gave me a pair of opal earrings as a souvenir from their trip to Australia. Long ago, I lost one and was never able to bring myself to toss the other— it was too beautifully deep blue. So I was hoping to find a suitable mate for it.)

Gary said that my opal earring was what he called either a doublet or triplet: thin layers of opal glued together, strong, but not investment quality. He will make another earring to match and will have it for me tonight—for $80A.

Kathy Samuels Devine guides us in as a professional manner as we've ever seen. Not only does she point us to the currency exchange which doesn't charge commission, but she finds the Garys and the Colin Joneses to speak. She knows just where to look for a particular artist's work, and to whom to speak about it. She has firm friendships all along the itinerary and they pay off in the high level of service that we get. Bob and I agree: we'd follow her anywhere.

In addition to the good nature and authority of our guide, we are with a congenial bunch of fellow travelers—not a clunker in the bunch, unless you count the peculiar, nose-dripping Buddy. He's worn the same mustard colored blazer and green pants since we flew in. Travels light. Sits alone. But he's harmless and, though a terrible joke-teller, fairly inoffensive. That is to say, he's a teller of terrible jokes.

Today we take a bus tour of the city.

4/18 Sydney, Australia

The city is new—the Europeans arrived here as prisoners in the late 18th Century, they were followed up by a more respectable community mid-19th century, and developed Sydney just over one hundred years ago. It reminds me of Toronto or Vancouver—pretty, clean, and white, built by the sea, with both spectacular views and housing prices.

I didn't write much about the Opera House because information on it is in every guidebook. Listing its year of birth, its architect, and its square footage would be boring.

We toured the famous Opera House. Its white-winged roof makes it look like a huge bird nesting at water's edge. The building houses four theatres. But for all its outward drama and size, the individual theatres are small and none seats more than 2700 people. No wonder the ticket prices are high.

I should have included the names of streets in The Rocks.

We ate lunch in the area known as The Rocks, where the convict population first settled upon arrival from England. It's hard to imagine a starker contrast between then and now. Stone buildings with a bloody history have been tarted up into cafes, coffeehouses, and shops with atmospheric prices, and the place is downright cute.

Most restaurants are serving "specials" from $12 - $20 each. At the suggestion of the bartender at the Hotel Orient, we bought takeaway sandwiches at a deli, then returned to his bar for beer and wine, carrying everything on a tray out to the Orient's garden. It was quick and delicious and cheap.

At The Rocks' Information Center, we watched an informative video of Sydney's brutal beginnings and subsequent development; then we walked around the narrow streets, popping in and out of the pricey boutiques.

"Dryzabone" gear, including those extra-long rubbery raincoats suitable for Outback survival, has become fashionable among the set which buys four-wheel drive, off-road vehicles to take their kids to school. A Dryzabone raincoat offers an exotic, slightly-menacing appearance (wearers look like the Jesse James Brothers), comes with its own swagger, and prepares one for monsoons, all at the same time.

So there are lots of those for sale, as well as the broad-brimmed Akubra felt hats for men and the wildly-striped, wildly-colored handknit Oogi sweaters. These items cost many hundreds of dollars each, but the Aussie look is in and no doubt will become more so as the year 2000 Olympic Games come closer.

We walked down George Street from The Rocks to the "QVB," the Queen Victoria Building, a lovingly restored, three-block, brown sandstone behemoth with a stained glass dome, which houses four floors of expensive shops.

Inside, we fell back onto Victorian benches, exhausted from our long walk and from the non-productive shopping, and waited for the famous QVB clock to strike. When it did, we pulled ourselves up and Bob took videos while I shot stills. In the belfry were scenes of British crown history—from William the Conqueror at the Battle of Hastings, to King Henry the Eighth and his wives.

Alas, I can't remember the other scenes, or even if all the wives appeared with Henry, because I didn't write it down at the time. Bad Susan.

Then we dragged ourselves back onto George Street and walked to the new McCafe. This is an upscale McDonald's which sells cappuccino and biscotti. How about that? A glitzy McD's. But it is a sensibly-priced oasis on Sydney's main street (only $1A—about 80 cents—for cappuccino).

Today we go to the Blue Mountains and then to an animal park to see an actual kangaroo at last.

4/19 Sydney, Australia
Yesterday's trip to the Blue Mountains (so-called because of the color of the blan-

keting eucalyptus tree, known locally as a "gum-tree") with a stop for lunch in Leuka (pronounced "loooka") was fun. The mountains only rise to a height of 3400 feet but the deep-green canyons and the rock formation of the Three Sisters are dramatic, especially after the long suburban stretch driving west out of Sydney.

It was hot in Sydney (about 80'), but cool and comfortable in the mountains. Lots of traffic clogged the narrow main streets; there's plenty of construction in anticipation of the Olympics.

I kept puzzling over why these signs made a place look boring and sort of run-down. Finally, I realized it was because of the plain-wrapped-package effect which projected no invitation to explore within.

Leaving town, we passed through an urban sprawl of small, square houses, undistinguished shopping centers and the same large, plain signs with black print that we saw in Cairns. (It's a small thing, but colorful graphics and a variety of print really do add visual interest to a place. I never noticed how much until we came here.)

Our local bus driver, Capt. Bob, kept up a steady patter of information regarding housing prices (high), taxes (30%: "reasonable"), average annual salaries (around $30-$40 thousand per year), Aboriginal fables (e.g., Three Sisters), during the two-hour ride to the Blue Mountains.

It's autumn here, and the leaves of trees in the mountains are turning red and gold. Everything is upside down in Australia—we left budding cherry trees at home.

After pausing at a couple of overlooks and a long photo op-stop at the point where the mountain formation of Three Sisters was most visible, we drove to the village of Leuka and bought sandwiches and drinks, then wandered around for an hour.

I wouldn't have remembered the names of the animals had I not written them down in my notepad.

Capt. Bob drove us from Leuka to the Featherdale Animal Park, a small compound of Australia's peculiar wildlife—kangaroos and wallabees with lots of babies ("joeys"), fat sleepy wambats, snarling Tasmanian Devils, two noble-looking Dingo dogs, an echidna (looks like a porcupine), a cassowary bird (small blue head, huge body), the yellow-masked kites (birds) screeching and tiptoeing around their cages. I'm not a big zoo-fan, but these animals and birds were so weird and wonderful that I was mesmerized by the place.

Returning from the Blue Mountains, traffic into Sydney came to a new standstill. It took thirty minutes to go two blocks. This, according to Capt. Bob, was normal for a Saturday night, when locals pour into the city center. What will they do with the onslaught of Olympic revelers?

Encounters like this next one are best shown, not told about

Back at the hotel, we hooked up with Pat and Ted and walked to Chinatown's Marigold Restaurant, which was recommended by Kathy. Our fine meal was marred by a contretemps with a surly waiter, who charged us for an unordered dish.

"You eat dis food," he said with a pout.

"No. We ate this food," I told him, pointing to the items on the menu. Instead of acquiescing gracefully, he repeated, "You eat dis food!"

"But we ordered and thought we ate this food," said I, again pointing to the menu. We went through another few rounds of this, until the little twit was convinced that we weren't about to pay for his mistake. He flounced away and was replaced by an apologetic hostess. "So sorry," she said, "so sorry" and handed us the corrected bill.

So far, I haven't been tempted to buy anything in Sydney. T-shirts for $30 don't cry out to me and most are in the $29–$50 range. True, some are Aboriginal designs, but pleeeeeze, $50?

Other clothing prices are high, too. For example, coordinated wool blend shirts, tops, etc. at the QVB may represent a terrific concept: Pack a carry-on bag of these flimsies and you'll have enough to wear for three months of any weather, any occasion. But the garments are shapeless and cheaply made—unlined skirts and pants with elastic waistbands and a price of nearly $3000 for the hypothetical three-month trip.

Souvenir boomerangs are $35 and up; didgeridoos can run many hundreds of dollars. Local apples cost about $3.00 (US) a pound and they're in season.

Bob is collecting small pins from each stop for his Aussie hat, around $3.50 each. It's beginning to look pretty impressive and he is the envy of those guys who didn't think of this earlier.

Today, we take the Sydney Harbour cruise in the morning and have the afternoon free. We leave Sydney tomorrow for Christchurch, New Zealand. I must remember to pick up the opal earring at Gary's shop, which is nearby in the Marriott Hotel.

By Golly! We just checked—the water DOES flow counter-clockwise here in the Southern Hemisphere.

4/19 4:15 a.m. Sydney, Australia

Yesterday, our whole group trooped to the monorail station looking like a herd of aging sheep surging around Kathy, who led the way. We rode around twice, like kids on a merry-go-round, then got off at the Harbour and boarded a sleek boat with cloth-covered tables and tea set-ups inside its cabin. The cruise was a satisfying two and a half hours and gave close-up waterside views of the Opera House and The Rocks, and much more.

Back at the pier, we decided to check out Paddy's Market, a Saturday/Sunday-only affair with hundreds and hundreds of stalls inside a huge warehouse building. The stalls predictably sold both good quality things and terrible schlock. We had fun searching out bargain t-shirts (found some for $5, $10), and another pin for Bob.

From there, we strolled over to the extensive and peaceful oasis of the Chinese Garden, a recent gift from a wealthy Chinese businessman, and walked through an outdoor Thailand festival of crafts, food, and a musical performance.

It was warm in the sun. We sat on the grass and listened to the music, drinking water from my canteen and eating bread we'd bought at Delifrance.

Later in the afternoon, I remembered the opal earring and rushed over to the Marriott to retrieve it, a perfect copy. Set next to the old one, we can't tell the difference. I wore them to our gala "Farewell to Sydney" dinner at a restaurant called

Wolfies, which is in an old stone building on the waterfront near The Rocks. Lots of new opals appeared at this party: in ears, around necks and fingers, on lapels. This is definitely a crowd of buyers.

4/21 Christchurch, New Zealand

Remember to write down your initial impressions. They may change radically by the time the trip is over.

First impressions: The land is spectacularly beautiful, but the people are not, at least so far, anyway. New Zealanders do not strike me as the outgoing, friendly, enthusiastic folks who seemed to be everywhere in Australia.

Ted and Pat sat next to a man on the plane who pushed Pat's elbow off the armrest and put his feet under the seat in front of her. When she objected, he snarled, "Get lost" without a hint of irony—our plane was then leveling off at 35,000 feet.

Not a lot of smiling happening here. This is something we probably wouldn't have noticed if Australia hadn't been such a jolly place in contrast.

We landed first in Christchurch on the South Island of New Zealand. Of the two, this island has the more dramatic landscape with the fjords and the Southern Alps mountain range which looked like rows and rows of pointed white teeth from our airplane window.

The city of Christchurch has about 300,000 inhabitants but looks like a large English village—lots of little houses cuddled up together with patches of rose gardens between, and much sloping, slate-roofed architecture. It strongly resembles Miss Marple country.

Our first activity after arrival was to visit the Botanic Gardens. We milled around our guide, Richard, as he pointed out the specimen trees—gum, cedar, redwood and the odd Monkey Pines which look like squat palms but have needles instead of fronds. The fifty-seven acre site lies along the Avon River which flows through the center of Christchurch.

This is included so that I won't forget such emergency items in the future.

The sky was overcast and it looked like fall. Well, it is fall here. I shivered in my linen suit until I remembered the anorak which folds into its own pocket. It was stashed (in case of weather unimaginable back in hot, humid Baltimore) in my backpack along with a pair of those eighty-nine cent stretchy gloves.

The weather in Australia was hot, not uncomfortable but requiring cool dress. Here it is cold. We are lucky that the snow and cold rains of last week have stopped. It looks like November (back home), with late leaves swirling around in shades of rust and gold.

Downtown in Christchurch, the occasional (fake) Elizabethan half-timbered buildings and the red and white-checkered pattern of brick on the public buildings confirm the comment of our bus driver who told us that New Zealand is reputed to be "the most English of England's former colonies."

Yesterday was Sunday, and Richard had come in from his home to guide us. He is an old friend of Kathy's and another example of the advantage of her connections to people in these parts.

Our driver is unknown to Kathy, a mumbler of facts who sent most of us dozing off during the short city tour.

He drove us, also, to Lyttleton Harbor; or, rather, to the mountain tops above it, from which we could see the Harbor and the South Pacific Sea. "Next stop," said Kathy, pointed out to sea, "is Antarctica." In New Zealand, we are at the southernmost spot in the Southern Hemisphere, where the Scott Expeditions and all subsequent Antarctic expeditions have begun.

Last night we ate dinner at a local "carvery" for $24 NZ (the New Zealand dollar is about .70 US). We had two plates piled deep with roast chicken and lamb, carrots, peas, potatoes, and squash, plus two beers and a glass of wine. It all tasted wonderful after Quantas' low-fat meal, the aforementioned gray slab of boiled fish and fishy-tasting et ceteras. Got it again for breakfast. Yum.

This gossipy info, I think, gives context and adds interest to a journal, I think. I wanted to chronicle the group's "personality" in the kindly way Buddy was treated.

We are midway through the trip and finding much camaraderie and joviality among the group. Except for poor Buddy. He seems to be a professional eccentric, intent upon being odd and shocking with stories of his abuse at the hands of his despised mother (the man must be in his late seventies at least) and other tales of woe. Buddy continues to wear the same mustard colored jacket, green pants, tie, rayon print shirt (ripe after ten days) and dainty little scuffed brown oxfords, daily. He tests Kathy's good nature with his constant whining and complaints and sits alone on the bus. Several people have tried to have normal conversations with him...and failed. (I am not one of those good souls. I find him extremely irritating.)

As to the growing congeniality among the rest of the people, it helps that Kathy encourages us all to wear our Grand Circle name tags; we can address each other by name and that is a surefire way to feel more friendly.

Last night we went to the church service at the Anglican Cathedral in the center of town. Kathy had told us about the 7 p.m. contemporary service with music, so a bunch of us walked over from Noahs Hotel, where we are staying, and sat together.

Like all cathedrals, this one felt like an airplane hangar to me. The jolly woman curate spoke clearly, but the priest was nearly incomprehensible, so I'm not sure what the sermon was about. The music came from a local choir and was standard church fare, but with exceptionally good voices.

April 22 Christchurch, New Zealand

This was a free day, which began with a brief walking tour behind Kathy, orienting us to the location of Noahs Hotel (central) and the Avon, a narrow winding river lined with weeping willows. She told us that later in the day, there will be punters in straw hats digging into the water with tall single oars, moving their narrow boats along the river. It will look, Kathy said, like a scene in Cambridge or Oxford in England. Our tour stopped at the shopping area around Cathedral Square.

Ted, Pat, Bob and I decided to walk to the Museum at the edge of the Botanic Gardens to view its Antarctic room. This was a compact, well-displayed exhibit of artifacts from the Scott Expeditions, the sad details of which were supplied by a ruddy-faced and voluble guide. Scott was in a race to the South Pole with the

Norwegian Amundsen. The guide filled us in on some back story. "I've been reading Amundsen's book," he said. "Contains all his notes and letters."

I thought this information from the guide made the exhibit much more interesting. It's the kind of story that makes me want to learn more about the events.

Scott, he said, was "a bit arrogant," an upperclass British officer who enjoyed both hero's stature as well as movie star good-looks. He left home a day after his only child, a son, was born and embarked on his ill-fated expedition to the South Pole. Scott had no expertise in skiing, used horses to pull the gear, and was foolishly unprepared for the dangers of the journey. He packed provisions for four people but required a fifth non-officer to accompany them because none of the four knew how to tie knots or do other practical wilderness-types of things.

Of course, the Norwegian Amundsen made it to the Pole first. He used dogs to pull the sleds, then ate them. He knew how to ski. In a letter home, Amundsen described Scott as "inept."

He and his entire party perished.

Back in the town's center, we wandered the shopping streets and found prices to be high. The ubiquitous woolen sweaters cost hundreds of dollars. A paperback book well-reviewed in the morning paper was selling for $24 NZ, about $18 US. The clerk brushed aside my surprise, saying, "It's the same price you'd pay in your country." She looked doubtful when I told her we'd pay less than half that amount.

In Cathedral Square, vendors hawked gyros, hot and cold drinks, and ice cream treats. A juggler occupied the attentions of a group of young children and a musician played his guitar, seated on a fold-up stool, his case open at his feet for contributions.

I was feeling dreary and decided to go back and soak in the tub at Noahs. Bob chose to ride the little trolley which leaves from Cathedral Square and tools around the city. He reported later that, indeed, the punters were on the Avon and looked picturesque as well as cold.

4/23 Queenstown, NZ

With all the hacking and sneezing going on, it was inevitable that I would catch the "Group Cold." In spite of extensive vitamin intake, my throat grew raw. I slept badly last night; none of my potions worked.

Yesterday, we rode the bus with Capt. Dave McDonald, from Christchurch to Mount Cook for lunch and then on to Queenstown. The ride took us through flatland plains that stretched neat and green for miles, squared off by thick hedgerows and an occasional square of dense pine forest.

Sheep grazed everywhere, cows and domesticated deer, too, both raised for food. Agriculture is highly developed, the largest industry in New Zealand. But the wool industry, Dave said, is on the decline. With such enormous prices, no wonder.

It has already snowed in the mountains and the air was cool yesterday. Glaciers were visible in the distance. We rode past a small airport and a huge lake, empty of people, boats, houses. No signs of life at all. Our bus was temporarily halted by a flock of sheep and its shepherd, then we moved on to the Hermitage, a famous hostelry with an unobstructed view of Mount Cook, at 12,348 feet New Zealand's tallest. Everything looks sharper-edged here, more brightly-colored and clear, the result of un-polluted air.

At the Hermitage, we ate a huge buffet lunch. A few days after our visit, a "cyclone" closed the road and blew out the windows of the small airport. Guests at the Hermitage were confined to quarters, we heard.

I sat next to Ruby and asked her about her family. "Tom and I had six children," she said. "Two were mine, both adopted. And four were Tom's." I wondered at her use of the past tense. She paused, looked down at her plate and then off into the distance.

"My daughter was murdered in 1978 by a jealous boyfriend," she said in a low voice. Her daughter's body had lain undiscovered for a year, until the murderer led police to the grave, Ruby went on to say.

"Tom's youngest daughter died two years ago of breast cancer. She left two kids." Later, Ruby gave me a sheaf of papers which she carries with her on her travels. It is their daughter's life story as told to a friend while she was dying of

cancer. I wrote down the poem with which the story ended. Its author is unknown.
> *"Do not stand at my grave and weep.*
> *I am not there, I do not sleep.*
> *I am a thousand winds that blow.*
> *I am the diamond glints in the snow.*
> *I am the sunlight on ripened grain*
> *I am the gentle autumn's rain*
> *When you awaken in the morning hush,*
> *I am the swift, uplifting rush*
> *Of quiet birds in circled flight.*
> *I am the soft star that shines at night*
> *Do not stand at my grave and cry*
> *I am not there; I did not die."*

4/24 Queenstown, New Zealand

Our hotel, the Lakeland, sits on the Esplanade overlooking Lake Watapaki. Our room is large and clean, with new-looking, nondescript furniture and the ever-present electric water boiler for tea and coffee.

I had a hard time communicating the drama of the New Zealand landscape. My words were simply inadequate to the job. So I gave up trying to write the perfect word picture and did what I could.

Yesterday we took a boat trip of about forty minutes across Lake Watapaki to Walter Peak, which is a sheep station on the lake's western shore. This was the best of touring experiences: unusual, visually stunning, memorable.

Along the opposite shore, the Remarkable Mountains jut straight up out of the water like skyscrapers. We were told that the herd of 25,000 Merino sheep graze high on these mountains in the summer, low in the winter. They must have hooves like suction cups to stay grazing at that angle.

At the sheep station, a rambling one-story homestead has been converted to a restaurant available only for catered affairs. Next to it is the pretty white cottage of the station's manager, a hearty, ruddy-faced fellow named George. His wife, George told us, tends the thicket of roses and he watches out for the trees and shrubs, as well as caring for and shearing the sheep.

We got a quick demonstration of his skill. While carrying on a running conversation, George flipped one large fellow on its side, whipped out an electric razor, and stripped it of its coat in about five minutes flat.

Back in the paddock, George promised that his border collie, Jill, would demonstrate her skills at rounding up stray sheep. He muttered a few words to Jill, who listened raptly, then turned and trotted off. She was soon out of sight. We watched the distance where she had disappeared.

Time passed. George chatted on. No Jill. We were getting embarrassed for George. Jill, it seemed, had taken off for parts unknown. Then, about eight to ten minutes after she had been sent on her mission, a small crowd of eight sheep scurried out from behind a distant clump of trees, skittering nervously this way and that. Even at our distance, we could tell that they looked worried.

Behind them, running back and forth, concentrating her gaze at their hooves, was little Jill.

She brought her quarry home to our enthusiastic applause, though George gave her only a pat on the head. "Don't you give her a treat, or some kind of reward?" someone asked.

"These dogs don't need a reward to work," said George. "In fact, we have to be careful or they'd work themselves to death. Loyal and hardworking to a fault, they are," he told us. "The border collie is the only reason that New Zealand was able to develop a sheep industry."

After tea and cakes with clotted cream, served up in the homestead, we returned by boat to the pier across the water. Queenstown is a resort town with auto-free shopping streets, boats moored in the town center's marina, hawkers selling bungee-jumps and jet-boat rides (even during the off-season of autumn), tea shops and restaurants. We loved it.

Bob bought a handmade white wool sweater for his friend Peter, who is watching Bob's accounts while we're away. I bought a rain-resistant suede hat, called a "squashy," which folds into nothing and fits inside its own small bag.

Today we take a long journey to Milford Sound. Snow is predicted in the following fashion by the local radio station, "Snow today, down to 500 meters." Translation: From the elevation of 500 meters on up, snow will fall, and we will be considerably higher than 500 meters high.

4/25 Queenstown, New Zealand

Once again, words are inadequate...but all I've got.
It is surely a challenge to find the words to describe yesterday's sights. Standing on the deck of the cruise boat, our faces damp from the spray of the cascading Fairy Falls, one of our group named Otto said, "For years I've heard people say that New Zealand is beautiful, but they never said why..."

We arrived at Milford Sound after four hours through the Remarkable Mountains. Our journey was punctuated by our astounded "oh"s and "ah"s, and "did you see that?"s. Everywhere we looked, there was a photo-worthy sight. We passed long blue lakes, the glassy Mirror Pond in the Wetlands, steep gorges, quiet streams, roaring rivers. The adjectives were flying around like the harrier hawks overhead.

The bus ahead of us looked like a matchbox toy in the distance as it wound around the hairpin curves descending from the mountain. Nature is big here. The topography on this South Island of New Zealand is so dramatic and so compact. It's as if a giant hand had gathered these awesome sights together and squished them into this small space.

At Milford Sound, we boarded the Red Boat cruises and sailed out into the fjords leading to the Tasman Sea. The air was cold and misty. The sky, streaked with swiftly moving clouds, almost disappeared from sight as the cliffs rose on either side of our little boat. We moved slowly through the deep black water in the crotch of the steep canyons.

On bare rocks jutting out of the water near the cliffs, we saw seals and walrus flopped and sleeping. The little boat was able to maneuver close to the rock walls for a damp view of the waterfall crashing down from hundreds of feet overhead, and it was there that Otto made his statement.

Milford Sound is the sort of place that, if it were set to music, it would be something impressive and classic, like Mahler or Beethoven. All parts of the orchestra would participate, from kettle drums to cellos to every kind of wind instrument to harps to...is this making sense?

The light of the day had nearly disappeared by the time we boarded our bus for the ride back to Queenstown. After a pit stop at Te Ainu, where we bought sandwiches and sodas, Kathy popped a videotape of "The Man from Snowy River" into the overhead player at the front of the bus. The film stars Kirk Douglas and was filmed in Australia. All the actors wore Dryzabone coats and Akubra hats and rode in spectacular scenery, but nothing was as gorgeous as the scene fading from view outside of our bus windows.

4/26 Ian and Betty MacCarthy's house, Queenstown, New Zealand

Here I go again, omitting important details like FULL names because I was too lethargic to check it out. What will I do with me?

Yesterday was ANZAC Day, a memorial day to the soldiers who fought at Gallipoli in World War I. We watched a celebration on television early in the morning before breakfast. ANZAC is an acronym for Australia New Zealand Allied Something, but exactly what I can't remember. (Perhaps the missing word is "Cause" or "Command".)

We began the day yesterday by packing, ironing (there is a laundry room near ours in the Lakeland Hotel), eating breakfast in the large buffet dining room and then walking the few blocks to town for the famous gondola ride up the green rocky side of Bob's Peak. Yes, the sight to see here, along with all the other sense-assaulting wonders, is a view from the top of "Bob's Peak," which you reach via another Skyline Gondola.

And it might have been so, had not the fog crept in during the night and stayed. The ride was, therefore, not harrowing at all, since I couldn't see anything but craggy rocks and green shrubs clinging to them.

At the top, in the restaurant/shop/theatre, we were shown a marvelous 30-minute video entitled "Kiwi Magic," highlighting the scenic wonders of New

Zealand, including the stomach-churning "shotover jet" ride, which some of our party took. (This is a nerve-shattering zip through narrow chasms of a raging river, with enough 300' turns and near-death experiences to make at least one member lose her lunch. I'm glad I passed—didn't sound like fun to me.)

After lunch, we all stood around the lobby waiting for our assigned hosts to arrive for our "home-hosted stay." Grand Circle and Kathy arranged for us all to be dinner and overnight guests at various homes, in and around Queenstown. It was like a group blind date. The houses are apparently large enough to accommodate two rooms of guests because we were assigned to Ian and Betty Mac-Carthy along with two jolly sisters from California, Dora and Enid.

Enid is a chiropractor, widowed with grown children. Dora's husband doesn't like to travel so she and her sister take trips together. Both are curious, friendly, outgoing, and good-natured. Bob and I were relieved at being matched with them.

The two big, largely-unspoken questions among us were: Who will go with Buddy? And will Faye and Charles go quietly or feuding? As it happened, Kathy had arranged for a sober-sided doctor and his wife to accompany Buddy to the home. Buddy belongs in a Home! And Charles and Faye seem to have patched things up for the moment.

The MacCarthys are former sheep-farmers who still own their farm but others now manage it. Betty tends a healthy, prolific garden which rings this split level house on a hill overlooking Queenstown. Even now, in late Autumn, her garden blooms red, pink, and yellow with roses. Both Betty and Ian appear to be in their late sixties. Both are rosy-cheeked and sturdy-looking.

Bob and I had bought a fine local wine for our hosts. To our dismay, it was stashed away upon arrival and a sweet Mogen David-like brew was served instead. Betty bustled about the kitchen. "No, no, you talk to Ian. I've got this under control!" she called in answer to our repeated requests to help.

Talking to Ian was a challenge. He is pretty close to stone-deaf and speaks in a thickly-accented mumble. Who knows what we talked about? Or Ian talked about, while we stared hard at his mouth and tried to figure out what he was saying.

It was pretty clear why Betty encouraged these events. First of all, we found out that they get paid for hosting us. (And why not? I'm sure the meal was expensive to prepare. But knowing this made the strong encouragement to bring gifts seem inappropriate.) But more important, she had people to talk to and who would talk to Ian. Or at least, to listen to Ian.

The meal was meat and potatoes in gravy, vegetables in sauce, buttered rolls and a dessert blanketed with sweetened whipped cream. Heavy? You bet. So why aren't Ian and Betty?

Enid and Dora shared a room upstairs while we were ushered to a suite in the lower level of bedroom, bathroom, and office. I had plenty of space to boil the water and make my coffee this a.m., but blew a fuse doing it.

Back at the Lakeland Hotel, we boarded the bus for the cute little Queenstown Airport. Bob was annoyed with me—furious is more accurate—for getting in line and boarding as soon as we were able. For reasons I never understand, he likes to hang back and board just before the doors close. Maybe it's his version of living on the edge, pushing the envelope, whatever. In any case, we agreed to hold our own boarding passes and meet at the seats, which I like to get to before all the overhead space is taken by those folks moving three-room houses in their carry-on luggage.

4/27 Auckland, New Zealand

First impression time, again.

We are in the stately, red marble Carlton Hotel on Mayoral Drive in downtown Auckland on the North Island of New Zealand, directly across from the Music Center. Auckland is New Zealand's largest city—one and a half million people— and a stark contrast to cozy Queenstown and the village atmosphere of Christchurch.

The land here is flat and, after the astonishing terrain of the South Island, pretty dull.

Our room is luxurious, capped off by a marble bathroom of awesome size and splendor. I love a tub that scrubs six, and the addition of a phone (with dual lines and hold buttons) evokes an image of important deals being consummated while one performs ablutions. The bathroom's best missing feature: A scale.

I loved this scene of "Mother" losing her cool. It describes Buddy better than anything I have said so far.

Buddy has driven one of our group around the bend. The sweet little lady, whose husband calls her "Mother," turned on him in rage today when he refused to leave his aisle seat on the plane, blocking her exit to the bathroom. She reached under her seat, retrieved her pocketbook, and slammed him over the head with it. By Auckland, as the story moved swiftly through the plane, she had achieved heroine status.

Buddy was pouting so badly that at the airport, he refused to move his suitcase to the bus. Bob walked over to him, leaned down and snarled, "Get that bag on the bus and do it now." At this, he moved quickly. Kathy thanked Bob profusely. How does she stand it?

I've been thinking how much the success of a trip like this depends on the tour's guide. We know from experience that you can have a non-congenial group of fellow passengers and still enjoy a trip if the guide is good. Kathy has done so much extra for us. She photocopied recipes from the Riverwalk plantation dinner near Cairns. She bought us boxes of local "biscuits" (cookies). She prepared sheets of information for every stop, called "Fast Facts." She found us city maps and included tour stops not on the itinerary.

Kathy has been especially sensitive to bathroom needs, stopping the bus whenever necessary. (On our way to Milford Sound, Capt. Dave stopped for one poor guy who has prostate problems. He had to scuttle off into the woods but was obviously relieved and grateful.) She's authoritative, too. Whenever she sensed group sleepiness on the bus, she declared "rest time," and doused the bus lights or just retired to her seat by Capt. Dave.

She has been kind to Buddy, in spite of his provocations, when I know she'd rather he take a bungee jump to hell. Her advice on currency and shopping and eating has been sound, accurate, and sensitive.

And best of all, Kathy is very funny. Witty in an ironic way, not a joke-teller.

We laughed and laughed, up and down Australia and through the South Island of New Zealand.

April 28 Auckland, New Zealand

A few random facts here.
Auckland reminds us that New Zealand is a prosperous country. This hasn't always been so. When Britain entered the European Economic Community (EEC), it took trade away from New Zealand and gave it to its fellow EEC members, which threw this little country into a kind of economic depression. It is still recovering from that blow by diversifying its agricultural exports (e.g. raising domestic deer—venison—for the German market) and beefing up tourism.

Auckland bustles. Shiny glass buildings stick up like reeds along the waterfront. Stores and sidewalks are crowded with shoppers and the harbour is dense with boats, small, medium and large. Actually, there are two harbours—one on the South Pacific Ocean, the other on the Tasman Sea. This, according to Kathy, makes for unpredictable wind currents and rapidly changing weather patterns.

The Maori (pronounced "mow-ree") population, at 80,000, is outnumbered by the Polynesian (90,000). In the whole country, only 300,000 Maoris remain. None are pure Maori. All have mixed-blood from intermarriage.

Last night we visited a "marae," which is a Maori village, named Te Ngira. With advanced tutoring we went through the required "challenge ceremony" in order to enter the village lodge.

We chose the magisterial Charles to be our "chief." He took the role seriously and went through the greeting phase with aplomb. The welcoming party sang to us and we responded with a shaky rendition of "God Bless America," which I found moving in spite of our poor command of the lyrics.

Susan, Susan, Susan—you didn't get the NAME of the CHIEF? Or her husband?
The chief was a handsome dark-haired woman (don't you love it?) of about sixty who wore a long purple velvet dress and a large greenstone pendant around her neck. She and her husband are tall and equally handsome. As we watched a

small group of young people perform traditional dances, they stood regally. We then filed by and touched foreheads with each—the local handshake.

Dinner was cooked in the backyard. Actually, I should say that, in the backyard, a hapless pig was buried in the ground and fired up for barbecue. We ate it at trestle tables along with peas, corn, pumpkin and potatoes, homemade salads and cakes. The chief and her husband oversaw the meal, replacing dishes and serving drinks of water and lemonade.

I suspect the chief's spouse isn't altogether supportive of the whole native-thing. As she removed her shoes for entrance into the lodge, he muttered to Ruby, "It's barbaric to make you do that."

We talked later at length with the pair. Why didn't I get their names? At departure time, she gave me a hug—not the forehead-pressing but your standard arms-around hug.

Before leaving, we were led to a small glass case of local crafts, priced ridiculously low compared to prices in town. The chief explained, apologetically, that this little "shop" helped fund some of the activities of the community. We swept through like locusts, nearly depleting the entire cabinet of goods.

I bought a thick square of greenstone hanging on a black cord. "That's wha' oi call 'the choc'late box,'" said the woman behind the counter. 'Idn't it just loik a choc'late box, dearie? Sweet, idn't it?" Bob bought a little hand-carved tiki statue, which looks like a short totem pole. Both cost about $42 US.

About the New Zealand accent: It's spoken through clenched teeth, words squeezed out so that "yes" becomes "yis" and "no" is "noy." It's kind of like Cockney but easier to understand. The word "marae," the Chief explained, "is spilled em, eye, air, eye, ee."

This was not the glitzy evening of professional native dance that some of us expected, but a simpler, church-supper kind of night. It was this Maori village's way of welcoming us into their lives for a couple of hours, and sharing their culture. We enjoyed it a lot.

The following Journey Journal passage answers two of the most basic questions— "what happened" and "what happened next?"

This morning, most of the group went off to see Rotorua. We abstained and, mark my words, it will turn out to be the "best field trip yet." "You didn't miss Rotorua, did you?" I can hear the incredulity now. But eight and a half hours in the bus to view glow worms and thermal rock for about thirty minutes each just didn't appeal to us.

We want to ride the ferry to one of the small islands, visit the street markets, and possibly revisit the museum. On yesterday's tour, I saw everything from stuffed birds to a reconstructed marae but missed the second floor World Wars exhibit that Bob said was terrific.

We have also begun to search in earnest for a medium-sized "squashy" for Bob. That's the suede bush hat that folds up into its own small bag. Mine had been the envy of many, and squashies are showing up on heads all around. We haven't been able to find Bob's size, though he lusts after one himself. Today might be the day.

Yesterday, during our city tour, we visited Kelly Tarlton's Antarctic Encounter and Underwater World. This sounds hokey, but it isn't, or maybe I just like "hokey." Inside the building, which is in an old water and sewer facility, is a detailed reconstruction of the ill-fated Scott's encampment in the Antarctic. After walking through it, we rode in snowmobiles through ice-packed rooms of cute penguins, splashing and hopping and waiting for their lunch. Then we stepped onto a moving staircase. This glided us through a plexiglass tub around which swam fish of all stripes, including sharks and rays. We thought the place was wonderful.

The tour took us through Albert Park and into the aforementioned museum, as well as around snazzy neighborhoods of multimillion-dollar homes and down to Waitemata Harbour.

In the morning paper, we see that there is an opportunity to sign up for "Urban Rap Jumping" from the high-rise Novotel a few blocks from our hotel. This is a 50 meter rappel down the side of the building—walking, hopping, or diving bungee-style. What can you say about a tourist population so bored that it turns to this kind of stunt for recreation? New Zealand is full of these treats. Remember the Shotover Jet Rides? (Did I mention that we stopped at the Queenstown bridge where the very first lunatic—back in the eighties, I think it was—hooked his heel to a bungee cord and leaped off?)

4/29 Auckland, New Zealand

This is our last day in New Zealand. I'm so glad we elected not to go to Rotorua. The group didn't return until 8 p.m. Most restaurants and all stores close by 5:30 p.m., so people had nowhere to go to eat. Their tales of the long journey were not full of joy, either. We had a lovely day.

We got up late, walked to the nearby casino to change money and then on to the Victoria Market. Bob bought a belt with a kiwi (the bird, not the fruit) on the silver buckle; I got some greenstone (nephrite) earrings to match the Maori pendant. Imagine my pleasure when at least two salespeople fingered my necklace and murmured, "Very nice. Very nice. A good piece of jade. Where did you find this?"

We walked from the Market to the waterfront, popping in and out of stores searching for the squashy hat for Bob. None to be found in size medium. At the water, we hopped onto a waiting ferry (a "fast cat") and sped through the blue water into the vast harbor, past many green islands. Our destination: someplace called Waikeki Island.

The weather alternated rapidly from cloudy to rainy to sunny to warm to cool. I pointed one out to a little girl. She glanced at it and said, "Oh, yeah. The end is over there," casually waving over her shoulder. Rainbows occur with such frequency that they don't bear mentioning here.

After a forty-minute ride, we embarked at a deserted pier, next to a parking lot crowded with cars. A sign read, "Your fellow Waikeki Islanders are parked here. Please do not pinch their petrol." We walked up the hill to a small village of wooden buildings housing real estate offices, down-at-the-heel cafes, and souvenir shops. Handwritten notes like those you find on refrigerator doors at home were taped to doors and walls and community bulletin boards, advertising "end of season sale," "off-season rental," "palms read," "second hand book sale."

The populace seemed to be Aging Hippy: Women with graying hair in long flowing tie-dyed garments and Birkenstocks; gray-bearded men in heavy handknit sweaters with leather-patched elbows. Very Cape Cod. Very Maine. They look sort of intrepid, the kind who flourish in the off-season cold. Seaside hearties who stay the winter after the weenies have gone home.

Using dialogue makes trip scenes—like this next one—more real.

At the nearly deserted information center, Bob went off in search of a men's room. I waited next to a sign that advertised "Antique Musical Instrument Museum." Peeking inside, I saw a large room of organs, pianos, and harpsichords with about twenty folding chairs set up on the available floor space.

A tall thin man with a narrow bearded face hurried up to me and asked, "Are you here for our performance?" in a hopeful tone. I shook my head. He turned back and said to the air, "Who'd have thought that no one would come. Ah, well." As he closed the door, he added, "We've got one person anyway. So we'll give it a go."

I was all set to give it a go with him, but the $7 each price tag and Bob's reluctance to be the sole audience (plus that "one") discouraged me. Also, it was time to return to the pier and catch our Cat home. We walked back down the hill.

In Auckland, there was still plenty of shopping-time left, so we began to search for the squashy. We hit the mother lode in a small shop at the Centra Hotel. Shelf after shelf were piled high with suede hats and, sure enough, many were "medium" sized. Bob snatched up a hat, put it on his head, and the clerk and I both began to giggle uncontrollably. He looked like Buster Keaton in a porkpie, not my handsome Bob at all.

"We have lee-tha, too," said the proprietress, helpfully. It looked considerably better, but Bob, put off by our hilarity, said no. His heart had been set on a squashy.

April 30 Korolevu, Fiji
Here we are at the free, post-trip extension in Fiji, which is a collection of three

hundred islands that are a part of Micronesia. It has been raining here for days. A mud slide killed three people on the other side of this, the largest island.

We crossed a bridge to get to our hotel, the Warwick Fiji on the Queens Road, about an hour from the Nadi airport. That bridge, Kathy told us, is frequently closed due to heavy rains. To our relief, she also pointed to a newly constructed bridge that opens officially tomorrow, replacing the old, unreliable one. The weather report promises more rain and we're due to fly out on Sunday, crossing (we hope) that bridge when we come to it.

Television technology has just arrived in Fiji, about two weeks ago. With four days of possible rainstorms ahead, it's comforting to know we can tune into CNN and the local channel, which features Japanese documentaries on nature and old "Leave it to Beaver" re-runs.

Our room has a balcony overlooking green lawns and the swimming pool, with the sea just beyond. It's a lush and tropical scene, with tall palms, deep green hedges, and fragrant white flowers everywhere.

Reminder: Noting the actual names of flora and fauna would have made reading about them more interesting AND educational.

Kathy had suggested a stop at the grocery in Nadi to load up on snacks and soda for our stay, there being no such place around here. I hurried up the street to a currency exchange and traded New Zealand dollars for Fiji dollars. I think I had about $50 US in Fiji money.

We fanned out in the stifling hot, low-ceilinged grocery store, pushing our carts past displays of unfamiliar foods. In spite of the strangeness of the goods for sale, nearly everyone found something to buy. We got some salty snacks, beer, coke, and apples and stashed them all in the room's mini-bar fridge.

We have today, tomorrow, and Thursday here to read, swim (in the warm rain—why not?), walk on the beach, and think about re-entry. We're winding down now and thinking about home. Three weeks is long enough to be away.

With no sightseeing scheduled, I am able to write more about the people I encounter, and even the seemingly insignificant stuff of day-t-day travel.

May 1 Kovelu, Fiji

Did I mention that it is raining? Rained all day, all night, and still it rains. It has been raining for three full weeks. Kathy is concerned that the road itself will wash out at low spots between here and the new bridge. She is resourceful, so I know we're in good hands.

The air is warm and everything is dripping. But we can sit comfortably on the balcony under an overhanging roof and read our books and drink tea.

Yesterday, there was an explosion of shopping at Jack's, a little emporium inside the hotel. Someone—I think it was Ron Gliot—discovered that its prices are reasonable and we all descended, wallets in hand. Such is our boredom that I bought three large bags of souvenirs including hand-carved bowls, tapa (which is actually a printed paper made locally) cloth purses and t-shirts. It was the highlight of the day.

Down the hall from Jack's is a clothing store called Tiki Togs, which are designed and made here on the premises. I bought a cool cotton sleeveless dress and wore it right out of the store.

Buddy is wandering the hotel lobby, playing the eccentric, but nobody is paying any attention to him. It goes without saying: He's wearing the same rumpled outfit, and it reeks after three weeks of travel.

Confinement has re-created the rift between Faye and Charles. Charles sat in the lobby reading his paperback during most of yesterday. Faye moved into a room of her own, down the hall from us, in the late afternoon.

Earlier in the day, Faye was called upon to rescue a bird hopping helplessly on the beach with its little legs tied together by drinking straws—somebody's idea of a good time. Who else but Faye would you think of in such a crisis? She strode off, happy to be of use, but by then, the bird had hopped out of sight.

"Soozahn," said my new friend Vinny, the saleslady at Tiki Togs, "Vinny is not saying this because she wants to sell dresses, Soozahn. But Tiki Togs are worn by our Fiji leaders and by the ladies of our leaders to big big events, Soozahn."

Her voice is soft and her smile is gentle. She folds piles of newly arrived men's shirts as she speaks. "Only can they buy them here, Soozahn. Nowhere else on Fiji."

May 2 Korelevu, Fiji
Today we can see a hint of blue between long strips of gray in the sky. The breeze has turned into a stiff wind and seems to be blowing the weather out to sea—not a moment too soon, as roads are washing away and more mudslides were reported on last night's local news.

After dinner, our group milled around the lobby for a while, then trooped into the large ballroom to see the Culture Show. We sat at round tables and waited and waited and waited.

We were there for more than an hour, listening to a four-piece ensemble seated on the floor in front of us play the same medley of songs over and over.

There is a local drink served here, called kava, which has some tranquilizing effects and tastes a lot like milk of magnesia. It is made of pounded (used to be chewed) root with water added; the pulpy root is then strained through a cloth.

Next to the ensemble, a man sat straining a huge cauldron of kava. It looked for all the world like he was washing out his underwear. Cups of the noxious stuff were passed but there were few takers.

This resort is a little loose around the edges, results of both the recent storms and the generally laid-back Fijian attitude. The people are worth any minor inconvenience, though. From my favorite, Vinny ("Where is Soozahn?" she called to Bob yesterday from inside her shop), to folks tending the coffeeshop and Jack's Emporium, to the attendants on the front desk. Happy smiles, soft voices, calls of "Bula!" ("good morning," "good afternoon," "good evening," whatever) said with genuine pleasure each day. The men are handsome and helpful; the women competent and motherly. All are dignified and have great posture. I'd come back to this place in a flash, in spite of the weather.

Finally, the participants in last night's show arrived. It was an entire village of men, women, and children bedecked in flowers, tapa cloth and grass skirts. A contingent of small boys performed a dance with spears and clubs—I can only imagine the chaos trying to rehearse that one. The others sang and danced with enthusiasm for the next 45 minutes. Everything ended up cheerfully with the final song, a Micronesian farewell, bringing tears to Kathy's eyes. "My favorite," she said in explanation. "I always hate to leave Fiji."

May 3 Korolevo, Fiji

Last night we had our Farewell Dinner at the small structure called locally a "bure," a thatched-roof hut which stands at the end of a short rock causeway on a tiny island in front of the hotel. It was a grand affair in spite of the wet weather. We sat at long tables and laughed loudly, taking each other's picture, writing down addresses, and drinking and eating tray after tray of food.

Ruby and Tom showed up in Full Fiji, matching Tiki outfits in a geometric print of brown, black, and gray. Bob said, "You look like wallpaper!" and so they did, but cute. In fact, they wore their new outfits all day, trudging through the damp sand and down the hotel halls in their black Nikes, white socks and Tiki Tog shorts and shirts.

Today was pretty low-key. We listened to Matthew, a local storyteller, who told us some local legends while weaving a long basket. Another man, named Soni, sat in the corner of the hut and carved something called "raintree" wood into turtles and masks. We bought one of each. The mask looks like Soni himself.

We leave for the airport at 5 p.m. although our plane doesn't leave until 10 p.m.

5/4 Los Angeles, CA

Our last hours in Fiji were spent sweating out the possibility of a cyclone striking before we caught our plane home. With this threat looming, Kathy gathered us together for departure by 4 p.m.

"In bad weather, the cattle, horses, and goats tend to stray into the road. If we don't leave before dusk, our driver might not be able to see them clearly." She got no objections to this line of reasoning.

We arrived at Nadi by 5:30 p.m. and found it in total chaos. Three trainees stood behind the check-in counters, sending people and luggage God knows where and doing it very very slowly. It took two hours to get through the line.

Kathy was wait-listed on the last flight to Honolulu and managed to get on it, saying her goodbyes to each of us before taking off. And, in a final gesture of good-guiding, she asked Faye to keep a watchful eye on Buddy. "Make sure he gets on the plane," she said. Faye assured her that Buddy would have full advantage of her skills as a police escort.

Kathy also enlisted the aid of her old friend Solo to shepherd us through the departure process. "Solo is reliable," she assured us. "He once swam across the river to be here for me. You can count on him." I guess so.

Solo is a large dark Fijian with the indigenous gentle smile and soft brown eyes, who stood at the counter rectifying the errors of the Air Pacific trainees and passing out our departure tax stamps. He was with us until all of us had group-hugged one another, made our promises to keep in touch, and handed our boarding cards to the attendants at the gate. Just the kind of devotion to duty shown throughout this trip by Kathy. It was especially comforting to have Solo there because of the possibility that the airport would close if the cyclone came much closer. Ours was the last flight out that night.

May 10 Baltimore, MD
Reflections:

I've just received an e-mail from Ron Gliot that made me laugh as much as he did on our recent trip. We've also heard from Vendetta (never did get the story behind her name), Ruby and Tom, and Ted and Pat Mandeville. It was a lovely group of people and I hope that our paths cross again someday.

As to the content of the trip, it was culture overload from the first day in Cairns. How could I have been so naive about Australia, thinking it was USA Down Under? And the mental picture that I had of New Zealand—green pastures, white sheep—was wrong, wrong, wrong.

The cleanliness and simplicity of life in both countries seem to be drawing a wave of immigration. The lack of crime and the clean air are appealing, too. I'd like to learn more about the Aborigines—their music and "songlines" and art. But the place is so far away—from everything. Isolation is the good news and the bad news.

What I take away from this trip is a pocketful of addresses of new friends and a sense that there's so much more to learn.

Russia by Riverboat

In this section, I've reproduced the journey journal I wrote during a trip sponsored by Grand Circle. "Russia by Riverboat" is an example of using both the "Notes, facts, what happened?" guide and the travel "segments" concept to record a trip that was long by our standards (18 days) with plenty of memorable occurrences. It begins with a brief answer to an important question: "Why did you go there?" Laying that out is part of the "reflection" process.

(By the way, the names of the most offensive and peculiar people on our trip have been changed to protect them—and me.)

Introduction

A couple of days ago, we returned from Russia. People wondered why we had gone there. "Of all the places to go, Russia is the last on my list," said our neighbor, Jane. "It's not even on my list," said another. "I hear crime is terrible there," a co-worker told Bob. "Whatever made you choose Russia?!"

So why did we go? Well, why do we go anywhere lately? To tell you the truth, I think we are a little travel-crazed at this point, willing to consider just about any destination if the price is right and our time is free. We are opportunistic travelers—going where we haven't been before when the best deal to go there presents itself. Russia proved to be an immensely enriching trip, a worthy destination.

We traveled with Grand Circle, an organization most often associated with retired people because it once served the AARP exclusively. Neither of us is retired but Grand Circle has expanded and is now available to anyone, regardless of age. The quality of its travel offerings has been praised by many, including my parents. This was our first experience and we chose this trip because it seemed different.

Even more compelling is that it was incredibly cheap. This is a riverboat trip, plying waters between Moscow and St. Petersburg and ending up in Helsinki, Finland. We flew FinnAir to and from; the price of airfare was included in the cost of the trip.

During the flight and at the Moscow airport, I wrote sketchy notes in the small spiral notebook that I carried in my jacket pocket, but they enabled me to remember pertinent details. Because my notes are frequently in a kind of shorthand, legible only to me, I only include them for illustration of the first entry. The morning after the first two segments of the journey (departure transition and arrival), I settled in to write the first entry in the "Russia by Riverboat" Journey Journal.

This trip was unusual in many ways, one of which was the time it allowed for extensive journaling. Be assured, it isn't necessary to go into this kind of detail in order to write a useful, evocative journey journal.

Travel schedules may preclude writing much more than a few sentences about each segment of the trip. To review, the segments include:

1. Departure-transition

2. Arrival

3. Meeting fellow travelers (Note: on the Riverboat Russia trip, we met fellow travelers over a period of time, not all at once, as on other group tours)

4. At the destination: What happened? Encounters, interactions, events, observations, highlighting sights, sounds, and tastes.

5. Return-transition

6. Reflections

To remain true to the precepts and intent of Journey Journaling (which is to pay attention and be present at all times during your journey), try to cover all of the segments. Find something to say about each, however brief.

5/23/96

Notes: Nina blonde blue eyes, Lena long brown hair, man in line France/Morocco/India 2X clean blondes raisin woman "get me a form this instant" pink men "calm down lady take it easy" airport toilet: rural gas station crumpled pink paper beggar woman

5/24/96 On-board the MS Lenin, dockside Moscow 6:30 a.m.

This begins the segment on "Departure-transition." As you will see, during this riverboat trip, some of the segments overlap with each other. For example, we were meeting fellow passengers throughout the entire journey. The purpose of segmenting is to remind you, the Journey Journaler, of the components of interest and to alert you to the Journal potential of each, particularly the "events, encounters, and interactions" that make up each day.

Yesterday was our first day in Russia. We are traveling in the cocoon of Grand Circle, shepherded by two young Russian women who were waiting for us at the check-in counter when we arrived at Kennedy. They introduced themselves as Nina and Lena, both born in Moscow but now living in Aspen, Colorado with American husbands.

Nina is slim, freshfaced and thirty-something with short blonde hair, large blue eyes and a broad smile. Lena, shorter than Nina's medium height but just as thin, wears her brown hair long and loose. Her eyes are sky blue and she laughs a lot.

Sometimes you'll get a random thought while journaling, which is a kind of assessment of things that are happening. When this happens, write it down. These insights enhance your experience, and committing them to paper acts as a commitment to the thoughts. As the trip continues, you will find yourself paying attention to things that might refute or confirm your insight.

Here is an example of what I mean: Bob and I were impressed that our fellow travelers had been to so many exotic places. They had worked their way through the continents and were taking this trip, if not as a last resort, as one pretty close to the last. It flashed on me that Russia is not at the top of most people's lists when it comes to pleasure trips. During the trip, I often returned to this thought and tried to understand why. It became part of my "reflections."

Several people in the group know each other, have traveled together multiple times. Russia, it appears, is not first on anyone's list. I asked a man we met on line where he had traveled before with GC. His brow furrowed. "Oh, my," he murmured. "Let's see. There was France. Then Spain. Then Morocco. Then we went to India." He thought briefly. "Twice." He still hadn't covered the list when his turn came to check-in.

The flight wasn't long by our recent standards. Slightly more than seven hours to Helsinki, we switched planes for another hour and a half to Moscow. Fine Finn food on both flights. Clean, blonde people with high cheekbones attended us, delivering my special low fat meals, as requested some weeks ago.

Direct quotes are more interesting to read and, I believe, can actually be "heard" by the reader. I also like to include color ("pink-faced") in order to "paint" a scene more vividly and simile ("raisin") to help a reader to connect what I see with something more ordinary.

It was an uneventful flight except for one peculiar incident. In the middle of the flight, we were handed customs forms to fill out. As Bob was signing ours, we heard a loud guttural voice from the seats a few rows behind us. I twisted in my seat to see a short tanned woman—so tanned, so short that she looked like a raisin—standing in her row and gesturing angrily as she barked an order to the startled attendant in the aisle. "Get me a form this instant!" she hollered. "NOW!"

She was in the seat on the aisle. Her two seatmates, white-haired, pink-faced men, cowered in embarrassment until one touched her waving arm and said, "Calm down, lady. Take it easy." She pulled her arm away, and gave him a murderous look, but finally sat down. An odd breach of good conduct, we thought. People are usually pretty well-behaved (in coach class) on planes.

These paragraphs include the "Arrival" segment with "Meeting fellow travelers" segment interspersed, as it is throughout the trip.

Capturing first impressions ("fresh-faced," "poorly lit," "disgustingly dirty") requires concentration and returning-to-the-scene via your imagination. In this case, I did not describe the woman in the bathroom in detail. Her physical description wasn't important to the stand-out first impression of the filthy bathroom.

With limited time to write, it's best to focus attention on the things most vividly recalled: here, the look of the public restroom. How to quickly convey it? What did it remind me of? Ah, rural gas stations with their never-cleaned restrooms.

Again, the woman's words are quoted directly. I wanted readers to hear her voice, to feel her dismay at my breaking covenant and actually using the place, as if I had left the world of decent people and had joined them, the indecent locals.

This next scene of the "heavy-set elderly woman" with her rapid changes of expression was the first interesting encounter with a Russian that I witnessed. I wanted to convey her "now I'm going off to work" attitude with her putting on the look of "desperate need," its quick disappearance and her "now I'm on break" expression when she had finished working the room and returned to her bench.

The general reaction among the group to the woman's expression—her muttered words and outstretched palm—confirmed my belief that we were among world-weary travel sophisticates, hardened to local hardships.

Trying to capture the facial characteristics of the first Russian people that we saw in the airport and on the streets, it struck me how much they looked like people at home—tired working people from blue-collar neighborhoods.

As she came to the fringes of the milling Americans, the flat expression on her face slipped suddenly off and was replaced with a look of desperate need: furrowed brow, downturned mouth, sad eyes—as completely different as if she had put on a mask.

The old woman tugged at the elbow of a tall, gray-haired man who was chatting with someone else. He turned and looked down at her. Palm outstretched, she muttered something to him, probably the local equivalent of "homeless—need work." His eyes flicked over her briefly. Then he turned back to his companion and continued his conversation.

For a second, the desperate look nearly slid off her face, but she pulled it back on and moved to the next person. I watched her go unsuccessfully from one to another to another. Nobody gave her more than a momentary glance. People seemed to notice her not at all as she moved among the crowd.

Eventually, the old woman left us and hobbled back to her bench, where she sat fingering the clasp on her purse, waiting for the next group of tourists to arrive. Her sad expression was gone—just another day at the office.

People here look a lot like East Baltimore housewives, manicurists, cabdrivers. A lot of Russian emigrés live in Baltimore, now that I think about it.

Here I throw in a few facts—the location of the pier and the name of the canal station and ship. Again, by "connecting the dots" with transition sentences, I tried to convey the impression of emptiness and distance from the Moscow action, while setting the stage for our arrival at the ship.

The buses dropped us off at a pier alongside a canal. This is the Northern River Station at the Leningradsky Prospekt. There is a large park next to the pier and we seem to be several miles from the center of the city. A huge granite building, majestic in design, stands empty on the broad cement walkway. Our ship, the MS Lenin, was awaiting our arrival with ramp down and staff looking out expectantly from the ship entryway.

The next two paragraphs describe our cabin's location and its physical layout. I knew that people would be curious about this form of travel and would want to know about the adequacy of the accommodations.

We received our key and found our cabin easily. It is on the entry-level deck, directly across from its only source of drinking water. What good luck! It is a huge metal drum with a hot water spigot on its top half and cold water spigot near its bottom. We were cautioned—no, ordered—not to drink the water in the rooms. Our cabin is supplied with several large glass jars.

The cabin is clean. The whole ship is clean. Everything gleams. The contents of our two suitcases fit into the two closets and drawers, and we stashed the cases themselves behind the door. We have two large portholes, one over each twin bed, from which we can see the park and that big empty palace. The bathroom (head) is compact and one of those arrangements where you close the door, tuck toiletries behind a short plastic curtain, and the room becomes a shower stall. There is plenty of hot water.

To capture first impressions on board the MS Lenin in this initial Journey Journal entry, I mentally returned to each event of the evening and recorded it, in the order in which it occurred. I wanted to keep descriptions spare, highlighting only the most memorable aspect of the event. I saw no need to describe the ship's dining room, or the waitresses, or anything else. My most vivid first impressions that night were of the food and the Cruise Director, only. With fourteen days to go, there would be plenty of time for other details.

Dinner was served immediately upon our arrival, and a good thing, too, because most of us were faint with hunger and nearly comatose from lack of sleep. Dinner itself was not a particularly good thing, except for the homemade black bread—thick, chewy, with a nutty flavor. Food swam a half inch above Bob's plate

Our first glimpse of Russia was the poorly lit airport. Once inside, I left Bob, and headed off to find the restroom. It was disgustingly dirty, reminiscent of certain rural Exxon stations back home. The toilet—cracked porcelain streaked with dirt—stood in a pool of what I hoped was water. It didn't flush; indeed, hadn't flushed for a while. And was that used paper? Rough pink sheets lay crumpled on top of the empty dispenser. I fished around in my bag for the kleenex pack.

A woman from our group walked out of the restroom just ahead of me. She said in a low, conspiratorial voice, "Isn't this horrible? Did you go?"

When I said yes, I had gone, she was horrified. "Well, I'm waiting until we get to the boat," she huffed. Maybe it was due to lack of sleep, but I felt suddenly un-hygienic in her eyes. I was tempted to see if she would shake my hand, but she hurried away.

A note on "candor":

As you will read in the following Journey Journals, there have been times when our fellow travelers do not become our new best friends. I believe it's a tribute to the magnificence of a place, a guide, an itinerary, the tour company, and so forth, that we can truly love a trip in spite of incompatibility with others in the group. I can say (with complete candor) that this has always been the case for us.

But I also believe that if you do find yourself traveling with people you'd like to see under the wheels of the bus instead of *on* it, you should be candid about this in your Journey Journal. Sometimes the best way to deal with the situation is to write about it. You can always change the names of the offenders (as I have in those circumstances).

To get from one situation or scene-segment to another, I wrote a kind of connect-the-dots sentence, setting the stage for the next event or encounter. To enliven it, a metaphor was thrown in ("...like a flock of dumb sheep"). By staying present in the next sentence ("I noticed..."), I reminded the reader that this rendition was from my point of view.

Following Nina, we passed through customs quickly and stood like a flock of dumb sheep as she left to locate the buses that would transport us to the pier. I noticed a heavy-set, elderly woman in a black shawl listing toward us. Her hands clutched a cracked black plastic purse.

in a liquid yellow pool. I had registered myself as a vegetarian when we signed up for the trip and so I was given a plate of potatoes and other things that grew in the ground. Eaten with lots of black bread, it was adequate. Bob, who eats just about anything put in front of him and with gusto, was pleased with his meal. I'm the food-fussy.

The orientation session was a scene with interaction and a beginning, middle, and end. I spent time on the physical description of the Cruise Director because it seemed to me that he was to be a major character in this journey-journal. It was his voice that thundered over the public address system, announcing dinner and shipboard locations of interest. I used his own words, trying to replicate his Russian accent, in order to bring him to life. His talk contained certain nuggets of information which I wrote in the journal because I thought they would be interesting to readers (e.g. cash only, no travelers' checks, the high cost of the opera and circus).

After dinner, we hauled ourselves up to the next deck where we sat in folding chairs, waiting for the orientation session—standard for group trips like this—to begin. The Cruise Director is a tall, sorrowful-looking man with dark bulging pouches under each eye and a nose so bulbous it looks removable, like a clown's. He introduced himself. "Good Eef-en ing, ladies and gennamen. My nahm ees Bo-Zho, spelled 'B-o-z-o'." Some of the audience chuckled softly.

He explained the basics of money-changing (no travelers' checks, cash only), the included daily excursions, and the cost of extra trips to the opera and circus (expensive). He finally stopped talking when he realized nearly everyone was asleep. We went back to the cabin and slept soundly for the next nine hours.

We will be in Moscow for three days. This morning after breakfast we begin our sightseeing with a Moscow city tour. Today, the ship is providing, according to Bozo, "peck-lawnch," which we will eat on the bus before visiting the famed Pushkin Museum.

May 25 , 6:30 a.m.

To introduce the second day's events, I used another connect-the dots sentence to set the stage, this one containing a tiny travel tip for outwitting jet lag.

One of the more effective ways for me to avoid jet-lag exhaustion is to change my watch to the destination-time as soon as we arrive. I think this fools my circadian clock into believing we haven't really missed a night's sleep. It seemed to work again as we chugged through our first day in Moscow.

I introduce and try to develop personalities of characters by using their own words. Encounters and interactions are more interesting when "shown" rather than "told." Here is where I get into "what happened" and, because I had the time to write more, I write about the the day's events in chronological order.

We disembarked the MS Lenin for the city-tour buses at around 8:30 a.m. Earlier, I was poking around this 300-passenger ship when I spied the ferret-faced raisin of a woman who had created the customs-form scene on the airplane. Talk about bad attitude. I smiled and said, "Good morning!" rather too brightly. But instead of saying anything in return, she fixed me with an angry stare and marched down the hall (er, gangway).

When she later appeared on the walkway in front of the buses, I grabbed Bob's arm and pointed. "Look, there she is!" I said. "Let's wait and see which bus she gets on." We watched her walk through the crowd and get on Bus #2 before we climbed aboard Bus #3.

And a lucky choice it was because Nina, our guide, is a witty woman with an ironic tone, a store of jokes on the local foibles, and excellent English, which is a huge plus.

Each encounter and interaction is part of a scene with a setting and characters. The characters in the Journey Journal are revealing themselves more each time we meet. Dialogue enlivens the scenes, makes them come to life. I want to turn each encounter and interaction into a story, keeping the journal interesting to read.

We sat behind the two pink-faced, silver-haired guys who had suffered through the flight with the crazy raisin woman.

"She's unbelievable," said the taller of the two, a cheery fellow named Fred. He's a widower who had planned this trip with his wife. When she died a year ago, his friend Ingvold urged him not to give up his plans and offered to go with him.

Ingvold wears a beard, and is heavier and much less cheerful than Fred. He smiles rarely but seems pleasant enough.

"Listen to this," Fred began. "She told us on the plane that she had claimed on her registration form to have a birthday during the trip so that she'll get free champagne and birthday cake." He laughed heartily. "Can you believe that?"

Ingvold scowled. "She's awful," he said.

Facts are inserted here to give a sense of our group's progress through the core of Moscow, as well as my first impression of the city's appearance. Nina's Muscovite assessment is meant to show her sense of humor. I avoided the obvious over-used "onion-shaped" for "bulbous" to describe St. Basil's Cathedral.

Our bus circled the inner core of Moscow, passing by the notorious Lubyanka Square—the still active headquarters of the former KGB—and dropped us off outside of Red Square. "Red" in Russia means "beautiful" not "communist." There is construction everywhere, with streets so torn up that people must zig zag over two-by-fours and through scaffolding to get around. According to Nina, center city has been in this state for years and no one can remember what it is they are supposed to be building or fixing.

In any case, we picked our way to the entrance of the enormous expanse and walked through to a setting made famous in news programs, papers, magazines, and movies. Dominated on one end by the bulbous multicolored domes of St. Basil's cathedral, and by the department store G.U.M (buff colored and palatial) on one side, the cobblestoned Square was shiny from recent rain and empty of crowds this morning. Facing G.U.M. is a low, dark-red granite structure which is Lenin's tomb. We headed for it and filed past the stern-faced teenagers guarding the entranceway in gray army uniforms.

An odd reverential silence descended on our crowd as we approached the tomb. Although no one spoke, the pimply-faced guardians hissed, "SSSHHHH!" at regular intervals as we filed past them and into the dark interior. Their requirement of silence was curious because Russia officially doesn't honor Lenin anymore.

Another fact not in the guidebook.

Against Lenin's own last wishes, a spiteful Stalin kept Lenin above ground and in view for the many decades after his death. The plan is to finally bury the guy, probably in the Kremlin wall which adjoins the Square and holds the remains of a lot of other notables—the American John Reed (of the film "Reds" fame), the astronaut Gagarin, the writer Gogol. For now, Lenin lies under a glass dome, waxy and glowing beneath pinpoint spotlights, wearing a white shirt, black and white tie, and a black suit and looking just like his pictures. He could be a figure in Mme. Tussaud's, so unreal is the whole scene. I loved the drama of the place. It lacked only background music, something martial or passionate like Tchaikovsky.

Out on the Square, we walked by the graves of other former Soviet leaders, marked by marble pedestals topped with their busts—Stalin, Andropov, Breshnev, all bad fellows, at least in Western history books.

We learned that the grand, palatial buildings like the one on our pier are from the pre-Communist era, the style dubbed "wedding-cake" because they are shaped like one. Some are pale yellow, some gray (Moscow University), and some are pink like the building which houses the Bolshoi Ballet.

Sometimes the best way to describe a place or thing accurately is to compare it to something else—Moscow to New York or Boston, as I did here.

Our city tour took place on Saturday and the streets and squares were empty. Where are the nine million people who live here? I thought of Saturday in New York City, in Boston and Philadelphia, teeming with shoppers and sightseers and restaurant diners.

Here follow four sentences to describe Muscovites, and four sentences to describe the subway system, with a little Nina humor thrown in. I'm not sure that I was successful in re-creating the scene. I wanted to convey the emptiness, the space available in this huge city, as well as the contrast between the quiet, colorless people and the grandeur of the state-built subway system. Things just didn't match.

Later, Nina took Bob and me and a few other people down into the subway system. There we found the Muscovites, dressed in brown, gray, black, and beige and looking like city people everywhere. They weren't jammed together, though, or carrying boxes and bags of purchases. They sat impassively, some reading, some sleeping.

The purpose for our subway trip was to see the grandeur of the stations, gorgeously decorated in mosaics and frescoes to represent various Soviet states. Huge crystal chandeliers lit the wide pillared halls, clean, litter- and graffiti-free. The trains run on time, too. Nina pointed out that subways are the thing Russians do best.

This "interaction" scene at the Museum shows the general disorganization of infrastructure in a very small way, as well as the petty thievery of Bozo who was collecting unusually large amounts of money for event tickets. By contrast, although I didn't see it at the time, the pocketbook scene shows the honesty of the women museum-goers—average citizens.

The day's tour ended at the Pushkin Museum, after we had eaten our "peck lawnch" of apple, boiled egg, and bread. On the boat, we had paid $10 to see the Trojan Gold exhibit, highly recommended by the Cruise Director. Inside, the local guide couldn't figure out where the exhibit was. She didn't seem to know that some of us had paid extra for it and herded all of us into a corner of the entrance while she disappeared to find help. It was hot and our group began to get surly, questioning why some of us had paid, and some hadn't. I slipped away to the ladies' restroom.

Inside women were jammed cheek by jowl listing to and fro and lurching toward the stalls very slowly. When I finally made it into and out of one, I saw a lone black pocketbook sitting on the shelf above the sinks. I gestured to it and asked the woman next to me, "Yours?" She shook her head. I shouted to a woman trying to get out the door. "You left your pocketbook!" She didn't turn around. I didn't know what to do next and was trying to decide if I should take the purse to our guide when a woman stepped forward and said in broken English, "Belong lady in toilet. She in toilet. She come out soon."

I tried to imagine the circumstances in which I would leave my purse unattended in a crowded public toilet—and it wouldn't be stolen. I couldn't.

Back in the museum, we finally managed to find and get into the Trojan Gold exhibit. Large glass cases held pieces of dull gold in shapes curled and bent, woven and plain, decorative things that once hung on necks and earlobes and wrists. It was a kind of dreary, pointless show. Just rooms and rooms of these cases of shaped gold pieces. I tried, but I could neither marvel nor get any sense of history.

This description of the Pushkin World War I and II paintings is included so that readers who plan to visit this museum will seek them out. Again, the size was impressive by itself ("long broad hall," "huge panels," and "floor-to-ceiling scenes") and in contrast to the little squiggles of gold in the special exhibit.

Bob, on the other hand, was studying each piece like it was talking to him, as he usually does in museums. So I wandered out of the Trojan Gold exhibit and down a long broad hall into exhibit rooms at the other side of the building. These held huge panels of paintings depicting the Soviet Union of World Wars I and II— marvelous floor-to-ceiling scenes of the proletariat hewing together in factories and fields, heroic figures doing the work of the masses, earnest devoted young faces and wise craggy old ones.

One painting in the World War II room showed Hitler in the throes of death surrounded by fallen, bleeding bunker-mates. Another room was devoted to the Soviet Union of the 1920s with its opera, dance, and theatre. All was terribly dramatic and much more interesting than the cases of Trojan Gold.

Here is another encounter/interaction that shows the emerging personalities of fellow travelers. People and their actions and reactions add interest to a journey journal. Also, writing about the encounter helped me get over my anger. With the recreation of this unpleasant scene, I tried to recapture the distress Bob and I felt.

Last night at dinner we sat with Ingvold and Fred. We had our choice of two sittings upon registration, 6:30 or 8 p.m., and took the earlier one. Grand Circle folks all sit on one side of the dining room. People traveling on their own or with other groups take up the other side.

I added this next paragraph because the clash in culture was so interesting: the Russian dining room crew trying to force the independent-minded, well-traveled senior citizens of Grand Circle to do their bidding.

Although the Russians running this ship—part of the OdessAmerica Line, a joint venture between our two countries—have ordered passengers to sit at the same table every meal, members of the group have simply refused to obey and for the three meals we've eaten so far, have sat with different people at different tables each time. The waitresses and headwaiter are obviously bewildered and dismayed by this total disregard of authority, but are powerless to do anything about this *exercise in free choice.*

We chose to sit with Ingvold and Fred. Ingvold, so friendly and pleasant during the day, fortified himself with vodka from the bar and ordered more at dinner. Expressing an interest in the investment business, he asked about Alex Brown, Bob's employer. Bob managed to get a few introductory sentences out, and I added a couple of items of interest, when Ingvold's voice turned into a snarl, his pink face darkening to red.

"You telling me that this company I've never heard of did that?"

I laughed nervously. "Yes," I said.

"Then you're stupid," he snapped. "You're both stupid." He muttered on about our measly, unknown, second-rate company. We were speechless, wondering what we had said that set him off. His tirade was embarrassing to his friend, Fred, who tried hard to change the subject. A few words into a new area, and Ingvold would be off again, charging us with lying about Alex Brown's position, about its underwritings.

What's with this creep? He's definitely a man who doesn't drink well. I told him he was offensive. Bob, ever the gentleman, laughed it off, but dinner fizzled to a close.

Still appalled at the scene, I formulated perfect retorts all night long, and a vow: I'll sit with the Raisin before dining with Ingvold again.

Below is a description of the famous Armory Museum from my point of-view, the way I saw it—no doubt in extreme contrast to the way it is usually described (especially since I missed its highlight, the Fabergé eggs). Once again, I want to find a story in each event.

Moscow, May 26

Today we rode back to the center of the city for a tour of the Kremlin. It began with a visit to the Armory Museum, which is the repository of the Czarist-era jewels, crowns, and armor, including the famous Fabergé eggs. Here I must confess to something shameful. I didn't see them. I got tired of hanging around while the Kremlin guide explained the contents of each glass case.

There were hundreds of them, filled with the most useless of luxury items.. One such bauble was a totally jewel-encrusted rifle (pearls, diamonds, and emeralds). Makes the Revolution seem like a reasonable response. Another was a pearl and ruby face plate for the horse-who-has-everything.

Glass cases of costumes of the 16th and 17th Century included boots and robes of Peter the Great. He was huge—well over six feet tall—and his brown leather boots looked like trees.

Unlike other Romanovs, Peter dressed plainly and was not as addicted to excess. He had lived in Western Europe as a young man and was determined to Westernize Russia, fearing its overthrow if he failed.

Anyway, I walked ahead of the guide and her band of followers into the next room and the next. When I returned, she was still expounding on the same case. So I left to find the ladies' room and wandered through the museum shop afterward. By then, the group had somehow managed to get through the glass cases and the Fabergé eggs and was coming toward me.

I fell into line and the woman next to me said, "Did you ever see anything so magnificent as those eggs!" I considered this for a moment and answered, "No."

Here is one of those random thoughts which will connect with the earlier one on Russia's position as a destination of last resort. If asked what surprised me about the trip, I'd say "I was surprised that it was so interesting." This is the beginning of that reflection.

The trip through the Armory Museum made me realize how little I know of Russian history. It seems full of mystery, violence, crazed rulers and murderous monks. Sort of a Grimm's Fairy Tales kind of history, but true. I vowed to read more about it when we get back home.

Again, I am surprised at something: the bucolic nature of the Kremlin.

We walked through the grounds of the Kremlin (which means "fortification"), amazed at its green grass and trees, flowering lilacs, wide paths and streets. Inside its walls are numerous churches, office buildings, guard houses and museums. It is not the dark, brooding place of imagination, at least not physically. We stood across the road from Yeltsin's office in a bright yellow building that has been frequently televised and photographed. He isn't there now, but somewhere else, recovering from ill health. (The election takes place two weeks after we leave and we expect to learn more about it soon from Professor Irina.)

I wanted to create this scene—another story in the day's chronology—as vividly as possible, and so I used sounds ("martial music"), smell ("we knew there was at least one animal act"), and dialogue along with my description.

In the evening, we went to the Moscow Circus. It is housed in a circular cement building which looks like a bunker large enough for the entire Russian Army. Inside, the crowd was sparse. The cost seemed high for a circus performance but, as someone standing at my elbow in the dinner line said, "How often do you get to Moscow? I hear it's one of the great circuses." So we peeled the dollar bills off our stash and paid Bozo the money.

At the entrance to the building, we saw the ticket prices prominently displayed. As nearly as we could figure, we paid Bozo about double what the box office was asking.

The amphitheater was stuffy and warm. A small group of musicians—heavy on the brass—played martial music from a section over the ring. We followed the barking orders of the stern-faced women who served as ushers but acted more like capos. If someone strayed off the march to the seats, say, to find a bathroom or buy a souvenir, they would shriek the offender back into line.

These ushers take their jobs seriously. A man and his little boy slipped down to sit in unoccupied seats near us—theirs were far away from the ring. The nearest usher/guard caught the movement out of the corner of her eye. She swung into action, signalling for backup from her fellow guards and charging the poor man. The whole collection of ushers screamed angrily while making shooing gestures at him and his son. The two grabbed their bags of popcorn, their plastic blowup dolls, and the little boy's sweater and stumbled back up the steps to where they belonged.

Satisfied at their triumphant rout of this "criminal element," the usher army withdrew, watching the rest of us with gimlet eyes, lest we stray, too, perhaps into the ring.

The show was heavy on acrobatics with only one animal act—tigers. We knew from the smell that there was at least one. This circus paled next to the Peking Circus from China. But Bob liked it, especially the tiger-act finale. He reached into his bag and pulled out the videocamera.

This movement attracted the attention of the ushers who converged on us from all sides. The one who had rousted the man and his son pointed angrily at the videocam and hissed something—obviously orders not to use it. Her finger waved back and forth in the air, her head shook violently. People turned in their seats to stare. Bob slid the camera back into the bag, looking as if he had just been caught tunneling out of the stalag. You don't want to cross these girls. Makes you wonder what their occupations were in the former Soviet Union.

Here I finally mention one of the trip's strange phenomena—outside light for nearly all 24 hours—which added to the foreign-ness of the place, so different from home. But I give it pretty short shrift. Must have been tired of writing.

We emerged from the hot interior into a cool evening, still light at 9:30 p.m., and didn't eat dinner until our return to the ship at 10:30. Somehow, it doesn't seem so late when there is still daylight.

Moscow, May 27

I included this update on the Ingvold-encounter to add interest and character-development of fellow passengers.

Today we boarded the buses early. Fred and Ingvold climbed on behind us and Ingvold shook his head and rolled his eyes briefly as he walked by us. "I can't drink," he said, softly. "I should learn my lesson."

At a loss for response, we both smiled uncertainly.

Using correct place name and location is necessary to the journey journal. Fortunately, the spelling of Zagorsk and facts about it were in my notes.

We rode out to Zagorsk, a village north of Moscow where the 600-year-old Trinity Monastery of St. Sergius stands. The area swarms with religious people—nuns, priests, monks. Graduates of St. Sergius are priests and, in order to find a church to serve, they must also be married.

This next little bit of information, given by Nina, lent human interest to the Trinity Monastery.

The story goes that mothers drive their unmarried daughters out to Zagorsk and hang around the monastery entrance at graduation time. Priests, at least according to local lore, make good husbands.

In this scene, I wanted to "show"—not "tell" about—the urgency with which Russians are pursuing capitalism, in small entrepreneurial ways. By starting with the colorful dachas and the request to stop, I wanted to make it clear that the scene was neither staged nor part of the regular tour to Zagorsk.

On our way to Zagorsk, we passed a row of old wooden dachas wildly painted in rainbow colors and looking like a Christmas display of gingerbread houses. Someone requested that Nina ask the driver to stop the bus so that we could get out and take pictures. As we trooped out, cameras in hand, a man ran from one of the cottages, holding in both hands a small table, a box balanced on top.

While we snapped our pictures of the houses, he set the table down beside the road, opened the box, and frantically began to arrange his goods for sale: dozens of painted egg-shaped dolls meant to nest inside each other. (They're called matoushka dolls and are as ubiquitous as t-shirts in tourist shops.)

I marveled at his industry. Did he sit by the window waiting for photographers, tourists? Was he on his way to some more obvious marketplace when we happened by? In any case, one of the group asked his price, in English, and, aside from Russian, he spoke only a few words of German. He had no idea how to respond in English. He just kept looking at us quizzically and repeating "zwei mark, bitte" and telling us that "mein frau hat machen"— the matoushka dolls were handmade by his wife.

Now I wondered, did the line of cottages attract mostly German tourists who couldn't withstand the temptation to stop and photograph cottages so reminiscent of German folk tales? People in our group scooped up his wares and, having no deutschmarks, handed him two dollars for each doll. With the busdriver impatiently revving his engine, it didn't seem appropriate to discuss the exchange rate. We left him stuffing money into his pocket, and carefully laying his wooden dolls back into the box. As the bus rolled away, I watched him pick up his table, box again balanced on top, and hurry back across the road to his cottage.

In order to include all this description, I must have had a lot of time to write the next morning. Sometimes, a place or event or encounter is so impressive in its foreign-ness or beauty that I want to take it step-by step, to see if I can convey its special impression in words. I think that these paragraphs were the result of having time to write and of seeing for the first time the sight of local craftspeople in numbers meeting the awakening buy-urges among us.

It was still early when we drove into Zagorsk. The sun was not yet above the thick trees and there was a clean chill in the air. Our busdriver stopped along the monastery wall and we stepped down onto a rough stone walk that led to the high wooden entrance gate.

Local craftspeople were unfolding tables and laying their work on top, hop-dancing in the morning cold, their breath standing in the air in front of them. This excited the bargain-hunters among us. Several from our group drifted over to the tables and peered at the goods, acquisitive instincts awakened now by the man at the dachas.

Nina rushed to their sides. "Not now," she implored. "We must go in before the crowds. Come with me. We can shop later," she assured us and turning, she hurried through the entryway into the monastery. Dutifully, we followed.

The only way I could adequately show this next monastery scene was to take it step-by-step. Remember, I had the time to do this kind of lengthy description. So I just closed my eyes and replayed the scene in my mind, then wrote it down as it happened.

Inside, Nina reached into her pocketbook and retrieved a fistful of head scarves which she handed out to each of the women. It is required that we cover our heads.

I whispered in her ear, "Is there a restroom here?"

"Yes, yes," she said. "I'll show you." She called out, "Please be back at the bus by noon" and then gestured for Bob and me to follow her. We snaked our way through the growing crowd of visitors, monks, priests, and nuns, past Russian Orthodox churches (small, medium, and large) topped with onion-shaped domes of gold and blue, until we came to a plain white stucco building.

Nina dipped inside and we followed. She led us through halls and down staircases until we came to an old woman wearing black felt slippers and apparently swathed in scarves. She sat in front of the w.c. doors, a basket marked 500r on a table beside her. We thanked Nina. "You'll be all right?" she asked. We assured her that we could find our way back and she hurried off.

Does it seem that I am inordinately interested in bathroom-culture? I wonder at my conclusion below, but bathroom availability does become an obsession with us on the road. I also liked and wanted to include Nina's funny story.

The w.c. was spotless, its sink gleaming white, floor swept clean, and stalls stocked with paper—well worth the fifty cents. Later, Nina told us that she took so many people through the halls and stairways to that bathroom, the old woman told her, "You can go free."

I thought this was another culture-clash scene: Bob and I as participant-observers trying to figure out what was happening. But now I think that it doesn't really show enough to be informative.

In the main yard, we saw a line of people outside of the largest, most ornately painted church. Wondering what was so interesting that it would create such a line, we stepped into it and edged forward toward the church door to see for ourselves. Inside, the church was dimly lit, but we could see that worshippers were leaning over and kissing something before being blessed by a black-robed, bearded priest. We stepped out of the line and watched.

In the half-dark, I could read in my guidebook that they were kissing the bones of St. Sergius. (Uh-huh) While we watched, a sextet of pale blonde teenagers appeared from a door next to the priest, four young women in cardigan sweaters and shiny skirts and two young men in black jackets and pants. They began to sing in harmony while self-consciously staring at the floor. Strangely, their lips didn't move at all. They looked like six ventriloquists.

Outside again, we both began to snap pictures. There are photo ops everywhere: the dramatic domes, the carved wooden doors, the black garbed priests and nuns.

Here I was able to find a simile ("...like blackbirds") which described the priests'

flight perfectly.

We discovered that one way to clear a path of priests was to point the cameras at them. These folks do not like to have their pictures taken and they flutter away like blackbirds if they suspect you might do that to them. One pair turned from us and crashed into the bushes rather than have their photos taken.

I like to record the circumstances surrounding a souvenir purchase. We usually take pictures of the craftspeople from whom we buy things and I write down anything that will bring them back to mind after our return home.

When we had seen our fill of the monastery grounds, we walked out to the lot where the vendors were now open for business. A forty-ish woman, with a sweet face and the tiniest of shy smiles, stood next to a folding chair draped with woven scarves. A boy of around eight played with a wooden toy on the grass beside it.

She held in her arms a long, delicately woven white shawl. I could barely hear her whispered words when I asked the price.

"Twenty dollars?" I repeated. She nodded and then by waving her arms and pointing to herself, she assured me that she had made the shawl herself. Ever the cheapskate bargainer, I worked for fifteen but finally paid the twenty dollar price, convinced that it was worth the money for its beautifully intricate design.

Looking at it now, I marvel at how utterly insulting I was to offer less. It is a wonderful piece of work, worth much more than I paid.

From another vendor, much more confident in his pitch, we bought a simple picture of dried flowers for $16. As with the scarf-maker, he started and finished with his price.

Another one of those random thought-insights: lack of bargaining interest or skill show the lack of experience with capitalism, I think.

Bargaining—the tug of war for price—doesn't seem to be the thrill for these people that it is in other countries more used to the tourist shopper. The capitalist system of making and selling your product for money is thrill enough, I guess. This is fine with me. Fixed prices are comforting, especially if they stay fixed.

This is "what happened next."

When we returned to the ship from Zagorsk, we ate a late lunch and then fell *into our beds for a long nap. The MS Lenin left its berth at 5:30 p.m. to loud piped military music—it seemed to be coming from that empty wedding-cake building— and began its float down a quiet canal.*

This passage into the countryside of Russia called for straight description. The contrast between the grim, gray streets of Moscow and the tranquil outskirts was startling. I wanted to get its "look" in words.

The city quickly receded and soon we were rolling by thick green birch forests, edged with narrow paths for walkers and picnickers. Small villages appeared from time to time as well as large homes under construction, a reminder of the proximity of Moscow and the concentration of its wealth. Near these new houses were marinas and boats, not unlike prosperous waterfront developments in the U.S.

The technology of these locks fascinated Bob and Fred, both former Navy men. I found them interesting but not galvanizing. For general reader interest, I think I should have included more facts about them.

After dinner, we passed into the first of sixteen locks and dropped about 50' at a stately pace.

I'm not sure why this random thought popped into my writing at this moment, but it did, so I wrote it down.

Russians don't smile much. They have a collective sad look. An expression of permanent longing for greener grass seems etched on the faces of men and women of all ages.

May 28

Still no technical details about locks, but this is what the operation looked and felt like.

This morning when I woke, we were in another lock, penned up and sinking as the water pours out to the lower elevation. The ship floats smooth as a leaf on this waterway. Only the passing scenery shows that we are moving. But at daybreak, we were not moving, the dark gray cement walls were rising, and the cabin was dark. I tried to peer up out of the porthole. The sun and shoreline were high above us. Men's voices, calling out to each other, echoed in the deep chasm. Then, slow-

ly, our ship glided forward again. We rose up along seamed and cracked cement walls, past huge rusted hooks and scaffold pipes to the iron grill railing. From entry to exit, the lock negotiation took only about 15 or 20 minutes.

Along the shore, purple and white lilacs, pale green birch trees, and lacy aspens reminded us that here in Russia, it is spring. We left home with summer firmly in place and we are able to see spring again. What a treat to have two springs in one year.

A few of the interesting facts not covered in the guidebook, as well as a glimpse of the cruise itinerary.

Stalin had these canals dug to connect Moscow with the Volga River and the Volga with other waterways, all the way to St. Petersburg. Our first stop will be at Uglich, which we should make at 3 p.m. this afternoon. Its name means "corner," which described its position on the Volga until the canals were built. Now it is on an extension of the river, the canals having straightened out the waterway north. So our trip will take us down this extension to Uglich and then back to the intersection of the canal and the river and north to our destination, St. Petersburg. But lots and lots to see before then...

On-board activities and the teachers were such a highlight that they required detailed description. Fortunately, I had plenty of time to write. Instead of describing the Russian culture teacher as "young and pretty," I wanted to give details which would more accurately replicate the way she looked. Hence, "delicate, nervous...", "wide frizzy hairdo", etc.

Because we don't land at Uglich until later this afternoon, we were offered — on-board—both Russian language lessons and a lecture on Russian culture. The latter was delivered by a delicate, nervous woman who appears to be in her early twenties. She has a wide frizzy hairdo and under it, her face is shiny and round like a new nickel. For the occasion of her lecture, she dressed up.

So did the language teacher, another young woman who also has other duties on the ship. (I saw her drifting around the dining room earlier in the day.) The lecturer, Professor Irina, teaches at a university but hasn't been paid in months. How do they live, we wonder?

Dos this sound mean? I wanted to re-create the appallingly awful sense of fashion which pervades.

About dressing up: Last night, the Captain held a reception at which he introduced his staff, including two women. It was obvious that everyone had dressed in their finest, pulling out all the wardrobe stops in order to look their most elegant. The results were awful. The women wore gauzy blouses, limp and shiny rayon skirts in vivid dyes of orange that almost glowed, yellow, brown, and purple shades that weren't meant for the togetherness of a pattern, large plastic "decorative" buttons and bows, seams that pulled the material into little ripples.

All of the women's outfits looked as if they had been built for higher waists, smaller hips, and flatter chests, even those worn by our very thin language teacher and Professor Irina. Visible panty-lines seem to be part of the fashion statement.

Bob accused me of being uncharitable. "They can't afford any better," he admonished. But that isn't what's amiss. It isn't the cheapness of the clothes that I find offensive to the eye, but their tastelessness. They are too garish, too dinky. If they faded in the wash and were three sizes larger, the effect would be less jarring.

The men's suits—mostly double-breasted—were no better, except the seams were less obvious in shiny dark material. The buttons were large and pulled the jackets out of shape. Too wide trousers, pleated like dresses, hid their shoes entirely.

Here is another of those random-thoughts. Re-reading it now, I wonder if the garishness, the over-decorated, too vividly colored hair and clothes constitute some sort of first step Russians are making into the world of fashion. I don't know why the almost aggressive ugliness was so appalling to me, but obviously, it was. Anyway, it may strike the reader as excessively critical, but in a Journey Journal, I believe you should always strive for your most honest reaction.

We haven't seen many beautiful Russians, here or in Moscow. Skin is pasty and spotted, hair is lank and colorless, or worse, dyed strange inhuman shades of magenta and yellow. These are not lovely people, but they might be.

Our guides with their smooth complexions and slim healthy bodies, dressed in conservative suits and fashionable draped scarves, show what a few dollars and good fashion sense can do. And their hair and skin demonstrate the value and effect of decent diets. They smile a lot, too.

At the reception, no Russian except the Cruise Director smiled during the Captain's introductions of them. The little band of staff members stood, self-conscious in their finery, arms crossed over chests, heads lowered. As their names were called, each stepped forward, the women bobbing and gripping their elbows, the men nodding curtly, before scurrying offstage and out the door like spiders.

At her lecture, Professor Irina wore another peculiar outfit—a short square bolero jacket in glistening red and an ill-fitting, very tight and short purple skirt, seamed stockings with rhinestones scattered from knee to ankle, and, strapped to her small feet like little electric chairs, thick-soled platform heels at least 3" high. They look like high-heeled combat boots. The outfit was distracting, but Professor Irina's voice is soft and sweetly melodic. After a minute or two, we were able to get into the rhythm of her accent and to understand her words fairly well.

I referred to my lecture notes (which I won't reproduce here) for this quick overview of Russian history. I didn't have the energy to write all the facts in detail and, besides, they're in the guidebook. Irina was more interesting to write about.

Irina began her lecture with a quote from Chekhov. "Russians," he wrote, "fear their future, hate their present, and deify their past." She told us that there were two dozen Ivans who ruled Czarist Russia, including the Great and the Terrible in the late 16th Century.

We heard about Boris Gudonov, whom she called an "apparatchik" (meaning a member of a political movement, not royalty) boyar (which designated an aristocratic class later abolished by Peter the Great). We also heard about "the false Dimitrios," who ruled after Boris.

She led us up to the last Romanovs with brief anecdotes and the observation that most died badly, at the hands of the next czar or those who wanted to be next.

I wanted to convey the fact that Irina's lecture had an ironic humor. Rather than say this, I included her direct quotes.

Irina concluded by telling us that Russia has been called "the most credulous nation in the world" and that "Russians prefer to be weak, underdogs for cruel rulers." "Ivan the Terrible" is not remembered as "terrible" at all, she said, but as strong, something desirable as a ruler, a fellow given to violence but overall, a pretty good tough-guy. "Ivan the Great" was great because he was more terrible than "The Terrible."

The lecture was excellent, and she wove so compelling a tale of intrigue, danger, violence and mystery that we can hardly wait to come back for the next installment. Professor Irina will be delivering several more lectures on-board. I think we'd better plan to get to the lecture hall early if we want to get seats. It was that good.

With time on my hands, I decided to write in detail about one of the important aspects of cruising: Food. This was most easily done by describing its physical appearance—color and texture.

Meals. Let's talk meals for just a minute. To make my meal vegetarian, shiny silver squares of fish or the brown pile of meat are removed and replaced with canned corn, chopped beets, green pepper strips, and potatoes, usually fried but sometimes boiled. There's a lot of yellow oil—and sometimes a pale gray gravy—on this stuff.

If soup is served, it appears in my bowl as the same canned corn, chopped beets, etc. with hot water poured over them. But the bread is chewy, black, and flavorful. Rolls at breakfast are stuffed with raisins or apples and served with seedy fruit jam. Fresh fruit is served every meal—bright green Granny Smith apples, oranges, and occasionally, bananas.

Actually, I've been happy with the food, sticking mostly to the bread, rolls, fruit and any vegetables that managed to stay out from under the greasy coating. Bob is satisfied with his non-vegetarian food as well. Mostly, people have been pleasantly surprised at its variety.

Again, with time to write, I am able to develop some ideas more fully. The people on this trip were an enigma and I was trying to work out an understanding of them. By using direct quotations as much as possible, I hoped to recreate my consternation for readers.

People. Let's talk people for another minute. I don't want to be cranky but these people are boring. We have gone along with the table-hopping, let's-sit-with-someone-new-each-meal, idea. But in these first few days, the ones we have sat with are mostly silent, uninquisitive, and dull.

I feel like Barbara Walters, pulling an interview out of reluctant guests. We ask question after question. "Where are you from?" "What did you do before you retired?" "Do you have family back home?" "Tell us about your children (grandchildren)."

Only this last question seems to inspire a spark of recognition that this is the stuff of dinner table conversation, not feeding-trough grunts. No one has yet asked us where we are from, what we do, or anything that would help us to connect and build a friendship with them.

One promising conversation was with a cute woman of about 75. Her name is Jane and she lives in Northern California. She is very funny. I kept complimenting her on her scarf until she said, "Susan, do you want to wear it?" She's one of those people that I liked instantly. She talked all about the books she's been reading and she seemed to be interested in us, too. We laughed a lot together.

When we left the table after our meal with her, both Bob and I said, "Let's sit with Jane again. Maybe we can get to know her a little better over a drink in the bar before dinner."

But the next time we met and I asked her to join us, she looked sheepish and said, "I would really like that but the people I'm with, well, they want us to stick together. I'm sorry..." and she drifted off. After that, I noticed Jane was always at a table with the same six people, (in spite of the Grand Circle-ers' group decision to move around), looking a little pensive, I thought.

So far, our travel companions aren't very companionable. Between the Raisin (who isn't traveling with Grand Circle, but is on each daily excursion), the drunken Ingvold, and the crushingly boring dinnermates, they are more to be avoided than sought after.

Finally, this conclusion popped into my head. As with other random thoughts, I wrote it down:

It is a measure of the wonders of this trip that this doesn't matter at all.

If there is a theme to this trip, it is Czarist Russian history. It seems bizarre, alien, and full of mystery—inaccessible to commoners. The story of the boy czarivich who

lived (briefly) in this little village is as ugly as the town's name, Uglich, suggests. The people the same. All this carping on ugliness makes me realize how much I take for granted the relative attractiveness of the world we live in, both of people and places.

At 3 p.m. we glided to the pier at Uglich. It was in this village in 1591 that Boris Gudonov had the 8-year old son of Ivan the Terrible, the boy "czarivich," murdered. His name was Dimitrios and he lived in exile in this small village far from Moscow with his mother Maria. A few years after Dimitrios died, another fellow appeared, saying that he was Dimitrios and that the wrong boy had been killed. History has named this wannabe, who was actually a monk and the former servant of a nobleman, the "False Dimitrios." In time, he, too, was murdered, as was a second Dimitrios imposter a few years later.

We walked up a dirt path to the town center where a political rally was in full swing: two rock bands simultaneously trying to whip the desultory crowd into some kind of enthusiasm for their candidates. It was warm and sunny. Couples—elderly and young—wandered from band to band, calling to errant children, pushing prams, and eating food from the vendors stationed around the square.

Now Uglich is not an ugly city. But it is a city of ugly people.(Oh, milk of human kindness, where are you? But I must tell the truth.) The consistent appalling ugliness is everywhere. These are not attractive people. Is it because no one smiles? Or because complexions are pockmarked or raging with acne? Or because the clothes are so badly cut—lots of shiny orange and thigh-clinging black taffeta over wide white legs?

All of these together were startling against a landscape of light leafy aspen, budding lilacs, and a carpet of violets along the broad dirt paths. People seemed even more menacing and hostile in this pastoral setting, managing to appear angry or surly even while they chatted or tapped their feet to the music of the bands.

We walked across the square and down another dirt path to the site where Dimitrios was murdered. Our local guide described the scene:

"Leetle Dimitri come out from heez houz there," she pointed at a wooden building a few hundred feet away. "'E was set upon and stobbed ofer and ofer by a bend of keelers sent by Ifahn da Terribul."

A small church was built to commemorate this event. Filled with vivid frescoes, floor to ceiling and wall to wall, it illustrates the famous murder.

Now this is really bizarre. The best way to tell about this odd overreaction by the authorities is to just write it down as I heard it.

During the attack on little Dimitrios, servants rang a large bell to alert the townspeople. They came running and killed the assassins. For this, sixty families were sent off to Siberia, 200 more people were executed, the remaining citizens had their tongues cut out, and the bell itself was punished by having its clapper cut.

And speaking of overreactions, how about the Church canonizing the little monster just because he was killed?

In truth, our guide told us, Dimitrios was not a delightful little boy, but acted out an inherited cruel streak by torturing cats and other small animals, slicing off the heads of snowmen with his sword (preparing himself for office, no doubt). But, due to the nature of his death, he was actually canonized in later years by the Russian Orthodox Church.

In trying to recreate the accents with direct quotations, I want the reader to hear the voices as I did.

When we walked back to the ship down the same broad path, it was lined with a double gauntlet of vendors, Russian-style, which means not rude or aggressive but gentle and shy. A band of adolescent boys pushed each other, vying for our attention and practicing their English in phrases like "what eees your nahm?" and "I geev you prazant." This latter turned out to be a blue and white medal for which the kid wanted a dollar. The boys were short, not scary, but nothing cute about them, either. They were already wearing the angry, me-against-you expression so prevalent here.

This was one of those scenes that I found so touching, I took the time to write it out in detail, hoping to recreate it accurately for readers.

The vendors, on the other hand, were an endearing bunch. They looked to be arranged in family groups—with each stand having an elderly member, a middle-

aged member, and a child anywhere from infancy to teenager.

At the top of the path, an ancient and wrinkled man sat beside a table of books. He wore a billed Army cap and dusty gray Army uniform on which were pinned several medals. His hands clutched his knees as he watched the crowd in silence. No customers approached his pile of books or spoke to him. A small boy crouched at his side, and every now and then, he jumped up and held a book wordlessly out to little knots of tourists walking down the path.

I sat across the path on a small bench, waiting for Bob to return from the men's room, and watched this scene—the old man gazing, the little boy trying to get the attention of passersby.

Two women in their thirties or forties arranged and rearranged cloth dolls on the table in front of them. They were both much better looking and better-dressed than anyone in the town square, wearing plain cotton skirts and blouses, their brown hair pulled back in scarves.

One of them caught my eye and, quickly turning, she plucked a boy-doll from where it hung on the bark of a large tree next to the old man.

"Hend-made," she called to me. "I do it." She held the boy-doll out for my inspection as I rose and crossed the path to her.

The old man spoke. "Ees balalaika," he said, pointing to the little handpainted triangular piece of wood in the doll's hands. I guessed, then, that he was a relative, maybe the father or uncle of the women. Probably he couldn't be left home alone. So they brought him everyday and set him up with his table and books where he could feel part of the action. I bought the doll. The old man nodded approvingly and smiled, his black and broken teeth showing.

Back on the ship, we proceeded our glide down "Mother Wolga" (as the Cruise Director calls it), past Yaroslavl where we will stop on our way back up this river extension. I am proud to say that, thanks to our brief instruction in the language, I figured out the city was Yaroslavl from the cyrillic writing on its pier building. Of course, it took until we were several minutes beyond the town for me to do this.

Reading cyrillic is like solving a puzzle. Each letter has to be figured out, then the whole thing put together to make a word. It's slow work but speeds up, I'm sure, with practice.

Here is another flash-thought about lack of good-looks. Maybe it will take on greater meaning later on when I have learned more.

In Uglich, it occurred to me that the oldest of the people were the most attractive. That seems to be fair. The really ugly get better looking as they age. The acne, and maybe the anger and despair, disappear; the large bumpy noses and flat cheeks are better concealed by wrinkles than cheap makeup. The broken and missing teeth look more appropriate on the elderly. They abandon the peculiar clothes and settle into large shapeless garments the color of tree trunks and rocks. The magenta, orange, and yellow hair turn to a soft frizz of gray. Everything matches.

It is important to record place names of obscure cities and rivers. Later you can find them on a map, recognize them in National Geographic articles and news items. Without writing them down, strange, difficult to-spell-pronounce names are quickly forgotten. Weaving parts of history into the journal also gives it added value.

Yesterday (May 30) we moved east silently and smoothly past Volga villages to Kostrama, where Czar Michael Romanov, first of his dynasty, was blessed and accepted as Czar by the Church. We walked through the newly restored church, admiring its ochre, deep blue, and gold frescoes. They completely cover the walls and ceilings, making the interior of the church look like some kind of tattooed lady. We snuck a peek at the gold icons in that secret little closet behind the altar, the iconostasis, where only the priests are allowed to go, but the frescoes were the star of the show.

By constant repetition, the history of this country is beginning to take shape in my mind. From the Ivans in the mid-1500s to the "Time of Trouble" (overseen by Boris Gudonov), which was followed by the Romanovs in 1613, starting with this Michael and ending in 1917 with the murder of Nicholas and Alexandra, it's colorful, bloody, and fascinating.

We wandered the square in Koctpama yesterday after visiting the open air museum of wooden architecture. It's my favorite kind of museum. Homes, farmhouses, and barns were brought here from the Russian countryside and spread *around green meadows to simulate life in the 17th century. Local ladies, dressed in period costumes, welcomed us into the houses and explained the interior designs and purposes.*

For example, each home had a "red" corner in which they displayed their most beautiful things—brightly patterned scarves, a carved wooden table, a candlestick or two. Honored guests were offered this place to sit. Others sat on a bench which was built along the walls of the main room. People slept in shelves over the fireplace (which looked similar to the beehive fireplaces of our Southwest U.S.) and stretched along these benches, the youngest and the oldest being closest to the fire.

I wanted to show Nina-at-work, an experienced and enthusiastic guide, who cares about the smallest details, such as finding the best location for picture-taking.

Nina is especially fond of this museum and has scoped out the best photo op from earlier visits. "Stend on dis britch," she told us, "and point at dat liddle shursh." A small band of photographers stepped forward, one by one, onto the narrow wooden bridge and snapped the scene, myself included. Bob, whose pictures are often postcard quality, was off finding ops of his own: interesting angles of the old log structures, and panoramas of the meadows.

What happened next: another small scene-story.

It was warm in the sun and people were sitting under the broad shade trees in the town square when we stepped down from the bus. "Be beck in an hour," instructed Nina. She pointed out a few souvenir stores and a grocery, and then waved her arm in the area behind the bus. "Da market," she said.

We headed for it and found a large expanse of food stands selling vegetables, nuts, spices, fruit. The cabbages were huge, like pale green basketballs.

People looked a little better in Kostrama, healthier and happier than the Uglich crowd. Maybe it's because no one was dressed up.

Packs of small boys followed us from the bus to the marketplace, demanding, of all things, chewing gum. One pasty-faced kid looked just like Oliver Twist. I said, "I don't have any gum." He pointed at the pin on my vest and demanded, "Giff it to me."

I was appalled that he expected success from this approach. I hate begging in young kids. These boys didn't look underfed or poor at all, just wanting something for nothing—like little bag men, Mafia-in-the-making.

They dogged our steps through the square, practically snapping at our heels, elbowing each other and shouting, "Vat iss your num¿" At first, we tried a little friendly conversation. "I'm Bob," answered Bob. "Susan," I said. "Giff me dat!" they all shouted, pointing at the pin, the pen in Bob's pocket, and the bag I was carrying.

"Nyet," we chorused, over and over. "Nyet."

Finally, an old man appeared and shooed them off. I burbled "SwabEEdo!" a word I thought I had learned in our language lesson to express gratitude. He looked bewildered. "SwabEEdo!" I repeated earnestly.

Perplexed, he wandered off. If it wasn't "thank you" I was telling him, what was it¿

In describing fellow travelers, I hope to convey the dynamics of relationships by presenting actual scenes and dialogue.

Fellow passengers are beginning to achieve identity. There are Fred and Ingvold, of course. Did I mention that Fred was born in Germany and is fluent in the language¿ He has found a friend, a German woman named Gerta who lives in New York with her husband, Alfred, whose voice I have yet to hear. Gerta does the talking for both. She is knowledgeable and interesting, a pleasant person. She speaks German animatedly with Fred who lumbers alongside her constantly.

Gerta and Alfred have taken to sitting with Fred and Ingvold at dinner. Alfred stares at his plate and chews slowly while Gerta talks. Ingvold drinks and remains blessedly silent, as far as I can tell. Fred smiles a lot, often laughs out loud at whatever she is saying.

"You gotta meet this woman," he said to me yesterday. "She's so interesting."

Gerta's wig-thing was interesting—a way to cope with the rigors of travel and its effect on hairdos.

Like many of the women, Gerta wears a wig. It sits on her head pertly, and in the wind, tips ever so slightly forward or sideways. I think it's too small and today I worried that it would fly off when we walked through the breezy open air museum. She and Fred were ahead of us, oblivious to the wind or the danger of losing Gerta's hair in their fascination with each other. Alfred and Ingvold trudged silently along behind us.

In the ship's ladies room, I heard women comparing their wigs. "It's not my real hair color, but I love it," said one of her blonde cap of curls. "So much easier than trying to fix my own hair," said another.

These women have lost sight of the fact that they look ridiculous. The wigs look like hairy bathing caps and, except for the varying shades, are all exactly the same. There seems to be a certain lowering of standards, a loosening of grip on the need for appearances among these people. They must not take a lot of pictures of each other.

May 30

Because I had time to look carefully at waterfront Yaroslavl, I wrote this detailed description.

This morning when we awoke we were already tied up in Yaroslavl. Across the river we could see a line of unpainted wooden dachas along the waterfront, with gingerbread trim and picket fences. The official buildings on the dock are large, crumbly, formerly grand pink things. Chunks of the stucco exterior have fallen off so they look like teenagers with bad complexions. Nowhere is the poverty more evident in this country than in its maintenance of public places. Grass isn't trimmed, wastebins are full, paint is chipping, peeling, or gone completely. But there is a raffish charm to the overall impression of neglect—"we're paintless but proud."

A few facts here followed by a memorable scene in the town's center. Events on this trip are so interesting to me that I am writing down virtually everything that happened during the day. In order to enliven long passages, I keep looking for the story potential in each encounter as if I were telling it as an anecdote to the folks back home.

Yaroslavl is known for its ceramic-tile production. Our bus climbed up a wide, linden-lined boulevard to the square, which is dominated by the Church of the Epiphany, a dark red, forest green, many-domed church decorated with this special Yaroslavl "Volga-tile." The city dates from 1010 A.D, has been a wealthy trading center—home to several industries—through both Czarist and Soviet times. About 650,000 people live here. Most of the factories are silent now. Prosperity seems to have abandoned Yaroslavl.

At the sight of this beautiful tile church, we all reached for our cameras and jumped down from the bus as soon as the driver pulled over to the curb. He, too, climbed out and walked to the rear of the bus which, in repose, was panting like a marathon runner. Its engine hood was missing and the innards heaved and coughed, naked and exposed.

The driver, named VeMHA3N (sort of) pronounced "Gim-NAH-Zee," poked at it with a stick, the seams in his face deepening like gorges. The panting vehicle responded with a deep sigh and then stopped.

Passers-by—other men with darkly-lined faces and soiled clothes—sauntered over from doorways and park benches to discuss this old, tired bus. They looked alike, the weary, sighing men and the poor engine, exhausted and covered with years of oil and grime. I watched while each took a turn examining it closely, then stepped back for the next observer. A brief conference and VeMHA3N was back in his driver's seat, working the ignition button.

By the time the photographers were seated again, the bus had roused itself and was once more ready to move. The little band of onlookers looked briefly cheered as they muttered a few words to each other and then disbanded for their corners and doorways.

How could I have neglected to get the name of this wonderful place? It isn't in the guidebook either. Readers will have to look for the white brick walk or ask for the museum in a former governor's home. Dumb mistake.

We stopped next at a small art museum. The bus parked at a square next to an imposing church built by a wealthy family in Czarist times. Faced with a block-long walk to the museum, several of the passengers chose to wait for us there.

We walked along a long brick wall painted white that concealed the museum's garden. It is early spring here and cold. The trees, visible over the wall, had only a hazy suggestion of green surrounding them like halos.

The museum itself was a jewel. It was formerly the home of the local governor, with spacious rooms and french windows and doors leading to the garden. This morning, a trio of silent women with lank brown hair and serious expressions opened the museum just for us.

One gestured wordlessly to the coat rack. Nina interpreted. "Please hang up your coats." Another woman stood by the staircase. "Zis way," she said through pinched lips, clutching her cardigan and shivering. We followed her upstairs to the main galleries.

It was one of the loveliest, most easily accessed art museums I've ever been in, well-worth a return visit and deserving of more time than we could take this morning. There were landscapes of birch forests, river scenes, villages scenes, including a dish of pink and blue lilacs so lacy and alive you could almost smell them—a huge winter Moscow.

Each room moved us further down the years, era to era, from classical to a kind of Russian Hudson River School and, at the end of the tour, into a room of Impressionists. We were enthralled, and as silent as our greeting party had been.

Milling around the coatrack, someone spied a lone glass case sitting in the dark hall by the ladies' room. This was the Museum Shop. Immediately, people converged on the women still in the entry hall, and tried to convey the message that we were buyers. But to no avail. The case remained closed to customers. Capitalist frenzy has not taken hold.

I thought this case of mistaken identity was hilarious at the time.

We returned along the white brick wall and I spied a benchful of babushkas (the name given to those elderly shawl-draped women) and peasants, huddled together in the morning sun. It was a perfect photo opportunity to catch eight locals taking the sun, perhaps feeding pigeons, and just being colorful. I was fumbling with my camera case when one of the women turned and called to us. Oh, my. They were the non-walkers in our group.

I tried to describe this encounter accurately, introducing the tough looking men first and then their gorgeous music, followed by the sale of those touchingly amateur tapes. When an event is so moving, the only way to recreate it is to do so,

step-by-step, as it happened, as you experienced it.

They roused themselves and joined us for a walk through the church, built by a noble family in honor of Elijah the Prophet. Outside the sanctuary, four men, dressed in terrible boxy black suits of rippled serge and looking like the lowest echelon Wise Guys, arranged themselves carefully in a corner of the narthex, probably where the acoustics had proven to be best.

Then they erupted in the harmonies of Russian Orthodox church music—deep bass, bell-toned tenor, with baritone and alto tenor in between, four people sounding like twenty-five. It was such a glorious depth of tone and such a fullness of sound that goose bumps formed along my arms and I almost cried.

They sang several selections and when they finished, one man turned away and picked up a small cardboard box from the floor. It held a dozen or so Memorex audio-tapes. Sliding each into its plastic holder with a blurry picture of the church on the front, the bass said, gruffly, "$10" and began to dole out tapes and collect money as fast as we could thrust it into his hands.

Again, I return to "what happened next."

Later, we drove to an ugly cement Soviet-era block of a building, decorated with peculiar cirliques and multi-colored gee-gaws which, I guess, were supposed to indicate that it was for children because it is the home of the Children's Theatre.

Inside, the director spoke to us in the 300-seat puppet theatre. Upstairs was a larger theatre devoted to plays performed by professional actors for children. Dazzling!

In the lobby were cases of retired marionettes, intricately built and elaborately costumed, and lacquered boxes, which were for sale. The quality was exceptional and the prices high. Some of the brush strokes were "as narrow as a wolf hair," said Nina. The prices ranged from $80 for the smallest, least detailed, to $600 for the most delicately drawn.

But since the proprietor accepted neither charge cards or travelers' checks, no merchandise was sold. Who would carry enough cash to drop that much money on a souvenir, no matter how lovely? No one in this crowd.

Anyway, we had heard from our guide that ceramics were the special craft of Yaroslavl. Therefore, on our next visit, which was to the 13th Century Spassksy

Monastery, several of us crowded around the wooden stalls situated near the entrance. Bob left me to wander around the grounds of this fortification, which proved impenetrable to the invading Poles during the "Time of Trouble" (Boris Gudonov's reign).

Fred and I fingered several different ceramic figures, trying to make our choices. That is, I was trying to make a choice. Fred just bought them all. He has many daughters, daughters-in-law, and I'm sure, with his charm, lots of other women for whom he is buying presents at every stop.

He talked me into asking for more to choose from and buying a couple of little angels with their skirts concealing bells. "You know you'll be sorry if you don't buy them," he admonished. And as I look at them now, I realize that he was right.

Another story, written in detail simply because I had the time.
Leaving the monastery, our driver, having parked his bus along the river, had trouble getting the vehicle to go forward and up the slight rise to the road. With every step on the accelerator, we shot backwards instead. A few people began to mutter anxiously as the bus lost ground with each try. The man behind us actually tried to get out the back door, but found it locked.

Gim Nah Zee didn't seem to be registering the fact that gunning the motor was bringing us closer to the water, not the road. With a final enthusiastic foot-to-the-floor, and several of us shouting "STOP," we shot backward again and ended up hovering precariously on the bank.

Perplexed, Gim Nah Zee studied his gearshift in silence. Finally, he grasped it firmly, and with his jaw firmly set, gunned again. This time we went forward in a shot and were up the hill and on the street before we knew what was happening. The whole bus erupted in applause.

Here is a random thought, which recurred again and again and was often remarked on by our fellow travelers
A person actually engaged in physical labor is a rare sight. There is a lot of leaning on walls, over walls, against walls, ambling, and contemplation. Women bustle more but the business of getting things done is not visible. Scaffolds hold no workers, construction sites are silent, factories and fields are empty. Policemen sit

in cars, smoking and chatting. There is little traffic on foot or in cars. Only the small group of vendors who set up shop near every stop of the bus are in the act of doing something productive that we can actually see.

I thought this scene worthy of writing because it showed the ship's crew in action, as well as continuing the saga of the Raisin.

After the ship left Yaroslavl and most of the ship's guests were resting or playing cards or reading on deck, I heard two long rings like a telephone, followed by the sound of running feet and shouts in Russian. Heavy spray shot from an upper deck outside of our porthole.

On the intercom, Bozo spoke shakily, "Ladees and genneman, plees moof immediately to the aft of the sheep. Plees moof widout panic to the REAR, the AFT of the sheep."

I pulled both life vests out from under the bed, found my wallet with our passports and left the cabin to find Bob. He was in the hall so we did as instructed, moving to the aft.

Other passengers emerged, some calmly turning to lock their doors before joining the throng. No one seemed unnerved, except the stewards who were calling to each other and pounding up and down the halls overhead.

We filed out of the hall and into the reception area. I smelled smoke coming from the staircase. A group of young women wearing chef hats and white aprons huddled together in a corner. One carried a spatula. Another was holding a wooden spoon. They looked dazed and uncertain.

We waited for more instructions. Bob said, calmly, "I was upstairs. There's smoke coming from one of the forward cabins."

We were standing next to the couple from the cabin next to ours. They are Greek-American, a retired physician and his wife named Peter and Elizabeth who have visited Baltimore and the Greek Orthodox Church Fair held in the city each fall.

"We should have had our fire drill by now," said Peter.

"I thought we were supposed to have a drill on our first day out," his wife said. "We've always had the safety drill immediately on other ships." They didn't sound *nervous, just irritated.*

In a few minutes, the voice came back on the p.a. announcing that all danger was past and that we were free to return to our cabins. "Zis vas not a drill, ladies and genneman. We will have a fire-safety drill at 1100 hours. Please remoof your life jeckets from your cebbins and go to your assigned steshun when you hear za alarm at 1100 hours. Steshuns are posted in your cebbin, behind za cebbin door."

There was a pause and the voice continued, darkly. "From now on, no one, that is no one will be allowed to use small boiling devices in zer cebbins. Hot water is zupplied on every floor. Zer is no need to use small boiling devices in your cebbins."

Later it was confirmed that someone using a "small boiling device" had left the thing boiling away while she ate breakfast and toodled around the ship, unaware that she was close to setting it on fire. Her cabin was burned black and, worse, her neighbor's things were ruined by the water from the firehoses.

The culprit? The Raisin! Her reaction? Fury that she was moved to a lesser cabin. Fred witnessed her railing at the Cruise Director and demanding that the difference in cost be refunded to her.

When thinking about the memorable aspects of a day, sometimes they have nothing to do with scenery or scenes or even people. The samovar—its importance as our water source, its incredibly-convenient location—was a large part of our life onboard the MS Lenin and, thus required explanation. Explaining it meant explaining my early morning coffee ritual which became ever more furtive as the cruise went on and "small boiling devices" were outlawed. Maybe we'd seen too many movies, but these paragraphs describe the atmosphere, at least from my point of view at 6:30 a.m.. Of course, it might have been the result of a guilty conscience, too.

May 29

The water barrel (I think of it as "the samovar") in the hall outside of our cabin is a 3' steel contraption set in a steel tray, with two spigots—one for boiling, the other for room temperature drinking water. It's the single greatest convenience on this ship. Water is drawn from it to brush teeth, make coffee or tea, and to drink. One step out of our door and I'm at the spigots.

Early in the morning, I step out to fill my small boiling device (I look furtive-

ly right and left, concealing the water boiler with a towel). This is one of those travel necessities like a notebook or an extra sweater or the canteen for water. I must have my coffee early in the morning. This is not negotiable. Rather than depend on room service or lobby service, and chancing the local stuff that is too often burned or bland, I pack up the water-boiler, a brown plastic cone with sufficient number of paper filters, and a plastic bag of Starbucks or Peet's finely-ground coffee.

For this trip, I have brought along the European bouillier which runs on the same current as the ship. (Elsewhere, I have an American one and a lot of little conversion plugs.) Usually, I'm a pretty good rule-follower, but I tried the hot water for tea yesterday and it was quickly tepid. Won't do. Won't do at all. As I said, this is non-negotiable.

To mask the wonderful rich scent of Starbucks-in-the-morning, I shoved towels under the cabin door, then dumped the grounds into the toilet. I felt like I was in one of those behind-enemy-lines movies, stripping cigarettes and grinding the tobacco into the ground, as I tried to anticipate any other clues that my coffee habit might have left.

I feel certain that Bozo calls attendants together each day to report on their charges. Our Lida is a gentle creature with a soft voice and sweet smile. Who knows how well she'd hold up under his questioning? Something about the atmosphere in this country—with its dark history of intrigue and oppression—establishes this mood, this suspicion that even the walls have ears.

More chronology followed by additional description of Nina, which adds a little information about money-changing. I should have written more about this procedure.

Afloat again from Yaroslavl to Irma, we spent the late afternoon listening to Professor Irina's culture talk and trying to spell our names in cyrillic at the language lesson. Lena and Nina hosted a Grand Circle cocktail party at 5:30, standing at the door of the lounge and greeting each one of us with a smile and a handshake. These two, particularly Nina, aim to establish themselves as friends, hostesses on-board both ship and bus. Nina's skill as a guide is great, she is knowledgeable about the history as well as current events, and her sense of humor prevails under the most trying of circumstances.

She does extra things for us, like the subway tour. In Moscow, she didn't just wave Bob and me toward an area where we could by film; she escorted us there and spoke to the clerk on our behalf. On that same day, she took the two of us to the bank branch where we could change some money into rubles and advised us on the complicated procedure for doing this in Russia. (For us, lots of filling out and signing of papers, and for the clerk, lots of stamping signed forms.) In our experience, this kind of hands-on attention is not common among guides.

Again, what follows was part of the day's chronology, but not important enough to detail. I only wrote these extras because I had time.

After the cocktail party and dinner, the musicians gave a concert in the bar, featuring the woman-singer with a powerful operatic soprano voice. She worked hard at expression and gestures, but the folk songs she sang all sounded alike and it was hard to get the down-home flavor from her big-stage voice. I would have preferred hearing her sing something more suitable for her, more operatic. "Moscow Nights" should be left to those with smaller ranges and lesser talents. When she took a break, we slipped out and went to bed.

In this next scene, using more color would have enhanced the description. Instead of just writing "marvel at the views," I should have described why they were marvelous. "Small squares" gives an accurate picture of the gardens but why don't the flowers have color and scent? I should have worked harder on this one, searching for simile to bring the day back to life more easily. I was probably saving energy for the scene that followed this one.

May 31

Today our ship docked near a village called Irma. This was called a "green stop" on the itinerary and what a pleasure to have one of those. We did nothing but hike the trails on the green hills, walk the dirt roads through the pine and birch trees, marvel at the views of the water, the little village with its neat wooden dachas and small squares of newly planted onion, potatoes, cabbage, carrots, and flowers. Lots and lots of flowers. It was cool with low clouds but the sun burst through regularly and the breeze was enough to discourage the mosquitoes (which, according to the guidebook, can be a true nuisance.)

The only way for me to tell about interactions like this one is to try to remember how it occurred, moment to moment, and just write it up.

While we were wandering around, Nina caught up to us and asked if we would like to visit a dacha—there was, she told us, a woman and her daughter who lived nearby who would like to have us in for a cup of tea. We said, wonderful! And followed her while she gathered up a few more people. Then we all walked farther down the hill to an unpainted cottage next to a large vegetable garden.

Inside the low doorway, an elderly woman stood next to her middle-aged daughter, both fluttering their hands and smiling shakily. The daughter, a librarian, brings her children here each summer to stay with their grandmother. She told Nina, who then told us, that there are 30 or so other children here, too, under the same arrangement. It's healthy here away from the polluted city and safe.

We filed into the little house. It had two small rooms and a kitchen alcove. In both rooms, wires from a bare bulb outlet in the ceiling fanned out to juice up toasters, lamps, and heaters. We dipped under this spidery array and placed ourselves around the second room, which held only a table, two worn chairs and sofa.

Hanging on the wall was a large black-and-white photograph of two mournful looking young people. The daughter, Anastasia, explained that it was a picture of her father and mother when they were first married and living far from Irma. Their village was destroyed by the Germans and her father died soon after, so her mother came here to this little island to live and raise her six children in this minuscule cottage.

While Anastasia was speaking (in Russian—Nina translated), the old lady began to weep, her poor old face collapsing into sadness, as if the death of her husband had occurred last week instead of nearly forty years ago. She disappeared into the kitchen. There was a brief silence in the room.

Then a woman standing next to me—one of the emptier heads in the group—said brightly to Nina, "Ask her if they have electricity out here." We looked at her in wonder, arranged as we were under the tent of wires protruding from the ceiling plug. Nina murmured that, yes, they had electricity. Just then the daughter signaled us to come into the next room and have some tea. We filed into seats around a picnic table where the two women had set carefully-arranged plates of cookies *and hard candy at each end. Care had been taken with the arrangement of sweets, too; the little brown sugar cookies were fanned in a circle around the edge of the plate, candies in the center.*

Nina explained the samovar which sat on a table in the corner. It is a tall, silver-metal device. A teacup sits on top of a container which holds water. Steam is generated from heated charcoal in the lower section. The hot water is tapped from a spigot in the side, and poured over the strong tea in the cup before serving.

Anastasia began to pass out china cups of hot tea from the samovar. Blessedly, she had left the room for more cups when the same dimwitted woman picked up a cookie and keenly observed, "This is store-boughten." It was hard to interpret her tone. Did she think that was good or bad? She said again to the man sitting next to her, "Harry? These cookies are store-boughten." This time, she sounded like she was accusing the women of some kind of cookie-fraud.

Anastasia returned with more tea. The rest of us began to compliment her and her mother lavishly, enthusiastically raving about the tea, the cookies, the candy, the house, the garden, the photos, the wires, the china cups. The visit ended in a babble of compliments and thanks for their hospitality. We left the dacha, hoping that our hostesses really didn't understand English at all.

This next little scene could use more color (the daffodils were yellow and white, as I recall now). But having spent so much time on the dacha scene, these sentences are sufficient for lodging this encounter in my memory.

Bob went off to take some pictures. I wandered through the little settlement followed by a large friendly dog of no known origin (at least to me). The sun was bright now and people were bending over rows and beds of furrowed dirt. A red-faced woman wiping her forehead with the back of a gloved hand saw me and her face lit up with a wide smile. She walked to the edge of her yard, plucked three daffodils, and shyly offered them to me over the fence. I took them happily, smiling back and trying to get those pesky little "thank you" words in Russian to come out right. Whatever I said, she nodded enthusiastically and went back to her garden.

Souvenir-buying is such a large part of many trips, particularly this one. Directly quoting Carolyn makes her more real than description alone would. This led to the

random thoughts about souvenirs themselves and the way in which Bob and I become buyers, and what we end up buying.

Carolyn, a quiet wraith of a woman who sat in near-silence while we ate with her and her husband Tom, is a frenzied souvenir shopper. She returns to the ship each day clutching plastic bags of amber beads, matoushka dolls, and painted boxes. "This is just crazy-shopping," she muttered to me as she boarded the bus in Yaroslavl. "I've bought what we need for gifts and now we just buy. I'll never use all this stuff."

Today vendors had set up shop at the top of the path from the pier. We walked by this little commercial center several times, on our way to Anastasia's dacha, to the spot where we photographed the view, to the little village. Each time, I saw Carolyn and Tom at the stands, heads bent over one display after another, holding amber beads up to the sun or opening folded woolen scarves and exclaiming at the colorful patterns.

I thought of our Mao caps, our Greek purses, Egyptian cartouches, Israeli bracelets, and Bali coolie hat, all those things we thought we "needed" to own. Souvenir-buying has a cycle: the casual first glance at whatever the locals are making and selling bus-side, then the stirring of interest as thoughts of folks back home pop up, in our imaginations wearing Mao caps, Greek purses, etc. and, finally, looks of delight and gratitude.

Another use for that small spiral notebook. Add "gift list" to "notes" and "expenses."

Names form lists in my notebook: the children, grandchildren, office people, neighbors watching the dog. Then the compelling vision of ourselves wearing these things. Suddenly, we need them, to complete an outfit, to decorate a dress or to shade the sun. Now we have purpose. We become buyers.

First forays are to establish price. Boarding the bus with a t-shirt having cost $5 is to be avoided if it can be found two for $5. Souvenir sophistication grows with each mile, each new city and sight. After a week or so, we know the best price to pay for this and that. I've often wondered if vendors can tell the difference between the naive well-pressed tourist who pays any price and the shop-hardened rumpled sophisticate ("You want what?") whose trip will soon be over.

For me, the best reminder of a place is music from the area, usually available as a souvenir cassette tape. This started when I followed the soulful sounds of a violin playing in mournful minor through the narrow streets of old Jerusalem. They were coming from a small store. The bearded forelocked proprietor stood in the doorway and smiled when I asked about the music. He produced a cassette tape.

"Ten dollars," he said. I paid and popped it in my purse. It has given me hours of joy since then, never failing to conjure up narrow streets, bearded Jews, and the brooding bustle of old Jerusalem.

On more recent trips, I have added t-shirts to souvenirs that I am likely to use myself, beyond the usual gifts for other people. I like it when people pause to read my chest or my back. These shirts attract other travelers ("Oh, you've been to Lombok! Didn't you love it?") or people who want to be travelers. Conversation starters.

After leaving Irma, we crept quietly into another lock on the Volga/Baltic Canal. By now we are veterans of this process. But it still amazes us how quickly and silently this enormous ship slithers into its designated spot, drops to the new level, and emerges into the next body of water. There is not a bump or a jolt, despite walls so close we could reach out and touch them without a stretch if we were on-deck.

The church spire was thought-provoking and dramatic. We'd read about it in the guidebook and had been told about it by Nina, but seeing it was most impressive. I wonder if my words properly conveyed my reaction. But all you can do is write it as you see it. In this case, the words do indeed bring the vision to life again—for me, at least.

We sailed this morning from the Volga River into the Rybynsk Reservoir. This huge body of water was created by Stalin by flooding more than seven hundred villages, as part of his plan to complete the connection of waterways between Moscow and St. Petersburg. A church spire juts defiantly out of the water, testimony to the life that once existed under it. Pine forests stand rotting just beneath the surface, stealing nutrients from the water, earning it the name "Fish Cemetery."

It is a powerful sight, that church spire. It is a sight common in small towns everywhere, a church spire on top of a church which stands in the middle of a square of houses and stores, a place where men, women, children, and animals live and work together. But now it sits in the middle of this huge reservoir, mute testimony to both the Stalin Era and the spiritual Russia that refused to die during the Communist reign. It isn't hard to envision the town which still surrounds it, deep under the black water. It is an image that will stay with me long after this trip is over, I am sure.

Again, I wanted to capture the feel of this village—with its dock and its schoolchildren. So I just closed my eyes and revisited it in my memory, writing down exactly what I saw there, step by step. The monastery's history was in my notes.

We docked at Goritsky, a small village southeast of White Lake. For some reason, we were warned repeatedly about wandering alone in Goritsky, although it looked harmless enough. Wooden houses huddled together along a dirt road. We can see paths in the grass leading around the inlets to other piers where two more huge white cruise ships are docked. Tourists seeped from them and fanned out like an oil spill to the little souvenir shops and stands. The entire fleet of Goritsky schoolbuses waited for us at the top of the path leading from our ship. Nina hurried us by the stands, assuring us that they would still be there when we got back from our sightseeing.

The buses were battered hulks. They looked like a parade of war-wagons. We were engulfed in fumes as we labored up and down the rolling hills to the town. It's hard to imagine these vehicles making their way through a Russian winter's ice and snow with a load of kids. But today there was a clear blue sky, warm sun, and a cool breeze.

We visited the monastery and museum of Kyrill, a wealthy man who had wandered Russia for years in search of solitude, and in escape from the fancy life of the city. By the time he got to the area of Goritsky, he was sixty. Kyrill lived as the head of the monastery until he was in his 90's. This was in the late 14th Century, powerful evidence of the effect of good diet and clean living. His monks were said to live an average of 100 years, tending their herbs and fasting.

The monastery was considered to be the richest in Russia. The Poles invaded during the 17th Century, as they did the monastery in Kostrama, but the double-fortified walls made them impenetrable, and set the standard for monasteries-worth-seeing, I guess. It is certainly the fact mentioned most in the guides' talks.

The museum inside the walls displayed Kyrill's clothes, his books and illuminated manuscripts. There was a tiny museum shop a step from the exit. We wouldn't have seen it at all, except that Carolyn and Tom, with their unerring ability to locate commerce, ducked into it ahead of us. Carolyn was already trying on stiff white lacy blouses by the time we stepped through the entrance.

We rode back to the pier and had hours onshore to wander the stands and shops. I caught amber fever today and bought a pin, a brooch, and a set of beads that look like a string of bad teeth.

It is the compulsory "work week" for schoolchildren, Nina explained. Schools are not in session, but kids are required to do something work-like. Near the pier there was a large fenced-in field, where we watched young teens haul dirt from one pile to another. A pretty blonde teacher, her baby playing in the grass beside her, directed these efforts. As soon as a group would dump the dirt onto the pile, another bunch would haul it back to where it started.

It was a stunning display of wasted time and effort. We watched in astonishment, imagining that some kind of educational outcome would magically occur, but no. They just loaded dirt, dumped, reloaded and dumped again, for hours. I kept leaving the little souvenir stands and going back to check on their "progress." They were still loading and dumping when we got back on the ship and sailed away.

Life (and food) on-board the ship is an important part of each day, so I tried to record what was happening and to reconstruct scenes as I saw them.

And speaking of oil spills, the one in the soup at lunch was so thick, the vegetables were in suspension on top. It was so unappetizing that I didn't even bother to fish out the carrots and potato. We scarfed down the entire tower of black bread, instead, and had to ask the waitress for more for the rest of the people at our table.

Late this afternoon, the kitchen staff held a "Russian Tea Party." Seven intricately decorated cakes were offered as prizes in a lottery, with chances going for

$2 each. The cakes were set in display on a large table under lights while a musical trio from the lounge wandered through, playing Russian folk songs. Everyone clapped in time to the music; it was a festive affair.

The woman who sat with us in the dacha—the one who wondered if it had electricity—was heard to ask if the cakes were actually made of ice cream. Somehow she has the impression that Ben & Jerry's started here in Russia. I think it's because an ice cream manufacturing facility was once located near here. Her own personal electricity is definitely dimming.

A random-thought here, inspired by having time to consider this peculiar bunch of fellow passengers:

But there's an odd lack of concentration among the passengers of this ship. People just aren't very alert when they're so well-cosseted, I think. The entire group falls silent during a p.a. announcement of, say, "the lecture will begin in 15 minutes in the lounge." Then they'll look at each other questioningly and say, "Does anyone know if we have a lecture today?"

In introducing two more fellow passengers, I wanted to conjure up their physical appearance before telling about Inez' difficult trip to Kennedy, in order to stress just how elderly they looked, then contrast that with Inez' energy and their general perkiness. In relating the following scenes at the pier, I hoped to convey their jaunty attitude, as well as to show the local populace in action. Direct quotes, as always, help to bring the scene to life.

Two exceptions are Beulah and Inez. Both in their eighties, they wear identical frosted brown wigs (Beulah has a pink bow in hers), heavy gray wool cardigans, and big brown lace-up shoes. Their old faces are lined with lots of evidence of past laughter; their eyes are bright with curiosity. These two are terrific dinner companions.

Inez lives in the west somewhere and had to change planes several times to get to Kennedy. Bad weather kept her overnight in the St. Louis airport, where she slept on a bench. She missed her connection, but undaunted, continued her journey the next day, meeting up with Beulah and the rest of us on the ship in Moscow.

As we filed out from the Russian Tea Party, Inez told us that the people in the little shop, the only building on the pier, were being watched by the police when she was in it. "But I was there when you were there," I exclaimed. Then I remembered the two men at the door.

"Those guys in uniform at the shop door...I thought they were protecting us," I said. "Remember how they kept telling us not to walk alone in Goritsky?"

Inez laughed. "Oh, that was ridiculous. Beulah and I took a lovely walk, didn't we?" Beulah nodded with enthusiasm. "We saw some fine gardens," she added.

"We weren't supposed to bargain with people," Inez said. "We were supposed to pay some sort of state-mandated price, I think. Remember how those cops kept watching us in the store?"

"Not state-mandated," corrected Beulah. "Mafia-mandated. Lena told me she thinks that's a mafia store, that there are a lot of mafia guys in this town."

I remembered the scene. The shop was crowded with people leaning over the glass cases, pointing at things, fingering the merchandise. Two women salesclerks were busy reaching into the cases, retrieving discards, returning them. They moved back and forth, case to case.

Behind them, a short, dark, thirty-ish man, standing alongside a battered desk, was rifling through papers most of the time, but stepped forward to help when the surge of souvenir-mad cruise passengers became unwieldy. There was frequent consultation in rapid Russian, eyes furtive and downcase. None of the trio looked pleased with the activity. We appeared to be more of an annoyance to them than a boon. This is not a culture where the customer is king, so that didn't seem unusual at the time.

I found the necklace that I wanted—irregular amber beads instead of the more expensive round ones ("they look like plahsteek," Lena said of the round beads when I showed them to her). I muscled into the crowd at the counter and handed the necklace to the dark-haired guy. The price was $15 but, out of habit, I asked, "Ten dollars?" and held out a $10 bill.

He shook his head hard, theatrically hard. "Nyet! Feef-teen!" he said, rather loudly, I thought. I was doing what I think of as "the ponder"—mulling over the choice of paying full price or leaving—when his fingers crawled toward mine, and he slid the ten out and replaced it with the necklace, now wrapped in cellophane.

He eyes were glancing about furtively, his brow was furrowed, he put a finger to his lips, and went about his business. I figured he didn't want me to tell all the people who had just paid full price about my bargain, so I became just as secretive, quickly dropping the beads into my bag, and slipping out of the store before anyone could ask, "Did you buy anything?" The two men in uniforms were snatching a quick smoke by the door as I pushed past.

I told this to Beulah and Inez, who were pleased at the confirmation—if that's what it was—of their suspicions.

After the Tea Party, I decided to walk the ship's decks for exercise. The Raisin was hurling insults at the receptionist for some infraction by her cabin steward. The other passengers have named her Miss Congeniality. Her reputation for sheer nastiness is firmly established.

The people on the ship were a large part of the overall experience. Some were downright peculiar. Marguerite was both peculiar and interesting. Physical description was important to seeing Marguerite as I did. The relationship between her and Ethel was worth writing about, I thought. Having the time, I remembered the little Kremlin-stop scene and added it, to show rather than tell about it.

Outside, I edged by a pair of women with whom we have sat on the bus—Ethel and Marguerite—said "Good evening" the way you do on this ship. Most other places, a "hi" would do, but, somehow or other, pounding around the outskirts of this boat, it seems more appropriate to say "Good evening," like someone in a British novel.

Ethel is an elderly black woman. On the bus, she says nothing, and sits in silence, listening to Marguerite, a very tall angular white woman with stiff, shoulder-length yellow curls, a long aristocratic nose, and a wide, curving back. Her resemblance to Big Bird is remarkable.

Marguerite is at least as old as Ethel but has told others that Ethel was her nanny or her mother's faithful family retainer, or some such thing. Unless Ethel is 120 years old and just looks to be 85 or so, I doubt her story. Marguerite has also told us that she is an opera singer, a professional photographer, and a ballet dancer.

By Fred, Ingvold, and others at dinner-time, Marguerite and Ethel remain the subjects of speculation. It is generally agreed that Ethel must be watching out for Marguerite, and probably has been doing that job for years and years.

Marguerite may be crazy as a loon but she is always in a good mood and friendly. She talks constantly in a cheerful voice with a cultured, upper East side New York accent. Ethel, when she speaks at all, is dignified and barely audible.

Ethel's only moment of exasperation came when they were late returning to the bus at the Kremlin stop in Moscow. She and Marguerite appeared after everyone else was seated. Nina was counting heads and obviously coming up short. I saw the two rounding the corner from the direction opposite where they should have been. Marguerite's stiff hair was pointing outward like the crown on the Statue of Liberty, her long bony elbows were pumping as she hurried toward the bus. The corners of Ethel's mouth were turned down, her brow wrinkled with irritation.

As they pushed past me to their seats, I heard Ethel say, "I don't know why I was following you. I knew you were lost."

Here I throw in some history and local color provided by the tour guide and not appearing in the guidebook. The Petrpzavodsk visit was a major highlight in a trip of major highlights and so, once again, I just ran through the chronology of the day and evening, not wanting to leave anything out.

June 3

We passed through the Volga/Baltic Canal after leaving White Lake and crossed over Lake Onega to the city of Petrozavodsk, which is the capital of this area called Kareliya. "Petrozavodsk" means "Peter's factory-town" and was the place where Peter the Great established a foundry to make munitions for his war with the Swedes. Because it's so close to Finland, it's considered today to be more Finnish in nature than Russian.

I wanted to capture the overall look of the city, so I closed my eyes, pictured it, and came up with the image of a "stale cake."

A boom/bust city, depending on whether Russia was at war or not, Petrozavodsk manufactured construction equipment during the Soviet Era. Now many of its factories are closed and it is crumbling like stale cake. Everywhere we looked, sidewalks, roads, pedestals of statues and buildings were flaking and breaking and splitting. Even one new construction looked dangerously cracked. The city is seedy.

The local guide ran down the list of industries which have flourished here—furniture, food-canning, and shoe-making. There's even a facility for manufacturing Ben & Jerry's ice cream here, too. She explained that this U.S. company was diverted to Petrozavodsk because the tariffs were too high in their first choice location: Moscow. We rode the buses into town and stopped across the street from a circular bunker, which was similar in architecture to the Moscow Circus building.

No longer a manufacturing center, the city now has a reputation for its fine arts. There is a music conservatory in town and the internationally known dance troupe, Kantele, is based here, in this bunker. A performance was scheduled especially for us.

Here is another of those step-by-step descriptions. I wanted to recreate this experience accurately, but I don't think I spent enough time on the dancing itself.
Inside, taped folk music was playing. I followed its strains to a table laden with cassettes, and bought a tape. Vendors were stationed at tables by the top of the staircase, in the lobby just outside the entrance to the theatre. Members of our group fanned out, leaning over the local offerings of jewelry, scarves, and matoushka dolls. Bob went inside and saved us front row seats for the performance. Eventually, the lobby lights blinked and the rest of us filed into the performance hall. The seats were arranged bowl-like, like an amphitheater.

There was no apron or elevation to the stage; the dancing took place on the floor in front of our seats. In the front row, we were so close to the action that if it had been a play, we would have had to know our lines.

Members of the company accompanied the dancers on "kanteles," stringed instruments which look like no-neck balalaikas. Everybody sang—solos, duets, trios, and the whole company in a chorus. The dances involved a lot of leaping and hopping around by both men and women. As close as we were, it was almost eery how soundlessly they leapt and landed. Not a foot-fall was heard, as close as five feet away from us. Their strength and grace was astounding.

The music was lively, toe-tapping stuff with an occasional ballad solo thrown in. I loved every minute of this unusual presentation. The company has recently toured the United States and often played in Europe. We were fortunate that they were in town when we were.

The first time I wrote this passage, it was loaded with adjectives like "very" and "beautiful." I crossed out all the empty words and it sounded better.

Back on the ship, Nina told us that some teachers from the music conservatory were coming after dinner to play for us. I don't usually go to the evening shows in the lounge (too hot, too long, too late) but didn't want to miss this one—a kantele-recital. You won't get that back home.

The music teachers—three men and three women—call themselves "Voices of Russia" and have toured, recorded, AND performed together for years. Plainly dressed and looking like your basic schoolteachers, they set up their folding chairs, put a stack of their tapes on a table near the door, and sat down to play various sizes of kanteles and mandolins.

The music ranged from sprightly to sad, from melancholy to playful. What I loved about the evening was that the group got such a bang out of each other. They were like musicians everywhere who get together for the sheer joy of jamming, loving each other's skill and sound, just awash in the pleasure of producing music. That we were there as audience was incidental. They would have had as much fun playing in the cloakroom of the local elementary school.

Musicians this good can't keep their instruments in their cases—probably pull them out on the bus home and noodle around for an hour or two after they arrive get there. For musicians, this is like a playground pick-up game of basketball.

Of course, I bought their tape.

June 4—our 16th anniversary

This morning, at the end of breakfast, Lena and Nina marched over to our table, holding a bottle of champagne and singing "Happy Anniversary to You." The rest of the dining room joined in.

Going through the step-by-step doesn't take much time but livens the writing.

Lena set the champagne down and Nina took a small package out of her pocket and put it on the table in front of me. I took off the paper and found a small, carved wooden box, just the size for earrings and at least one of the painted pins we've been collecting.

Why didn't I record Bill's and Ouida's last name?

We were so touched by this thoughtful gesture. We asked our tablemates, Ouida and Bill from Minneapolis, to join us for the champagne at dinner. Lena and Nina demurred. I think for convenience and their own privacy, they've made it their policy not to join passengers at the dinner table.

Bill and Ouida are happy people. Bill is a big red-faced man who has an explosion of a laugh. His eyebrows shoot up, his smile widens, and out it comes. Ouida's face is built for smiling; her cheeks and eyes are circles, her mouth is curly. They are cheerful to be with and so pleased to be with us at our anniversary dinner that Ouida slipped a pink enamel bracelet into my hand as they sat down.

"I have another one," she whispered. "And I want you to have this as a souvenir."

I divided this day-at-Kizhi into more paragraphs than usual because I thought the description and narrative was a little dry, and that by breaking it up, it might become more appealing to read.

During the night, we sailed to the island of Kizhi in the middle of Lake Onega, the second largest lake in Europe. It is only six kilometers long and one kilometer wide and is totally devoted to an open-air museum of wooden buildings, among which is a gorgeous, gray shingled church. The gray wood shone in the afternoon sun so brightly, it looked like it was made of sterling silver.

After breakfast, we disembarked and walked to the church along wooden planks—to avoid the local poisonous snakes in the long grasses near the waterfront. It is the Transfiguration Cathedral and it consists of 30,000 shingles on twenty-two cupolas in five tiers, a "summer-church" built entirely of aspen-wood and without a single nail. The legend is that it was built (in 1714) by one man with one axe.

On the approach, there are few trees, few shrubs. The cathedral loomed huge and solitary against the morning sky. The sun was still climbing up from behind it and the unpainted wood made the building look dark and forbidding, sort of Charles Addams-ish, as we walked up the rise shivering in the cool air.

Up close, we could see the construction detail of the individually hewn shingles on the cupolas. They looked like gray Necco wafers, an enormous gingerbread house left too long in the attic. The aspen changed hue in the sun, looking alternately silver, pink, and pale purple (licorice, peppermint, and grape).

Next door to the cathedral stands the smaller Intercession Church, which dates from 1764, and between the two is the bell tower. These are the original structures on the island.

Scattered around Kizhi's southern tip are more churches, homes, bell towers, and bathhouses. They were collected from the Lake Onega area and brought here to this open-air museum, which is officially called The State Historical, Architectural, and Ethnographic Preserve of Kizhi. It makes for a quiet ghost of a town—with its buildings connected by wide paths, lined with small trees.

We toured one of the larger peasant houses where several generations had lived, each with its own spacious room similar in design to the one we had seen in Kostroma—"red" corner, bench-lined walls, beehive fireplace with sleeping shelves—sort of an eighteenth century apartment building. The barn was built within the walls; a huge ramp for the animals leads from it to the outside.

We left Kizhi in the early afternoon and sailed by the Cathedral gleaming silver in the sun. We are on our way to the southwestern tip of Lake Onega, where we will sail the Svir River into the largest inland lake in Europe, Lake Ladoga. We'll cross Lake Ladoga at its southernmost end into the Neva River and up to the Baltic Sea. We are due to reach St. Petersburg by late afternoon tomorrow.

Interspersing this personal view with the tourist-type information (e.g., the history of Kizhi) is important to maintaining your presence in the journal.

This is the twelfth day of our riverboat trip and it may be just a teeny weeny bit too long for the crew. Our cabin attendant, Leda, no longer replaces toilet paper (I lurk around receptions until the crowds thin and then whisper, "toilet paper?" to whomever is there, who nods wearily in response. This is, apparently, a common request). Nor does she fill the water carafe as she did in early days.

Enthusiasm for service has waned in the dining room as well. The stack of black bread gets shorter each meal, the water pitcher is nowhere to be found and the number of glasses at the table doesn't match the number of table settings. We point all these things out to the waitresses each time and they scurry of, returning with the missing bread, water, glasses.

Obviously, the crew is not tip-literate. It is, after all, only the second year OdessAmerica has run this cruise. Russians are just waking up to the potential of capitalism, the marvels of marketing, the joys of pay for personal production. Here, on-board the MS Lenin, they are not yet aware of the value of beefing up their service and ministrations as we get closer to disembarkation, when those little envelopes stuffed with cash will cross from our hands to theirs.

That brings to mind a major irritation of ours—on this trip, the business of tipping everyone who is still standing at the end of a cruise. No personal checks, of course, no exchange of traveler's check, no credit cards—the requirement is for US dollars to be paid as tips to virtually every human being on-board, seen and unseen. (We are told, "don't forget the kitchen crew, the sailors who swab the decks," etc. etc.)

Why can't this honorarium be included in the original price and handled by Grand Circle instead of us? I will write them to find out. I doubt if there is anyone (except perhaps the Raisin) who isn't planning to do his/her fair share so why not just levy it to begin with, instead of requiring us to squirrel away huge fistsful of bills and then to parcel them out to this multitude? It is what I would classify as a Major Pain-in-the-Ass.

In fact, Leda is dangerously close to coming up empty-handed if she doesn't pull herself together and start replacing the toilet paper again. (Maybe "tp" was rationed. "Twelve rolls a trip and that's it" is written in some list of regulations somewhere.)

In spite of these minor inconveniences, this is emerging as one of the finest travel experiences we have ever had—educational, illuminating of the local history and culture.

You can catch up with things you've left out when time allows.

We are at sea ("at lake"?) most of today, sliding along the shores of Lake Onega and into the Neva River. We got to bed late last night because of the Talent Show. I guess I forgot to mention this event earlier. A couple of days ago, Nina called a meeting for anyone interested in participating in the traditional Grand Circle/cruise talent show. I went alone, because Bob would rather be keel-hauled than appear in a talent show.

I wanted to get across the fact that this talent-show was an integral part of the trip for these people; they had brought their costumes, and had their acts together. Marguerite even added an element of surprise.

Attendance was sparse but enthusiastic. I keep forgetting how cruise literate these people are. They are veterans of this experience. Some even brought music and costumes with them. Peter and Marie, the Greek American doctor and his wife, plan to sing Greek songs—not together, but each in solo. They asked for at least twenty minutes. George, an elderly guy with a bad limp, volunteered his whistling act. His wife said she would tell a little Bible story. Sound good so far?

Nina was writing down each offering, not questioning the time requested nor asking for any demos. She, too, is a veteran of these things. The only time she faltered was when Marguerite appeared without Ethel in tow.

She crept in, looking more like Big Bird than ever, in a yellow leotard, a rolled-up mat clutched in her hands, and perched on one of the banquettes, legs akimbo. She was prepared, Marguerite told us, to do her fifteen minute yoga demonstration for the talent show and would be happy to run through it immediately, if necessary.

Nina, looking slightly dismayed, stared at the mat in silence. We all did. The prospect of Marguerite writhing on the mat for fifteen minutes was daunting.

"Do you have music?" Nina finally asked. "No," Marguerite answered with perfect aplomb. "There is narration. I explain the moves as I go along."

The show was going to be lengthy enough so I declined to do anything but watch. I might not have done that except for the promise of Marguerite's yoga act. The woman is 80 years old (at least, that's what she admits to) and her rangy body looks better in a leotard than most women do at 30. Her good natured self-confidence was irresistible. I just prayed that no one would laugh.

I wanted to accurately capture the talent show scene, so I went step-by-step, putting down the events as they happened without much explanation or description.

The show began right after the first seating of dinner last night. The second seating has its own talent show so we had to be out of there by 10 p.m. We were late. Here's why:

Peter began with his Greek songs which he translated before singing. There were a lot of them (it seemed like forty) and they all had the same melody and nearly the same words. When he finally finished, Marie stood and sang her greatest hits, which sounded just like his, and by the time she sat down, the room had grown increasingly hot, and the audience was getting restive . We were thirty minutes into the show and had only seen the first act. Not a good sign.

The Whistler was really good—he told how he had learned to whistle lying in a hospital bed in the Philippines, recovering from a war wound. This lent a tone to his performance that engendered special appreciation. His wife's little Bible story was peculiar but short.

A few more rickety acts followed, including a hastily choreographed chorus line, a nervous trio singing "Moscow Nights" from a shaking sheet of paper, and a very funny comedy routine satirizing our Cruise Director and his "safety drill for ship evacuation."

This is what I wanted to get to: Marguerite's yoga act. The rest was just introduction, setting the stage. Color (the yellow leotard) and similes ("daffodil" and "ship's knots") helped with the description

And then came Marguerite. She stepped into the spotlight wearing her yellow leotard, transformed from the gawky Big Bird into a graceful daffodil. She unfurled her mat, talking all the time in her patrician accent about the benefits of yoga. With dignity, she folded and knotted herself into yoga positions that made her body look like a demonstration of ship's knots. The few who had started to snicker now stared in awe. Not even when, face on mat and on her knees, she presented her yellow-clad rear-end up for the big finish to her act, did they emerge *from their stunned silence.*

When she stood and bowed, the audience finally erupted into enthusiastic, grateful applause. Marguerite, a big blonde beacon, had shown what could be done with aging bones, a mat, a leotard, and a lot of self-confidence. She gathered her mats and, big shoulders hunched, she left the little stage.

When the applause died down, Nina stepped forward to say that Marguerite is eighty and has recently undergone treatment for cancer. The applause began again and this time, went on for so long that Marguerite came back to the center and took another bow.

"The White Nights" phenomena were among the many things that surprised me and made me know I wasn't at home. Here I once again mention their effect. I felt no need to write about their cause. Another journal-er, one with more knowledge, might have done so.

It is the time of year referred to as "The White Nights," daylight for twenty hours. It was still light when we went to bed and light again early this morning. I woke up once during the night and it was light then, too. When the four hours of darkness occurs is, therefore, a mystery. It's kind of eery but nice to have daylight around the clock. Amazing how darkness makes one shut down for the day and daylight keeps you open for business.

Here I insert a brief introduction to St. Petersburg, starting with the culture professor's surprising claim that it is a "satanic city."

Professor Irina referred to St. Petersburg as a "satanic city," telling us that it is now the Mafia's "capital." It is considered to be unique in culture, not representative of Russia at all, but of itself, in the sense that New York is not representative of the U.S. but is unique to itself.

The guidebook says that five million people live here amidst fifty museums, more than twenty theatres, sixty stadiums, and 4500 libraries. We arrived later than expected, and so our city tour was cut short, but will be made up tomorrow.

Again, using a simile ("huge bakery of cakes...") helps give the reader my visual impression.

Driving through the center of the city was like riding through a huge bakery of cakes with pink and white, green and white, and yellow and white frosting. An exception was St. Isaac's Cathedral, a big brown pillared- and domed- hulk on the outside. Inside, however, it outshone them all. Malachite pillars the color of emeralds, deep blue pillars of lapis, several stories high, flank the iconostasis. It is surrounded floor to ceiling with huge mosaic icons.

Earlier painted icons had flaked in the damp air and so it was decided that mosaics, small pieces of tile, would make the pictures of the saints last longer. We are told that 11,000 pieces went into their construction.

(This is the sort of guide-given information that is hard to grasp. Who counted, I wondered? It's hard to picture the mosaic-makers mumbling "nine thousand and one, nine-thousand and two," as they pieced them together.)

I had a hard time coming up with a good explanation of the mosaic until I remembered the difference in my computer scanner's low number of dpi and its fuzzy picture-production.

The tile bits in these mosaics were so small and numerous that the pictures in the icon wall looked as detailed as paintings, the effect of, say, a thousand "dots per inch" on expensive computer scanners.

St. Isaacs is a museum now, used by the Russian Orthodox Church only twice a year to celebrate Christmas and Easter. We had arrived only shortly before closing so we rushed around behind our local guide as she shouted out the specifications and particulars of the architecture and decor, things like its weight (30,000 tons) and the fact that serfs hauled and laid 20,000 tree trunks for its foundation.

I hate meaningless phrases like "truly awesome" but my ability to do justice to this place just came up short.

These silly facts aside, the cathedral is truly awesome in its splendor and proportions, shrinking the individual to mite-size in comparison. No doubt this was its builders' intent.

The difference in physical appearance between Moscow and St. Petersburg was so marked that I had to mention it—as one of those "first impressions."

St. Petersburg is where all the beautiful people live. Our guide Elena is a beige-blonde of about thirty, tanned and slender with eyes the color of the malachite pillars. She wore a herringbone blazer and beige skirt with polished tan leather pumps. "St. Petersburg has the most beooootifoool guides," Nina told us later.

Looking around at the people hurrying home in the afternoon rush hour, it seems that they could be plucked from the public at large in any U.S. city. The cold air (St. Petersburg is on the same latitude as Alaska) pinches cheeks and noses red. The predominant clothing size is sturdy but not Sherman tank. People are dressed in clothes the colors of clothes, not of dirt (like the clothes in Moscow)— blues, greens, reds.

June 5

An update on one of the players, Bozo. When a controversial character is introduced, it's interesting to the ongoing "story" to include follow-up.

There's been a bit of a rumble over Bozo's handling of the Kirov Ballet tickets. Passengers were offered these tickets as soon as we arrived on-board ship and many people forked over the $200 or so in cash. We returned from the truncated city tour so that ticket-buyers could switch into their finery for the ballet performance. Bob and I sat on the deck with our wine and beer and peanuts and watched them troop out, all gussied up for the evening.

Several things went wrong went wrong with the ballet-evening. The first bus took off on time. But the tickets bought from Bozo at orchestra-seat prices were for the last balcony, and no one could see what was happening on stage.

The scene as we saw it from the boat.

The second bus never arrived to take the rest of our troops. People waited, first patiently, then impatiently as the minutes ticked by and it became clear that they would still be standing on the cement pier next to the boat when the first dancer leaped onto the stage. Voices got louder. One man raised his fist. Bozo stood looking frantic and uncertain as the crowd surged around him. Finally, he stepped forward and began to call cabs. He dispatched the rest of the group to the show but they missed part of the performance and were surly and mutinous this morning.

I remembered our Moscow Circus ticket experience and thought Bozo had *pushed the financial-opportunity-envelope a little too enthusiastically this time. These people may not listen to the p.a. with the focus and concentration of more nervous travelers, but I'll wager they've attended enough operas and ballets and concerts to recognize ticket-scalping when they see it.*

The buzz at our breakfast table is that Bozo works with a mafia show ticket supplier, the Russian version of Ticketron, and his take from the price-gouging is a perk of the job. I suspect Grand Circle will hear about this. Nina and Lena are enraged.

A kind of "meanwhile, back at the ranch..." insert to the Journey Journal follows—with what we did with our evening, again divided into short paragraphs for easy reading.

While the ballet drama was unfolding, Bob and I hooked up with Nina and a few other people to ride the rails of underground St. Petersburg. We boarded at a metro station conveniently close to the pier. The escalator down to the tracks was steep and long, like riding into the center of the earth.

We stared at the ads and fellow passengers (one guy even videotaped them), and at some of the stops, the heavy steel doorways that the train door revealed when it opened. How could you read that stop's name, even if you understood Russian?

Nina said the steel doors were there to protect against the frequent flash floods. St. Petersburg, which is built on swampy surfaces, is actually composed of forty-two separate islands connected by canals—hence its name, "The Venice of the North."

Nina instructed us to count the five stops to the Nevsky Prospekt, which is in the heart of the city. It is necessary to count the stops because, of course, we can't read the names.

A random thought here.

(It makes you understand the horrors of illiteracy to be in a country where the writing can't be puzzled out from its root or sound. I took Latin in high school and can often pick out a common root in a foreign word and figure out what it means. But Russian—in cyrillic—defies that.)

Today is clear and cool; the sun is shining as it has for nearly all of the "white nights." As we rode into town for our tour of The Hermitage, the buildings looked even more whimsical to me than yesterday, frosted in pink, green, blue, yellow with gold and white trim, like Bermuda done up grand and palatial.

The Hermitage itself is a group of five pale green buildings, one of which was Catherine the Great's winter palace. Peter began the art collection with some paintings that he bought while living in Holland as a young man.

Catherine added to it in Czar-ish proportions, first with the purchase of 250 paintings bought from one person in 1764. From there, it grew to this enormous accumulation of some 1000 rooms. It dwarfs the Metropolitan (in New York) and is larger than the Louvre (in Paris). Strictly for the palace residents originally, this hoard of masterpieces wasn't seen by the public until 1917.

It was hard to find the words to adequately recapture the Hermitage. So I just put down the visual description, word after word, and hoped it would do the job.

The recently refurbished Hermitage is overwhelming, with its gleaming gold pillars, gold leaf trim on molding, and the blinding white, gold, and marble halls, filled to the brim with masterpiece paintings.

We were fortunate to arrive early and ahead of the crowd. Our guide took us to the more important rooms of each of the buildings, so newly renovated that we could smell the paint.

We saw da Vincis, Titians, Rembrandts, Raphaels, VanDykes, Rubens. Room after room of Manet, Monet, Van Gogh, Villard, Sisely, Gauguin, Picasso. We saw mosaics of precious stones in tables large and small. The entry to one room was flanked by huge pillars in deep red with a parquet floor made of such variation of wood in black, brown, silver-gray, and ochre, that it looked mosaic, too.

Exhausted from this visual stimulation, I walked to the huge glass wall in the third floor Impressionist wing. It overlooks the Square and was, by this time, a hive of activity. I stood there, picking out little scenes to study in this panorama of daily life at Palace Square in St. Petersburg.

In one corner, schoolchildren in uniform were grouped together and singing for a small crowd. Hawkers wandered up to knots of people, holding out their wares for sale. Vendors stood beside carts of food, steaming in the morning cold. Busdrivers huddled in groups in front of their parked vehicles, drinking coffee and smoking. It was like looking at an animated Brueghel or one of those gigantic scenes by the Italian Caravaggio (?), as much a part of the Hermitage visit as the Rembrandts and Van Goghs.

Later, Nina volunteered to take a little band of postcard-writers through the paces of buying stamps at the Post Office, while the rest of us ate our "peck-lunches" on board the bus which parked next to St. Basil's.

Russians haven't quite got the hang of retailing yet. Many stores don't have display windows but lurk inside brick walls, their wares unseen and unadvertised. Next to the bus was a small sign standing on the sidewalk, stating simply "art store." There was no indication as to where this art store might be.

We stepped down from the bus and walked back up the street until we came to a door that stood open. We walked in and lo! There was the art store. "Art," in this case, consisted of postcards, t-shirts, army hats, and matoushka dolls.

I bought a t-shirt and tried on some of the hats. I loved a Soviet Army cap and walked through the store with it on my head, looking for a mirror. When I finally found one, I could see the sales people behind me giggling and pointing, and one actually hooted. When even the clerks can't suppress their laughter, it probably doesn't look that great, right?

So I didn't buy it for myself, but for my son Trevor. I suspect he'll love it—in dark green wool, it looks like a little dunce-cap or a hat for an army of coneheads. There is a large red star emblazoned on one side.

The only way to describe things accurately here was to use similes. Silica gel and dried flowers were the driest things I could think of at the time.

We travelers are taking on an end-of-the-trip seediness now, wearing second-day and even third-day shirts and coffee-stained jeans. This morning, I tried to revive my hairdo with disastrous results. I promise my head that I won't use any of those hairstyle concoctions ever again. My hair feels like I sprayed it with silica-gel and has all the pliancy (and faded color) of a dried flower arrangement.

A note to myself here so that I'll remember next time about the amount of clothes to pack.

As happens with every trip we make, I have worn the same clothes nearly every day. No matter how I imagine I'm going to dress on the road, convenience and the press of tour schedules usually have me grabbing the easiest thing to put on, the most comfortable and the most squishable, in case the weather warms and part of an outfit must be peeled off and stashed in the backpack.

Except for on the plane, a skirt is superfluous on this trip. Pantihose seem wildly inappropriate and non-essential. Bottom-line wardrobe consists of jeans with denim blazer, short sleeved blouses, v-neck sweater, cotton socks and sneakers. Period. Call me colorless but it works. (Of course, because I am wearing the same thing in every picture, family and friends sometimes think we did everything in one day.)

More here on touring. In retrospect, I should have written more about the practical joke fountains that Peter installed. It would have told more about his unusual personality.

We rode out of the city this afternoon to Peterhof, the summer palace of Peter the Great which he approached by canal and the Baltic Sea. The grounds are filled with wide paths to wander under the trees and among the gardens, where Peter indulged his wit and built trick fountains—one that purposely sprayed people sitting on a nearby bench, for example.

The huge yellow and white palace was closed for renovation. But you could get an idea of its style by seeing the newly restored Grand Cascade Fountain. It gleamed in the sunlight with gold and more gold. The fountain water flows down a hill and is lined on either side by one shiny gold statue after another, with a huge gold Samson at the bottom of the Cascade. It was clear to me that opulence can be so easily overdone.

Sitting apart from the main structure is Catherine's Palace. In contrast to Peter's, it is a small jewel-box of a building, the wood parquet floors so delicate in their design and structure that we were required to change into felt slippers, leaving our shoes in an ante-room at the entrance.

160 PART TWO [JOURNEY JOURNAL]

Naming the colors of the wood furniture and tiles helps develop the word picture here. I wanted to contrast Catherine's Palace with the too-glitzy shine of the larger palace's Cascade.

Karelian birch furniture in shades of dark-gold and honey and locally-fired deep blue Delft-like tiles made this palace so appealing. It sustained heavy damage during World War II. Photos in the anteroom showed "before" and "after" the renovation process.

A random thought which will probably end up in "reflections."

It is unclear to me where the money comes from for these enormously expensive renovations. The Hermitage cost many millions of dollars, trillions of rubles. The people are selling their clothes, their books, and anything else they can turn into cash, in order to eat. Workers, like Professor Irina, are not being paid their salaries. Where does the money come from for the gold leaf statuary and trim? I wonder how high the resentment level is among the populace.

Here I just took the day step-by-step, not wanting to forget any of it, but not going into much detail, either. I could have written more about the canal boat trip, and Count Stroganoff's palace, but didn't—must have been tired.

This (June 6) was our free day in St. Petersburg. Bob and I took the metro to Nevsky Prospekt, managing to buy tokens at the window with a lot of sign language. We rode the escalator into the bowels of the earth to the tracks and then, carefully counted off the five stops to our destination. We walked its length, or rather, I did, while Bob sat in a park and watched people and pigeons. I was trying to find a souvenir store recommended in the guidebook, called simply #51 Nevsky Prospekt.

Of all things I could have described—trees, avenues, plantings—I picked the thing I thought of first when I sat down to write: the lack of marketing skills.

The shops along this broad boulevard are dimly lit, or not lit at all. There are no display windows and sometimes only an open door indicates that a shop lies within. Clerks can be surly and resentful. Some speak a smattering of English, though, and some even smiled at us.

When I finally found #51 Nevsky Prospekt, I discovered that my taste for matoushka dolls, wooden bowls, and scarves has been satiated. I'm done. No more.

I walked back to Bob and we found the only cafe where we could read the menu. It was, of all things, a former Subways and served good sandwiches, cheap. Our chore was not adventurous, but the other cafes were stifling hot and so crowded that we knew we would be hours in those steamrooms before finishing.

We bought some snacks at a small grocery store, took a canal boat trip, and visited the Stroganoff Palace, former home of the Count and site of his "invention"— beef in mushroom and cream sauce. It is now both a souvenir store and a small museum. (The w.c. was our main interest there.)

In the late afternoon, we dipped back into the center of the earth for the metro ride home, feeling pretty smug at having done the town on our own.

The farewell dinner on the ship consisted of brown things that looked like shoe heels (Bob thought they were beef), whipped potatoes, and a group of colorful but unrecognizable vegetables. Dessert was chocolate eclairs, sweet wine and oranges.

Our group (except me) has been pleased with the food, and particularly amazed at all the vegetables. This veggie-presence somehow convinced people that they were eating healthily. No notice seems to have been taken of the pools of fat in which everything swims. Dinners have been massive fat-transfers and now fellow passengers are dimly complaining about tight waistbands.

June 7

Today we disembarked the MS Lenin, waved goodbye to the tearful attendants (sorrowful at our departure or just the size of their tips?), rode buses into the city, and hopped out near the Grand Hotel. We were given a few more hours at our leisure to visit museums or just wander around.

This especially memorable place is described here in detail because of its spare mention in the guidebook. It shouldn't be missed. The writing is sort of colorless but descriptive.

Bob and I went to the Museum of Ethnography, which had been a footnote in our guidebook.

Again, an empty word, "wonderful." But the place really was full of wonder, so maybe the word isn't that empty after all.

What a wonderful place! It should have a chapter of its own. The rooms display dioramas of the many cultures that exist in this huge land, from the Russian Far East to the areas where we had cruised and the states to the south.

Room after room of life-sized figures hunting, farming, cooking, doing their cultural thing in native costumes, in fields and yurts, on carpets, with handhewn utensils—each scene was flanked by actual photographs of what was depicted.

The Far East was particularly interesting because we were led through it by an elderly woman docent, an enthusiastic woman who mimed every activity in the glass cases until we understood exactly what was going on. She clapped her hands and hooted with pleasure each time we connected with her sign language. I felt like we were playing charades.

We had so much fun puzzling out her actions and matching them with the scenes on display that I wanted to take her with us to the other rooms where less-antic docents barely managed to nod hello when we entered. But she was committed to her Far East room and looked over our shoulders as we left, her face broadening into a huge welcoming smile as another pair walked into the room. I slipped her a few dollars in gratitude and hoped it wasn't an insult.

A visit to the Museum of Ethnography could be compared to a visit to the Smithsonian by foreign tourists in the U.S., highly recommended for people who want to understand the scope and diversity of this country (now, collection of countries).

At a flea market near the Museum, we bought a cutting-board, so newly decorated that the paint was still wet.

This line so perfectly described Carolyn's (and lots of tourists') buying habits that I wrote it in my notes verbatim.

Walking back to the bus, Carolyn told me, "I bargain better for things I don't want." I pondered this all the way to the airport.

At the airport, we joined the surge and milled our way through passport control in less than an hour.

This travel tip from Nina saved us money on our "cocktail hours" in Helsinki.

I bought a cheap bottle of Rioja wine at the duty-free shop, having been told by Nina that drink prices in Helsinki are outrageous. We flew to Helsinki in a couple of hours and were taken by bus to the Ramada President II Hotel in the heart of town. In the minibar was a corkscrew, and there was a nice little sitting area where we can look out the window onto Helsinki.

Heat makes me crabby. I felt better after writing this.

Our hotel room is larger than the ship's cabin but extremely hot. We were told various stories by irritable concierges about the non-functioning air conditioner. Bottom-line: it goes on sometime during the night, maybe. Meanwhile, to lower the 85 degree temperature, we propped the door open with our suitcase and pushed the window as far out as it would go. It is White Nights and underneath our window is Where It's Happening here in Helsinki, at the ever-popular and always crowded Hard Rock Cafe.

A quick update on two characters introduced earlier, Beulah and Inez.

We ate the hotel's buffet dinner with Beulah and Inez and a couple named Alice and Simon who are ninety years old and just returned from the Galapagos. They highly recommend the riverboat trip down the Amazon River. Beulah was disappointed that she hadn't visited the Museum of Ethnography. She, too, is fascinated with the Russian Far East.

"Next January," she confided to us, "I plan to take the Trans-Siberian Railroad across Russia."

Why January? we asked.

"I think Siberia should be experienced in winter, don't you?" she said. When I told her that my son Trevor had done this, she gave me her address and asked me to let her know how he had arranged the trip. Whaddawoman!

First impressions of Helsinki: in contrast with Russia, it was squeaky clean—even "gleamed."

June 8

We managed a few hours of sleep after Hard Rock revelers went home early this morning. After breakfast, we walked through the city. Everything gleamed. Things are so clean: windows, cars, buildings, parks, people. Massive department stores display the works of well-known Finnish designers of clothing, jewelry, furniture, textiles. This is a prosperous country and so tasteful.

The outdoor market at the piers was bustling with sleek, beautiful people. The market itself was a collection of stands, vans, and small pickup trucks. One man was selling heavy seeded bread—thick and chewy.

Using the actual words and trying to capture the dialect enhances the description.

"Made from sunflowers and flax seed," he told us. "Is linen," he laughed. "My grandfodder's recipe." We bought a gigantic loaf and moved on.

There were displays of fish, meats, vegetables, hot coffee on one end and crafts—woolen hats, wooden toys, knitted sweaters, reindeer rugs, silver earrings and much more—on the other. Everyone seemed happy with us, smiling wide white smiles, ruddy cheeks dimpling with pleasure at our very presence.

We bought an albino reindeer skin, small and lightweight, to lay in front of our fireplace back home. Wandering through the remaining aisles, we heard someone running and calling, "Wait! Wait!" Turning, we saw the boy who sold the skin to us waving our credit card in his hand. We had left it on his counter. We took it, thanking him profusely.

"No worry," laughed the woman behind the stand we were beside. "Dis is Finland. Nobody steal da card here."

Walking back to the hotel through a park, we stopped and listened to an oompah band playing a Gershwin medley. We sat under a tree and ate our linen bread and some oranges I had saved from the ship. Absolutely delicious. Helsinki is a lovely place. Today, the temperature was sixty five degrees and sunny, brightened as much by the general good cheer as by the sun.

A few points of interest not included in the guidebook.

In the afternoon, we took a city tour with Nina and visited the neighborhoods of Helsinki and the grave of Jan Sibelius, composer of "Finlandia," which is not, as I had thought,, Finland's national anthem.

At the piers, we saw ships being built and learned that the Finns make most of the world's ocean liners. Something massive called "Radiance of the Sea" lay under scaffolding, its innards exposed and crawling with workmen. It is being built for the Royal Viking Line.

Helsinki is small in size and easily accessible by its tram system, which Bob and I rode in the late afternoon just for the fun of it. We have been issued two-day "Helsinki Cards" that entitle us to free tram rides, discount boat trips and lots of other goodies, for which we won't have time.

Today (June 9) we took a sightseeing boat tour of the islands in the Bay of Finland. We could see the cottages to which many Finns retreat for weekends and holidays. The day was piercingly clear and bright. The sight of trees, small boats, and cabins along the sparkling water was undimmed by pollution or fog.

After the boat trip, we attended a service at the Church in the Rock, a sanctuary hewn out of a massive boulder. It was in English, and many of the churchgoers were tourists like us.

Tonight, Nina and Lena hosted the farewell dinner at an elegant Russian restaurant on the water, the Alexander Nevsky. Inside, it is paneled and intimate. We tried not to be first in the door so we could avoid some of the more boring people as dinner companions.

We finally found seats next to a friendly, talkative, charming couple.

Who apparently shall remain nameless.

Uniformed waiters swooped down on us with Beef Stroganoff (for Bob) and (my choice) chicken breast. It was the best food I've had since we left home. The conversation was interesting and I hardly wanted to leave when the speeches of gratitude to our guides ended and the cameras stopped flashing photos.

June 10

We repacked our suitcases, managing to squish the reindeer rug in with the other souvenirs. Today we leave Helsinki and return to Baltimore via Kennedy. Once *again, the most valuable items that I packed for myself, without which I could not have done, were the water boiler/plastic filter/filter papers, Starbucks coffee and the water canteen. All are confirmed top-of-the-list. But I am dipping deep into the coffee bag and have only one filter paper left. The cap on the canteen has cracked and it leaks.*

Time to go home.

The Journey Journal ends here with no more departure-transition. The trip home was apparently totally uneventful but since I didn't write anything about it, we'll never know because I don't remember any more.

June 15 Final reflections on the Russian experience:
In the end, what surprised me? The sheer beauty of the country, the peace and tranquility of the rivers and canals, the drama and contrasts of Russia—people and places and cultures—all a big happy surprise. It was so interesting.

I feel like a door opened and I peeked into a room full of enticing things, then took a step in and looked around. I realize how ignorant I am of so much in the world. The richness of the glimpse we had of Russia and its history, culture, geography, people, diversity, makes me want to know more, to step farther in from that door and to study and to return someday.

Also: The surly attitudes and unhappy faces, the terrible clothing and make-up and hair colors in Moscow and Uglich—is this the result of early capitalism? Sort of an embryonic, baby-consumerism?

Russian faces are not impassive. Their ridges and lines are evidence to me of expressiveness. Like their dramatic, romantic, emotional music, Russians faces look capable of wide ranges of emotion and humor. I hope the Muscovites and Uglichites make it to another, happier level.

I am listening to the tape of the men singing in the cathedral. The little boy-puppet holding the small wooden balalaika is hanging on our wall. And I think, we know more—about Russia, about a large part of the world—than we did a month ago. A lot more. And there's still so much more to learn.

[CHAPTER FIVE]

COMPARING STYLES: THE BEST OF EASTERN EUROPE AS WRITTEN BY BOB AND SUSAN

The Journey Journal which I wrote during the "Russia by Riverboat" trip was longer than most because I had more leisure time to devote to it. With one or two exceptions, I wrote each morning for about 30 minutes. This comes to a total of roughly ten and a half hours of writing time—spread out over nearly three weeks—or less than two days' work. I seldom have the time to write, which traveling by riverboat afforded me.

My other journals have often been considerably shorter. The following is an example of a journal written on a recent trip to Eastern Europe. The trip was not as long as the Russian journey (16 days). It was not tightly scheduled and offered plenty of time in each city for a good overview of its charms. But I wrote for much less time, no more than 20 minutes a day or about five and a half hours total—or less than a day's work. This is a kind of mid-length Journey Journal example.

To prove how possible it is for *anyone* to write a Journey Journal, I asked my husband Bob (a stockbroker who finds writing even phone messages tedious) if he would keep track of the things that interested him most each day. He was mildly enthusiastic about the idea and agreed.

During each day's excursions, Bob carried a small notebook in his travel vest pocket and intermittently wrote a word or two in it. Each night after he heard the market reports on CNN (and I had gone to bed), Bob faithfully took up his notebook and filled out his notes with his memories of the day. For all his protestations that he can't write and that any journal of his would be excruciatingly dull, his entries are excellent: brief, (not wordy, like mine) and to the point. As you'll see, Bob's journey journal demonstrates the truth of my belief that writing is as simple as talking.

Not much here on transition-departure phase. I tried to be alert to first impressions upon arrival.

(Day 1—Susan)
Schipol Airport, Amsterdam

Lots of Midwest-, and Western-American accents swirling around in the cigar and cigarette smoke. We're sitting in a glass box—the departure lounge for Gate 36—waiting for our connecting flight to Warsaw. I'm on the floor to escape the stench. Somewhere I read that smoke rises.

> Overheard conversation: "You going to the You-Krane?"
> "Yuh."
> "Ah've been there two, three times. Pretty nice. Good restaurants."
> "Any McDonalds?" Silence. Again, "Any McDonalds?"
> "Yeah. Couple. Not many."
> Our flight is called.

(Day 3—Susan)
Warsaw, October 24

This would be Friday. Thursday was "day 2" on our itinerary. We arrived in "Waszawa" (pronounced "Vah-shah-vah") yesterday. The airport was clean but spare, and we made a quick exit through customs. On our flight were only four other passengers traveling with us on this tour. Two are sweet, two sour. The former are two older ladies from Wisconsin. The latter pair frowned and frowned and finally decided not to take the GC rep's offer of cabs to the hotel.

They elected instead to wait in the orange plastic chairs for an unspecified length of time until the next flight (it was delayed) arrived with more tour members. They looked unhappy at the idea of doing anything, yet certainly chose the least attractive option.

We and the Wisconsin ladies took two cabs to the hotel, ours chasing theirs and both darting like butterflies through the downtown traffic. Bob and I cringed with one seat belt between us, but we all arrived safely.

The hotel and center city were only about 30 minutes from the airport. Warsaw gives the initial impression of being composed of cement bunkers, Soviet style. But as we came closer to the inner city, we found ourselves on avenues of stately buildings, including an enormous wedding cake of a "culture center." The cab driver tried awkwardly to mime the concept of "gift" which it was, from Communist Russia, by handing us first the contents of his pockets, then everything on his cab's front seat, finally items from his glove compartment. At last we understood.

Warsaw is lovely, lovely, lovely.

There's a lot of leather here, on the backs of craggy, dark-haired people with seamed, serious faces. The mode of dress is ultra-casual, surprising for such a bustling place. The populace looks like they all carry lunchboxes and work in a mill. I only saw a couple of sleek Euro-types (both men) in those long dark loden coats with tan leather collars, carrying smart slim briefcases. Warsaw looks working-class, down to earth, old shoe. But it is bristling with business.

Signs for office rentals and apartments are in English (guess who's coming to lunch?) and rents are high, if I did the conversion right. (The zloty is at 3.4 per dollar.)

The hotel lobby was sleek—a snazzy black and glass bar rising in the middle of its vast floor. At the edge was a lounge-full of deep, inviting soft mauve sofas and chairs. Although it was before noon, our rooms were quickly made available and we fell onto our beds for a long nap.

We met the guide in the late afternoon. Her name is Halina "Something Unpronounceable." She looks to be in her forties, wears glasses, a bright red coat and has wild hair. She took our group for the standard, brief orientation walk of the neighborhood, pointing out landmarks ("You turn at ze yellow shursh—left going to, right coming back...!") with which to work our way over to the Old Town and back and to the nearest grocery, liquor store, and drugstore. These orientation tours are enormously helpful.

Most of the group lumbered back to the hotel behind Halina—they were without our benefit of nap, and looked dazed and glassy-eyed. We walked on to the Old Town, through narrow alleyways into a wide, cobble-stoned square, lined with tall, narrow buildings of different hues, shades of yellow and red and blue with heavy wood doors and designs painted on some exteriors. This is Warsaw's Market Square.

There are several inviting restaurants with white curtains and dark mullioned windows through which we peered onto cozy scenes of small wooden tables, candle-lit with open fireplaces and lots of happy diners. It must have been some kind of mealtime but because of my screwed-up, jet-lagged clock, I couldn't say which. I thought it was about 4 p.m. Maybe they take tea here in Warsaw.

Our hotel, the Victoria Intercontinental, sits on another huge open square. An elaborate pillared building, the Opera, is across the square (north, I think). On its west side, in a small white marble structure, an eternal flame burns as a war memorial. The names of battles fought through the centuries are etched on its walls, floor to ceiling. Apparently, there hasn't been much down time for the soldiers of Poland.

Last night, after the "welcome dinner," we took a walk. It was the blackest night. We were walking across the marble expanse of the square when we heard martial steps and squinted to see the silhouettes of soldiers backlit by the lights from our hotel. They goose-stepped by us with quiet ceremony, exchanging themselves for the guards at the little war memorial.

As to people: our fellow group-travelers look pretty good, so far. Milling around in the lobby before dinner, people introduced themselves, asked where we are from, made little bits of small talk, efforts to connect quickly. It seems to be the Grand Circle Travelers' Way and we hope this bunch is as compatible as the Australia/New Zealand group was.

Dinner was excellent: potato soup, fresh tomato/cucumber salad, rare beef, steamed broccoli, and a meringue and cream dessert. Good red wine—I drank both Bob's and mine—and tea to wrap it all up. CNN is in our spacious room. There's a deep coffin-like tub and herb bath sachets that smell like mint and look like giant teabags. What a treat! By 7:30, I was into a 12 hour sleep.

It's cold here. The air feels fresh and invigorating. All of our layers are working—from long underwear through shirts and sweaters to jackets. (After that dinner last night, I think I've added another layer.)

(Bob's journal entry—day 1)
10/22—at the airport

It's now 6 p.m. and we are leaving "Dullest" International Airport in Virginia on the way to Amsterdam, a seven hour flight. We left our house at 1:15 p.m. in order to be at Dulles 3 hours prior to departure. I always find the most stressful part of international travel is getting there and getting home. Susan insists that we arrive as early as possible so we may be assigned good seats. (And I always fuss at having to arrive so early, but I must admit it has proven to be good strategy. In the past, we have been able to solve some unexpected problems easily by being early.)

Bob is much more succinct, gets the facts on paper without a lot of frills. He's not quite ready to embellish yet. He chose to write at the end of each day instead of first thing in the morning.

(Bob) Day 2
10/23—Warsaw

Our flight arrived in Warsaw, Poland at 10:30 a.m. after an hour stopover in Amsterdam. The advantages of group travel became evident immediately after leaving customs when our tour guide met us outside. She gave us a choice of waiting for another group to arrive in 45 minutes or taking a cab to our hotel. Since the waiting area looked very austere, we elected to go by cab, as did another couple (in another cab). The fare, including tip, was paid by Grand Circle. What a blessing to have these logistics taken care of.

After a brief nap, our tour guide Halina took us on a brief orientation walk to the Old Town. She left us mid-way to return to the airport to greet another group. So Susan and I explored some shops and examined restaurant menus for another hour. It is quite cool and we were glad for our warm jackets.

The group had an early dinner at the hotel. It was a nice meal of potato soup, beef and potatoes, broccoli, salad and dessert. Then a short after-dinner walk around the large plaza. We were in time to see the changing of the guard at the "tomb of the unknown soldier."

The subject of the slacks isn't all that important to the trip, but does emphasize how cold it was. And I thought it was funny.

Susan:
Warsaw, October 25

One of Bob's pairs of slacks turned out to be mine. When he tried getting them on, he thought he had put on a lot of weight. "I can't get into these anymore," he said in a rueful tone. Then he looked at the label—Land's End. "Are these yours?" he asked, dismayed. "Yes," I said. Now I have a nice extra pair of warm, lined corduroys, which works out perfectly. It is bone-numbing cold here with a body-piercing wind. But Bob is left with only two pair of pants for the next 2 1/2 weeks.

Introducing fellow travelers who look like they'll be our pals for the next couple of weeks is best to do as soon as congeniality becomes evident. It's awkward to do later.

Yesterday morning we bent against that wind and walked back to Old Town with new friends Beattie and Clayton Stephens from Marblehead, Mass. Clayt is witty, makes us laugh a lot. Beattie is good-natured and walks briskly, like me. (I hate to saunter. Sauntering makes me tired and cranky.) They've traveled extensively, lived in both London and Paris, and are fine conversationalists. Goody.

Yesterday afternoon, we took the city tour. Except for those gray cement rectangles on the outskirts of town, Warsaw is gorgeous—filled with stately 19th Century-style buildings, completely rebuilt after World War II, which totally reduced the city to rubble. Streets are clean, trees are still green in spite of the cold and the slight dusting of snow.

How could I forget to get the name of the "large park"? Or the specifics about the monuments? No excuse for these omissions.

We walked in a large park, formerly owned by the royalty on duty during the Austro-Hungarian Empire. Around a large reflecting pool, where a statue of Chopin dominates one end and Chopin concerts are played every Sunday until November, hundreds of tattered, wind-blown garnet-red roses hinted at the splendor of warmer seasons.

School children are everywhere in tight, well-behaved groups dressed exactly as kids are dressed in the U.S. but without the hip-hop low slung jeans or earrings. Just clean khakis and cords, ski jackets and heavy sweaters.

Dialogue helps enliven a Journey Journal. Here it illuminates the Polish attitude toward Warsaw.

This city is the nation's pride, rebuilt after the War by citizens who worked without pay. Halina's father said to her, "I had my soup and tea and bread. It was enough." The expense was borne by taxes levied on all Polish citizens: nothing from the U.N. or Marshal Plan was accepted. Old photos, old memories, and paintings by the great Italian painter (and Warsaw fan) Canaletto were used to recreate each block, so each looked just as it had before the Germans blew it up in the Warsaw Uprising (1944).

Capturing a random thought adds to one's storehouse of reflections. I try for insights on-the-road. They may turn out to be false or meaningless later, but so what?

It seems to me that this must be what comes from generations of attachment to place, to one's home. Warsaw must have been so much a living part of themselves that its citizens rebuilt the city in its original form without compensation, in order to have their lives back again. (They didn't get that wish—they immediately found themselves under a Communist regime.) This would not happen in the U.S., I think. At home, new styles would rise from old rubble. In America, recreating the old is rarely as important as creating something new.

There is a huge bronze memorial, a set of statues of the fighters in the Uprising, just outside the walls of the old city. Individual figures crouch in battle-stance around a tank. Maybe it's the Soviet-style of huge human figures and strong stalwart faces but this is an unusually impressive and dramatic monument.

The Warsaw (Jewish) Ghetto is also memorialized in a large open space where it once stood.

Sad to say, it was snowing and bitter cold, so we didn't get any useful photos of these monuments.

Ha! Another thought.

The thought came to me today that, convenient and reasonably priced as it is to be traveling with a group, there are disadvantages. It's more difficult to actually be here. When we travel alone, we are immersed in the struggle to find our way around, understand local culture and customs enough to order food and appreciate the setting. That struggle removed, we are a little island of America on wheels, looking at the sights through bus windows, listening to the voices of English-speaking guides. There is no context to what we see. We don't participate, just observe.

Now, that is not to say that the huge advantages of having the guide and the bus through traffic and the great hotel don't far outweigh the disadvantages. They definitely do. It's a far more convenient, more efficient, and cheaper way to get an overview of foreign countries—a sweep through their cities enables us to determine which we would like to revisit. You just have to work harder at absorption.

Using Halina's—and Wocusz's—actual words makes them seem more real.

Last night we had dinner at Halina's home. It was the advertised "home hosted meal." Sixteen people ate at the apartment of a friend of Halina's and her two daughters. (Halina said, "My friend has two bee-yooooo-ti fool daughters-uh." She has a funny way of ending a word emphatically with an "uh" sound like she just fell on it. "Who wants to eat there?" Male hands shot up all over the bus.)

The remaining 26 people rode on in the bus to a suburb of Warsaw, to a duplex home in which Halina, her husband and three sons, her mother and sister live. The whole family bustled about the kitchen preparing the meal.

In the little living room, sixteen people wedged themselves into chairs at two tables. The other ten, including Bob and me, sat at a large table in her sister's small apartment on the lower level, hosted by Halina's 20-year old son, Wocusz (pronounced "Woe-koosh"). He is a tall, handsome, dark-haired young man who smiles a lot and speaks excellent English.

"My mudder make me learn," he said. "I practice and practice, but my grammar not so good." It was, in fact, just fine. (Better than some in our group.)

There is a large garden in the back from which the vegetables we ate were harvested. The rest of the huge dinner came from the animals and produce at Halina's mother's farm. "Even the cherry vodka is homemade," she told us proudly—her mother made it from her own cherry trees.

We ate piroshki (little ravioli-like pasta curlicues), tomato soup with homemade noodles, something called "galumpka" which is cooked cabbage wrapped around a ground meat and rice mixture, and a light dessert of whipped cream and jello.

"It's made by my fahder," said Wocusz proudly. "Is his cooking spesh-ulty." Wocusz is a happy, voluble host, telling us about his pre-law university classes and his ambitions for the future. To the inevitable cracks about lawyer-ing from the group, he said, "Hardly anyone knows Western law, only Common-ist law here. There is a need for many, many people who know Western law.."

He gave us a helpful hint. "Don't ask directions from anyone over 25. They never learned English under Common-ism."

It's bitter cold today, we hear on CNN. Outside, I see people in heavy coats and scarves, leaning into the wind as they walk. Our plans include seeing Old Town again, the free market in front of the Culture Palace, and, if time allows, also checking out Chopin's heart, which is buried in the Holy Cross Church not far from here. I don't know where the rest of him is.

Bob writes a lot about prices, percentages, and food. I think it's a guy-thing.

(Day 3—Bob)
10/24 Warsaw
I always look forward to the wonderful buffet breakfasts that our tour hotels provide. Besides the usual items, the host country adds foods unique to its culture. Here we had dark bread and three varieties of sausage—I love sausages but recognize their high fat content, so I reluctantly passed them by.

After breakfast, our tour guide Halina described the optional tours that are available for the remainder of the trip. Here one must decide which are worth the time and the cost. The rest of the morning was spent on another shopping tour of the Old Town. This time we bought something: a unique porcelain candleholder shaped like a small cottage, for $15.

For lunch we bought two small sandwiches and a loaf of dark bread at a little grocery. The bill was 5.6 zlotys, less than $2.

At 1 p.m., we boarded the bus for the city tour, stopping at the Chopin statue and in the Old Town, to see a short movie on the reconstruction of Warsaw. Having been 85% destroyed in 1945, the amazing thing is that in Old Town, the buildings have been rebuilt exactly as they were before WWII. Truly incredible.

We had supper in the home of our tour guide, where the group was divided into two. Her 20 year-old son Luke (not his real name, but he said we could call him that) acted as our host. Wine and vodka (no beer) and good Polish food. Tomato soup, ground meat in a dumpling, ground meat in a cabbage wrap, boiled potatoes and salad.

This is one of those step-by-step renditions of a day. What happened? And what happened next?

Susan:
5 a.m. Warsaw, 10/26
Yesterday: Sunny blue skies faded to gray-white midmorning and snow flurried around us as we walked to Old Town with the Stephens couple. We all bought amber earrings for gifts and I added a pendant and chain for me.

Not sure why I didn't include the prices of amber here. It would be helpful to have them in the future.

Amber is the thing to buy here. Not only is the selection of hue wide, from milky white to pale gold to deep rust, but the settings in sterling silver are gorgeous—far superior to Russian settings in design and quality and still reasonably priced. Other interesting local crafts include wood carvings and dolls.

After the amber-buy, we all trooped back to the cobblestoned square in front of the reconstructed Royal Palace at the entrance to Old Town. Bob snapped a few photos of the picturesque scene (several horses with carriages and carriage-drivers stood in the swirling snow below flickering gas lamps) while we stamped our freezing feet and blew into our clenched, cold fists.

Halina had told us that in the rebuilt Royal Palace, one entire room is devoted to the display of Canaletto paintings. An Italian painter, he was on his way to Russia when he stopped for a visit to Warsaw and never left.

Bob and I love Canaletto's paintings. There's so much to look at in each picture, so much activity going on. So we bought tickets to see the Palace and made our way straight through the gilt and marble and parquet to the Canaletto Room and behold! There must have been 30 or more, hanging Louvre-style, floor to ceiling. It was a treat to see, a real highlight.

After lunch, Clayt and Beattie pled frostbite and went back to the hotel. We walked on to the department stores and "free-market," which refers to the open stalls in front of the towering gray Culture Palace—a gift from Soviet Russia in the Wedding-Cake style of architecture. Inside of this building, which looks like a squat overweight Empire State Building, there are theatres and offices. We didn't go in, mainly because there doesn't seem to be any obvious entrance.

Instead, we stepped over puddles of melting snow and walked through the crowded stalls. This is where the locals are: buying boots and shoes, coats, sweaters, and other clothing. Across the street in the department stores, there was an equal bustle of buyers. Warsaw certainly acts prosperous.

Our brief stay in Warsaw was topped off with a private piano concert of Chopin music by pianist Jerzy Romaniuk. It was held in another rebuilt palace, in the park where we saw the statue of Chopin. We sat on gilt chairs, under a vaulted ceiling, surrounded by panels of floating cherubs carrying garlands of flowers, all newly restored in pastel pinks and greens and blues with gold-leaf trim on white. Outside the French windows, the afternoon light was fading and the sun slanted on the green leaves tipped with snow.

As we listened to the stirring romantic chords of Poland's favorite composer, I thought, "It doesn't get better than this."

We leave soon for Krakow.

Ah! Bob remembered to include the price of the necklace.

Bob:
10/25 Warsaw 10 p.m.
After breakfast today, it was back to the Old Town for Susan to shop for

amber. Success! She bought a nice pendant (about $60) on a silver chain ($22). It is quite cold and a light snow fell.

Bob dispatches the day far more efficiently than I. I'd like to read more details about what he saw, and about his impressions of things, but that comes with practice.

We visited the palace museum (completely rebuilt) primarily to see the collection of Caneletto paintings there. Clayton and Bea from Marblehead accompanied us and also had lunch with us: soup and bread all around. Then Susan and I hit the department stores and bought a small blue bowl and a ceramic pitcher, for gifts.

The highlight of the day and perhaps the entire tour was a Chopin piano recital performed in the palace by Jerzy Romaniuk, a professor of music here. I hope my videotape comes out. As insurance, we bought his CD and cassette tape.

Dinner was at an Italian restaurant with Clayton and Bea. Tonight, daylight savings ends. An extra hour of sleep.

Susan:
Krakow, 10/27
Our hotel room has rough white plaster walls, and is trimmed in dark wood. Its sliding doors open to a balcony overlooking a river. Across it is the panorama of Krakow, a postcard-of-a-place, with the towers and turrets of Wawal Castle on one end and a large white church at the other, all reflected in the quiet waters of the river.

Hey, Susan! Which river?

Yesterday, snow fell for most of our bus trip from Warsaw. On the way, we stopped at the Czestochova Monastery and crunched and sloshed our way to its entrance. It is the home of the Black Madonna, which legend says was painted by St. Luke. Do people believe this stuff?

Sometimes only the actual dialogue can convey an impression. I should have added more of Fr. Simon's talk, but I had left my notebook on the bus. Big mistake.

Our English-speaking guide met us inside and introduced himself as Father Simon. He has the ironic wit of the priest who showed us around Assisi in Italy a couple of years ago and had us warmed up and chuckling in no time. (I wonder if these fellows are chosen as guides by their Order, not only for their fluency in English but to show what hip folk priests can be.) He took us through a passageway, and stopped briefly at a large book, where, he said, "people who had experienced da blessed Mother working in dere lives wrote dere names as witnesses."

Among others to have signed—we weren't able to stop and flip through its pages—Father Simon said, was Heinrich Himmler. Maybe this is why the Monastery escaped destruction during the Second World War, even though the surrounding towns and farms were reduced to rubble by the Germans.

It was Sunday and the church was jammed with worshippers, all looking like people we know. The resemblance to fellow Baltimoreans—Highlandtown bakers, airport cabdrivers, Pikesville housepainters and manicurists—is remarkable. The sanctuary was thick with leather jackets, knit caps, and heavy-soled shoes. It didn't seem right to spend a lot of time snapping the painting (The Black Madonna) while worship service was going on, so we just filed through and out.

Waiting to follow us in was a group of fresh-faced mountain women, dressed in multicolored costumes. Their leader carried a large bowl in which three yellow cones sat. "Doz are cheeses," explained Fr. Simon. "Dey come to get da blessing for dem and to tank da Lady for da safe return of dere husbands" who had spent the summer and autumn months in the mountains with the goats.

In the Monastery's museums, we saw vestments for the Black Madonna, hanging in a case and looking like doll clothes, amid other elaborate gifts received over the years. Outside the church, Fr. Simon took us to a small building where Lech Walesa's Nobel Prize and his many other medals and seals-of-approval are housed. (It's hard to believe that this brave and honored man was voted out of office recently in favor of a former Communist.)

I walked with the priest, making small talk about the weather. He asked, "Are you Catholic?"

"No," I said. "Presbyterian."

"Are you happy?"

"Very."

"But you don't get communion," he said.

"Yes, we do," I assured him. "Presbyterians take communion."

He looked doubtful and then said, "But not confession. Not absolution." I said, no. He looked triumphant. It reminded me of the fried chicken restaurant in Frederick, MD which used to trump its competition with its ad, "But we give doggie bags!"

Our group left the Monastery with Fr. Simon's assurance that, whether or not we are believers, the Holy Mother and her son Jesus will be there to meet us in the next world. He took a moment to give us each little pictures of Mary and to flick holy water on the pictures held by the Catholics in our crowd.

The dynamics of group travel: Sometimes they aren't so good. I believe in candor on this subject. It doesn't spoil the trip to find that fellow travelers won't become your new best friends. Speaking of our crowd, there is not much congeniality, and more's the pity. Pairs who are traveling together tend to stick together and are not particularly friendly to the rest of us. Some don't pay much attention to what's happening. On the bus, Halina gave clear and concise information about our schedule. She spoke slowly but firmly.

"After da mona-stair-ee, we will stop-uh for our lunch-uh."

Not five minutes passed before someone asked, "Aren't we getting lunch?"

They don't make much of an effort to keep up physically either, sauntering slowly and chatting while the guides talk. Several aren't at all interested in the country's story. Halina was telling us about Polish history during the bus ride when one woman whined, "I wish she'd stop talking so I could sleep."

Thank heavens for Clayt and Beattie and one or two others who look promising.

After arrival at our hotel, Bob and I walked to the Old Town section of Krakow and had nice big bowls of soup at a cafe that was less smoky than most. (Some were so filled with smoke that we couldn't see the diners for the fog.) I also ordered the vegetable plate, which was a platter of cabbage, carrots, and potatoes—cooked and fresh—more suited for four than for one. Bob had fish and said *it was good.*

On the way home, we stopped at a little grocery store and bought a loaf of the dark bread, a bottle of wine for me, and some beer for Bob, which he put into the mini-bar fridge as soon as we got back.

Please note: As you'll soon see, Bob is of the "if you can't say something nice, don't say anything at all" school. Just the facts, no personalities, please.

Bob:
Warsaw to Krakow 10/26

We left Warsaw at 8 a.m., stopping at Czestochowa to see the Black Madonna. The countryside was covered by 2-3" of fresh snow. Father Simon at the church said it was the earliest snowfall he could ever remember.

The Black Madonna is not a negro but is painted on a black or dark brown wood, supposedly painted by St. Luke. It is a very famous icon in the Roman Catholic church and draws 5 million visitors a year.

How did he remember that? He didn't have his notebook with him either.

We had a nice lunch at the Hotel Polona in town.

Arriving in Krakow at 3:45 p.m. at the Forum Hotel, Susan and I took off for the Old Town, a good 20 minute fast walk. Only a few shops were open in the large market square (it is Sunday). We had a nice supper of soup, chicken for me and vegetables on rice for Susan. Her German saved the day, as the waitress didn't understand English.

I should have included the guide's name but without notebook, I didn't write it down and promptly forgot it back at the hotel.

Susan:
Krakow, October 28

Our first stop on today's city tour was the Castle on Wawel Hill in Old Town Krakow, which we walked up slippery, snow-covered cobblestones to see. This was the headquarters of the SS Nazi Hans Frank, who was the commandant of Poland for "five years and five months," according to the local guide. Thus was

Krakow spared destruction during WWII.

Our guide was an older woman, dressed warmly in a knit beret and fur-trimmed coat. She was without smiles and slightly impatient with us. On the hill, a group of teens was reluctant to move out of our way when she asked. She turned to us and said emphatically, "Dat's what capitalism has brought to us. Kids were nef-fer rude before. Nef-fer."

She took us through the Cathedral which shares the hill. It is the home church of the current Pope John Paul and the burial site of several great names from Polish history, a kind of mini-Westminster Abbey: St. Stanislav; Jan Sobieski, the hero of the Turkish siege of Vienna; and Kasimir the Great (who founded the University and encouraged cultural development). Among the notables packed into its nooks and crannies is Hedwiga, crowned King (not Queen). She married a prince of Lithuania when she was twelve and thus caused the entire Lithuanian citizenry to convert to Christianity in deference to their leader. For this mass collection of new souls, Hedwiga was recently canonized by the Catholic Church.

I'm reading Michener's Poland, an historical novel, so the story about Hedwiga was familiar to me. I was relating it to one of the women in the group and the guide overheard me.

"You know our history!" she cried in wonder. "Americans nef-fer know our history! It's WAHN-der-fool dat you know dis!"

"Well, I'm reading this book..." I murmured. Halina beamed in approval. It was a brief shining moment.

The book has been of immense help in putting all this history together and in understanding the importance of places like Czestochova. It was pretty dull stuff back home, but galvanizing when read in its own setting.

When we came out of the church, it was snowing and the cobblestoned road down the hill was slippery, but no one fell. We got back into the bus and moved on to the Jewish district of Krakow. Jews were expelled from the city, after one of their number was accused of setting fire to the business of a Christian competitor. (Imagine expelling an entire population today for the unproven crime of one.)

Many years later, the city opened again for Jews, so they moved back. Now the district is the site of some apartments, several restaurants and a tiny synagogue, which we visited. Stephen Spielberg used this neighborhood for his film "Schindler's List."

The tour ended at Krakow's Market Square which our guide said is the largest in Europe. It is mighty impressive, a vast open expanse of vendors, pigeons, portable puppet theatres, musicians and, in warmer weather, probably lots of people. But not today. Too cold.

At its center stands a huge brick building, the Drapers' Hall, the interior of which is lined with permanent vendors' stalls. Because of today's bitter wind, I rushed in and bought an enormous wool sweater ($13) to put over all my layers.

We trudged over to St. Mary's Church just in time to see a waif-like nun, who looked about twelve, pull back elaborately carved and gold-leafed wooden doors behind the altar. It opened to dozens of scenes in the life of the woman she called the "Holy Queen of the Earth." This would be Mary. Catholics here (maybe everywhere) seem to worship Mary as much as they do Jesus.

This story of the Trumpeter of Krakow was complicated for me to write. I wanted to include the hand-waving because it was so cute and unexpected.

After this impressive sight, we followed the guide out a side door and stood in the courtyard on the west side of the church. Looking up at a small window high on one of the church's steeples, she told us that from it and the three others facing north, south, and east, the famous Trumpeter of Krakow appears hourly and plays a melody that has been tooted from these windows for nearly seven hundred years. (Not sure I got the date right; I'll have to check this in Michener's "Poland.")

This is done every hour of every day throughout the year to honor the man who back in the 14th Century warned the city of an approaching army by blowing his horn from this very tower. That first trumpeter was struck in the neck with an arrow, mid-melody. So today, at the same spot, the song ends abruptly to honor his memory.

Sure enough, as soon as we had assembled in the courtyard, the little window opened and the song began. We couldn't see the player who wisely stayed back from the window and the cold. But when the playing stopped in the middle of the song, a hand appeared and waved bye-bye to us.

Coffee-drinking is an important part of my morning writing-ritual, so I include the details here.

Back in our hotel room, we scarfed down some of the bread we bought and Bob drank a beer. I had coffee left over from the morning. (I've been making coffee in my room early each morning by setting the Melitta cone, with filter and grounds on top of a thermos, and pouring water over them—using the electric kettle I bought years ago in France. It fits European plugs without all those little wiggly conversion things.)

This is a puny effort to convey horror in words.

Then we suited up for Auschwitz or Oswiecza, the Polish name for the village near the infamous concentration camp. It was about an hour and a half from Krakow and a dark gloomy afternoon with flurries of snowflakes and a cold wind in the air. A young woman whose graduate studies are on this camp guided us through it.

Auschwitz is an evil place. We passed under the "Arbeit Macht Frei" sign, one of the many ploys used to mislead the prisoners into believing they were at a place of work and not death. "Work" wouldn't make anyone "free" in this setting. The average life span after arrival was three months.

We walked through the barracks building known as "Canada" where belongings were collected from those immediately condemned to death. We filed by enormous floor-to-ceiling glass cases; one filled with suitcases marked with names and home addresses, another entirely of shoes, another huge case of brushes—for teeth, shoes, hair—and another filled with shorn hair, some of it still in braids and buns.

We stood in the one remaining crematorium, too small to be useful to the Nazis long-term, and looked at its oven doors. (The other crematoriums were at Birkenau, a mile and a half away, and were blown up at the end of the war.)

We stood at the Birkenau railroad tracks where Mengele made his decision for each arriving prisoner—left (for the gas chambers) or right (for a temporary reprieve from death).

We stood at the Wall of Death, where prisoners were placed and shot in the *back of the head. Candles flicker at its base, flowers lie in memoriam.*

What can be said about Auschwitz and Birkenau? One is struck dumb by the menace which still hangs in the air. And by the sheer stupidity of it all...the enormous amount of strategy and energy and resources that were poured into the goal of mass murder, the harebrained plan to eradicate entire populations: Jews, Poles, gypsies, homosexuals, enemies of the Nazi state. The plan was to murder every one of them. The concept is so hugely evil and brainless that it is hard to grasp even while looking at its evidence on-site. There are no words adequate to the task.

Some separation was required between the camp tour and the evening's festivities so I drew a line across the journal. The rudeness of the "dinner partners" could only be conveyed by using the actual words.

Last night we ate buffet style at the hotel with our group. After dinner, Halina announced a surprise, and in trooped a group of musicians and dancers, suited up for a program of folk singing and dancing. Their leader was a jolly fellow whose partner, fat and stern-faced, looked like she'd rather be home boiling potatoes than standing before us, singing silly songs. The other members were just as jolly as their leader and danced with us all before the night was out. It was fun—except for our dinner partners.

We sat across from four joyless people from New Jersey, two large pear-shaped men and their pale-haired, blank-faced wives. The two couples travel together frequently and apparently don't want to expand their social circle. My conversational gambits were unsuccessful.

"Oh, from New Jersey," I asked in a spritely tone. "Do you commute to New York?" Derisive snort.

"Commute to New York," one repeated. "Noooo, we don't 'commute to New York.'" A second derisive snort, as if I'd said something really stooo-pid. I won't be adding these folks to our Christmas card list.

Here's Bob with his facts-only, elegantly brief rendition of the day's activities, though he recorded his clearest memories of what happened. Next time, he'll add the details, he says.

Bob:
10/27 Krakow
We awoke to see a blanket of snow 1-2" deep. In the morning we had a city tour and visited the Coronation Chapel where all but the last two Polish kings were crowned. The temperature was above freezing, but walking on the snow- and slush-covered cobblestones required concentration.

Our next stop was St. Mary's Cathedral, where we arrived just in time to see the huge altar doors opened and the wooden carvings behind. We also stopped in the church courtyard and caught the Trumpeter of Krakow blowing his horn from each side of the tower. He does this each hour 24 hours a day.

In the afternoon, we visited Auschwitz, about 1 1/4 hours from Krakow. Although we had seen movies and pictures, there is nothing like seeing the camp itself. There were actually two camps, a death camp where Jews were gassed within five hours of arrival (no records were kept of their names; they were never "registered," said our guide) and a concentration (slave labor) camp where the life expectancy averaged three months.

I wore seven layers of clothing and still felt none-too-warm. I can't imagine how the prisoners with only one garment could survive. And this is only the beginning of a long winter.

On display in the barracks, now functioning as a museum, were 43,000 pairs of shoes, hundreds of pounds of human hair, mounds of pots and pans, eyeglasses, combs and brushes, suitcases with names on them.

We returned to the hotel for dinner (on Grand Circle) and were entertained by a local group of dancers.

Susan:
Krakow 4 a.m. 10/29
I'm up earlier than usual today. We're leaving for the Czech Republic at 7:30 this morning, a long drive of about ten hours.

Yesterday we gorged on souvenir shopping. The quality is so fine here in

Poland and the prices, Halina tells us, are considerably lower than in either the Czech Republic or Hungary. The tourist world hasn't fully discovered Poland—its excellent sights and history, its crafts and music and food and lodging—as yet. I'm glad we got here before the onslaught.

Halina took us all by bus to Market Square, where we fanned out. Bob and I went immediately to the Drapers' Hall, that medieval building in the center of the Square. We moved slowly from stall to stall, gift list in hand, poring over displays of amber earrings, pendants, pins, and bracelets. The damp, freezing temperature finally drove us out into the Square in search of tea and warmth, which we found at McDonald's.

Yes, just off the Square is a large, clean, stone and stucco McDonald's in which, down a flight of stairs, we found room after room of students from the University, reading, talking, eating. It was like an underground student union with clean, free bathrooms (unusual here in Poland).

Fortified with tea and baguettes, we returned to the Hall and went right down our list, buying something for everyone. On our way back to the hotel, we stopped in a department store and bought Bob some good sturdy shoes ($45) and me some warm boots ($13). We were shopped-out and exhausted. Last night I had to unfurl our extra folding bag to store and transport all the new stuff.

But the day wasn't over. We had signed up for the optional tour of the UNESCO-protected salt mine at Wieliczka, about twenty minutes outside of Krakow. It is one of the oldest such mines in Europe, built in the 15th Century and visited by Copernicus.

On our way, we passed a granite monument on a small hill by the side of the highway. It commemorates the site of the concentration camp whose inmates were saved by Oskar Schindler. His factory still operates in Krakow.

The tour of the salt mine was pretty dull. It began with a ride in a cage-like elevator that dropped a few floors in pitch blackness with a wssssh of cold air, to a level where we disembarked. From there, we walked down several more levels.

We saw no actual mining, but lots of hallways and stairs and statues carved out of salt. The final site was a huge "chapel" down a wide staircase made of salt, with chandeliers and floor "tiles" and biblical scenes carved in the walls, also of salt. Except for the white "crystal" chandeliers, the entire room was in charcoal tones of black and brown. It was odd and dramatic.

Another oddity: we were about 135 meters into the earth. Two levels below us is a sanatorium for asthma sufferers who benefit from breathing the iodine-laden air.

The corridors we toured were cold, and the rush of air as we ascended in the creaking cylinders was chilling. Packed seven, eight to an elevator and rising so quickly in the dark was frightening to some. The salt mine tour wasn't taken at all by a previous Grand Circle group. On seeing those elevators, they bolted and went directly to dinner.

We finished the evening with the best dinner we've had so far, at the Restaurant Krolewska, a short walk from the mines. We ate fat white bouncy dumplings, fresh cucumber, tomato and cabbage salad, and beef. There was plenty of vodka, good red wine, a light apple thing for dessert, and tea.

With all that vodka and wine (beer for Bob) came some camaraderie—our travel companions seemed a little less boring on the bus ride back. Shopping also helps. We bonded over purchases, found commonality in our search for bargains.

I tried to pinpoint impressions that might become hazy later on.

Overall impression of Poland: It is prosperous-looking. The stores are full, people drive cars, not bikes. (I saw only one bicycle rider, and he looked like the town eccentric.) Warsaw rents are ridiculously high, reflecting the world's interest in being there. Service is good, marketing skills are well-developed. There are young people everywhere, and while they may be under-employed, they are well-dressed and not surly.

Poland is a perfect example of the value of travel. Unknown to many tourists (at least in the U.S., or, at least to us), it is rich in history and culture, with picturesque and well-preserved cities, responsible stewardship of the terrible Auschwitz-Birkenau camps, elegant and sophisticated arts, and handmade crafts, all of which are still accessible for good prices.

Industrious, prospering, with clean unlittered streets and parks—I'm glad we *saw Poland in 1997. Western-style capitalism hasn't yet taken its toll.*

Bob:
10/28 Krakow
We spent the morning shopping at the market square in the Old Town. Susan made some good buys in amber earrings for gifts. I bought a hand carved wooden figure of a man holding two beer mugs.

Our feet were so cold that we ended up buying boots and shoes in a department store. My leather boots were $45 and Susan's $13.

At 3 p.m., we boarded our bus and drove about 30 minutes to the Salt Mines. Spent an hour in the mine walking well over a mile. We expected the walls to be white, like table salt. Instead they were dark, sort of charcoal gray. The lady guide said that the color was due to the minerals in the salt.

There were various rooms with sculptures all made of salt. The most impressive was the huge "cathedral" room with beautiful chandeliers made of white crystal salt. On the walls were carved scenes from the life of Christ.

Dinner was at a local restaurant and consisted of salad, soup, beef and dumplings. I bought a beer glass for my collection from the proprietor for 10 zlotys, about $3.

General observations and notes on Poland:
It's best to change dollars at the exchange booths called Kantors. They don't take travelers' checks. The best buys are amber, wooden figures, glass, and sweaters. Prices are very reasonable. Old Town square shops are best.

The restaurant food is good, especially the soup. Avoid the very small places. They tend to be filled with smoke.

Buy beer, wine, snacks in local groceries. Beer can be chilled in the minibar refrigerator in hotel rooms. There are no bakeries: good bread is sold in the groceries, though.

People are industrious and attractive. They don't appear to be overweight despite a diet heavy in meat and fat. The fattest people around are in our tour group. Public transport is easy to use and cheap. There are no black people anywhere.

Susan:
Prague, 10/30

Our guide is so important to this kind of a tour. I wanted to note the extras done by Halina so we could add them to our evaluations later. Also, I used to dread the inevitable l-o-n-g bus rides on trips through foreign countries. Not anymore, thanks to the journey journal. There's much to note on the road which makes the time go quickly.

Halina tried to brighten the long bus ride to Prague with little treats and and surprises along the way. She had risen early to find a baker who could supply us with "ponchki"—a filled donut which is traditional for the day before Lent. (It not being anywhere near Lent, I suspect Halina had a hankering for some off-season ponchki.)

The baker she found used a non-traditional filling so Halina offered a bottle of special Polish honey liqueur to the group member who guessed what the ponchkis were filled with (rose petals and lemon). The woman who won shared her booty.

After the bottle ran out, Halina brought forth extras. To us, it tasted like poisoned cough medicine, so when Halina went below for more (the guide rides separate from the group on a lower level with the driver), I carried both our cups to a guy in the back, who was only too pleased to get the extras until I accidentally tossed them all over him when the bus swerved. Poor guy smelled like a barroom floor for the rest of the trip.

At the Czech border, the lineup of trucks waiting to clear customs and passport control was many miles long. As far as we could see, trucks snaked over the hills. Halina told us that the wait can often be three days or longer. The radio regularly announces the "wait time for truckers at the borders." Prostitutes do a good business. Lots of books get read.

But we drove through with little delay. We weren't suspected of smuggling, which is apparently a thriving trade among the truckers. Inspection creates the delay.

Lunch was in a roadside restaurant in Brno, capital of Moravia—lots of slaw and rice and dark-roasted chicken. Afterward, it was back to the bus and the remaining 225 miles to Prague, the capital of both Bohemia and the Czech Republic. We arrived in the dark to heavy traffic at around 5:30 p.m.

Again, the important first impressions.

I loved Poland, and I now wonder if I'm ready for this bustling, sophisticated, up-market city teeming with cars and trucks. Czechs are Germanic in origin, says one of our group, the sophisticated Eduardo from Ecuador. Poland and the Slovanians are Slovakian. Eduardo explains the difference as between Austrians and Italians. The hotel staff (we are staying at The Diplomat) is actually Austrian, crisply efficient with hard edges and few smiles.

Prague was spared during World War II, Czechoslovakia having been ceded to the Nazis by the Allies (who, as Neville Chamberlain, Prime Minister of Britain, put it, hoped by doing this to gain "peace in our time").

The buffet dinner last night (included) was sizeable and delicious—the usual array of multi-colored slaws, a whole table devoted to cheese, another to fancy desserts, and still another to hot vegetables. There was, of course, a lineup of main dishes, too: dark meats with dark gravy, and fish. Behind the food stood the waitcorps, smartly garbed in black and white.

In the elevator, a man with a Texas accent answered "$13" when I asked Bob what 400 Czech crowns converted to in dollars. It was the advertised price of a concert ticket. He added, "You can get the best dinner you ever ate, both of you, including wine, for $13 here."

The doors opened at our floor. We stepped out. "Two big steaks," he called after us. His muffled voice continued as the doors closed, "...dessert, too." The car began its ascent as he added, "...best food you've ever eaten..."

We're here until Monday. I exchanged $50 for 1500 k. The exchange rate included commission of about $1 to 30k.

A little history: In 880 AD, Vaclov ("Good King Wenceslas") chose Rome over Constantinople for religious leadership and therefore, Latin over Cyrillic, Roman over Eastern Orthodox, Western over Eastern. He was eventually canonized for this choice. In the 13th and 14th Centuries, under Charles IV, Prague became the seat of the Holy Roman Empire.

I marvel at the economy of Bob's entries.

Bob:
10/29 Krakow to Prague

We left Krakow at 7:30 a.m. and arrived in Prague at 6:50 p.m. Stopped for lunch at Brno in the Czech Republic.

Halina tries very hard to make our journey as pleasant as possible. She arranged for a local baker in Krakow to bake "ponchkee," a type of jelly doughnut, which all Poles eat on Fat Thursday (our "holy Thursday"), following an old tradition. She held a little contest to see who could guess what the jelly filling was made of. The prize was a honey liqueur. One woman correctly guessed rose hips. We all shared in the bottle, but it was too strong for Susan and me.

Halina also played cassette tapes of international music for a sing-a-long. She gave a very thorough history of the Czech Republic as we rode along. Talking without notes, she is clearly very well-informed.

Our evening meal in the hotel was an excellent (included) buffet.

Susan:
Prague, October 31

Halloween today, but it's not celebrated here. All Souls Day (Nov.2) is the big day around these parts, says Halina. She's missing it this year to be with us.

The Czech language, like Polish, sounds Russian to me, although Polish is a little softer with more "zhuzh" -ing and "zizz" -ing. Czechs speak English with a kind of twangy sneer.

We heard from our local guide yesterday that the country is in political turmoil. At the least, it is unstable, with the social democrats moving into a position of favor. He believes that this will halt the forward economic progress made since the fall of Communism.

Our city tour took us from the gorgeous Baroque library of the Strahov monastery down the cobblestone street to the site of Jan Masaryk's supposed suicide leap from a window in 1948 (he was actually murdered by the Communists). From there we walked to the vast Prague Castle grounds, through the inner courtyards to St. Vitus Cathedral.

There's a lot more that I could have written about this famous place, but it's all in the guidebook.

Inside the Cathedral is a ceiling so high, it is distant. There's a lovely interior chapel with much gold, silver, and fabulous frescoes where Wenceslas is buried (murdered by his brother). But the most impressive sight is the group of stained glass window-panels, rising from the floor several stories high. These are recent additions; one is the work of the famous Czech art-deco artist, Alfons Mucha.

Again, only dialogue can truly convey this moment.

One of the four unsociables from New Jersey is writing down everything the guide says, but it's hard to imagine what she's hearing.

Yesterday the guide pointed out the Loretto chapel, built in 1626 as a shrine for a Catholic victory. The original, he said quite clearly, was in Loretto, Italy. Grasping her pencil and pad like a reporter out for the scoop, this woman asked, "Who was Loretta?"

"I beg your pardon?" said the guide.

"Who was Loretta? This is the Loretta chapel, you said. Who was she?"

"I just explained the connection," he said with some exasperation. "It is named after the one in Loretto, Italy."

"Oh." She looked down at her pad. Then up at him. "But who was Loretta?"

We left the group to walk over the Vltava River via the Charles Bridge into Old Town, called here Stare Mesto. On the bridge is a collection of religious statues, one of which is St. John, canonized for not blabbing about his Queen's confession to her enemies (or so goes the legend). A scene below his figure shows him being tossed into this very river to his death. The bronze here is bright gold from *hands which touch it constantly for luck, for blessings, for whatever.*

We waited our turn and Bob took a picture of me, hand on the statue for continued good fortune.

Bob, the former math professor, likes numbers. And he remembers them without notes.

Bob:
10/30 Prague

Our hotel is conveniently located near a metro stop and only four stops (about 8 minutes) to the center of Prague's Old Town. The morning tour took us to the library of a monastery in which we saw two spectacular rooms with painted ceilings containing 43,000 books. The library also contains manuscripts dating back as far as 1000 years.

Following the library (the monastery is still active with some 30 monks), we walked to the Prague Castle, the largest in Europe. Next to it, the St. Vitus Cathedral was awesome with its many beautiful stained glass windows, so designed that they appeared to have been lit from behind.

Susan and I elected to walk to the Old Town center across the Charles Bridge which was built in the 10th? 12th? 14th? Century. We had a good lunch of onion soup, beer, and wine. Total: about $20, including the beer glass which I bought from the restaurant's manager.

Later, we shopped for gifts and bought a pair of candle holders directly from the blacksmith who made them. His forge was on the Market Square. I finally found a wool muffler for a reasonable price: $2.

At 5:30 p.m., we left for a dinner cruise on the Vltava River. Another great day.

Susan:
Prague, 11/1

Yesterday morning, we all trooped behind Halina to the subway. The last stop is just outside our hotel's front door and the four stop ride to Stare Mesto took just eight minutes. Before embarking, you must time-stamp your ticket, which gives you

15 minutes for the 6k cost (about 56 cents). The subway station is well-lit and feels safe. A young boy about fifteen stood and gave me his seat. Wow!

We had the morning free of tours so we cruised the stalls on Charles Bridge, watched the musicians and puppeteers for a while, then walked back into Stare Mesto for lunch on the Old Town Square at its center.

This is a large open space flanked by sights seen in postcards: the huge old (14th Century) Tyn Church, which towers over the four-storied buildings in front of it; the Town Hall with its "Astronomical" clock (also of 14th Century vintage), which gives all sorts of information regarding positions of the sun and moon.

But the big draw of the Astronomical Clock is the hourly march above its face, of 12 puppet-like Disciples, followed by a skeleton-puppet ("Death") and a rooster crowing the time. We stood with the crowds to watch this as often as we found ourselves in its vicinity.

Vendors of velvet hats and painted wooden toys wandered among the people who were looking up at the clock's face in anticipation. A Dixieland band played in the Square's center, at the base of the huge bronze monument to Jan Hus. He was a reformer of the Catholic church (1402)—similar to Martin Luther in his beliefs.

Scattered around the Square are posters advertising musical events: Mozart's Requiem, Handel, Vivaldi, Bach. Not a rock concert to be found.

We bought tickets to a recital to be held in a small Baroque library just off the Square last night: Vivaldi's Four Seasons, Beethoven's Brandenburg Concerto, and something by Haydn.

We ate lunch at "Starometska Restaurace," in a pale green building on the Square. We charged through the smoke-heavy front room to a booth in the back with clearer air and had wonderful soup, fish, vegetables, wine and beer for about $10, including tip. That guy in the elevator was right.

We met up with the group again after lunch and went to the Jewish section to see the Meisel Synagogue, on whose walls are the names of 83,000 people who died in the Holocaust.

One of the rooms displayed pictures sketched by children at Theresianstadt, a concentration camp near Prague. Under each was the child's date of birth, date of imprisonment, date of death. Only a few of the children survived. Their pictures were simple line drawings of suitcases, barracks, railroad stations, skeletons, scenes of prison life through children's eyes. The horror comes alive in these rooms with names and drawings. They spoke to us.

The cemetery behind the Synagogue is lumpy with graves. People are buried in layers in its limited space, anywhere from seven to ten deep. The gravestones were tipped and crooked; some had fallen. The guide pointed out the family graves of I.B.Singer, the writer.

We stayed in town for the concert, which was played on Baroque instruments by seven young musicians—five women, two men. The setting was perfect: the room is newly restored to splendor, with stark white walls and cherubs—in pastel shades of blue, rose, and green—dancing all over the ceiling.

There were three rows of folding chairs and about fifty people in attendance. One man in the front row fell asleep as soon as the first note sounded. His glasses went clattering to the floor after about twenty minutes, but he slept on.

The concert lasted only an hour, after which we rode the subway back to our neighborhood and searched out the Cafe Obura, which Halina recommended.

People eat like farmhands here. Our dinner was enormous. I ordered the "vegetable plate" and was served a platter for 12. After I'd been eating for ten minutes, it still looked undisturbed, intact enough to serve to someone else.

Bob's meal was gargantuan, too. Again, the price astounded us. This mountain of food with drinks in a really classy restaurant came to a little over $20.

Bob:
10/31 Prague
Halina took us on the subway to "Mustec" stop and showed us where to meet her at 2:30 p.m. for the walking tour of the Jewish section. At Market Square, we watched the famous clock, where every hour two small windows open and the disciples slide by. When Peter appears, a cock crows. Several hundred spectators are present each hour.

The w.c.'s require money here, even if you are a patron of the restaurant. I guess the attendants must be independent contractors.

Our lunch of soup, fish, bread, with wine and beer cost only $10, including tip.

The trip to the Jewish section took us to an old synagogue, now a museum, then to a building where every interior wall was covered floor to ceiling with the names of 83,000 Jews who were killed by the Nazis—their dates of birth, dates of imprisonment, and dates of death. Before WWII, 114,000 Jews lived in Czechoslovakia, now only 3,000. The Germans did not destroy the Jewish buildings and cemetery—they were kept intact as a remembrance of a soon-to-become "extinct" race.

At 6:30, Susan and I attended a recital of chamber music by five women and two men.

Dinner was at the Obera Restaurant near our hotel. I had fish, potatoes, two beers. Susan had a huge plate of vegetables, wine. The whole thing was $23.

Susan:
Prague 11/2
Yesterday, Saturday, was another day of wandering the city. I've caught a cold and feel sodden and puffy from it and from the oily food we've been eating. There were no specific destinations for our day, no museums or galleries recommended to see. We rode the trolley with Clayt and Beattie to Old Town and walked along the narrow streets, admiring the painted exteriors and carved wooded doors.

The "skyline" at the west end of Charles Bridge is a cluster of Gothic towers, spires, and red tiled roofs huddled together like they were all trying to fit in one picture. On the Bridge, dozens of artists stood alongside their paintings, marionettes danced and sang, crafts people fingered their displays of jewelry, arranging and re-arranging pieces on black velvet.

The streets in Old Town were jammed with tourists and street musicians. On a sidestreet we came upon a wedding party hurrying down the cobblestones, laughing and calling to each other. They were led by the bride, a fresh-faced thirty-ish blond woman holding her white satin gown off the pavement and a bouquet of flowers in one hand and her veil on her head with the other.

She laughed when she saw Clayt and Bob point their cameras and called her group—young men, the bride, an older man, and a couple of women—to a halt. They smiled for the cameras, all said "Sank Yooo!" resumed their laughing and moved on.

This cheerful bunch lifted my spirits immensely. I had been popping Hall's and holding Kleenex to my running nose all day. I know I smelled mentholated and were it not for Co-Advil and the draw of the scenery, I would have stayed under that big puffy thing they call a "feather bed" and watched CNN for the day. (CNN, by the way, is everywhere, keeping us in close touch with the gyrations of the world stock markets and the "nanny trial.")

Several members of our group also have colds. So, even though I've been washing my hands like an obsessive/compulsive and taking daily vitamins, it was probably inevitable. Why doesn't Bob get these things? His good health inspires awe.

I forgot to mention that we took a dinner boat trip down the Vstula (called the Muldau by the Germans) a couple of nights ago. The dinner itself was pretty awful—lots of glue-y stuff in pans on a steam table. But the scenery of lighted Prague Castle and other massive 14th Century public buildings was gorgeous and worth the terrible food. Haven't we seen it a hundred times in the movies? Foreign intrigue, love stories, film noir. This city is so gorgeous—its assault on the senses so overwhelming, that it cannot be easily absorbed. It must be slowly processed.

But...am I being cold-induced-crabby? I want more. On a trip like this, I'm not set on "wander." The built-up adrenalin level requires more purpose to a day. We've bought our souvenirs and I'm bored with shopping. Today promises more content than yesterday. We are to go as a group to the Institute of Economics on Wenceslas Square and hear a lecture by one of its professors. This evening, we go to a Mozart concert at an estate in the suburbs where M. himself used to stay.

Last night we ate Asian with the Stephens couple, a very good meal at the

Dong Do Restaurant on the so-called "Round Square" (known before 1989 as "Lenin Square") near our hotel. Bob says the beer is excellent here and was good in Poland, too. The wine in the Czech Republic is far superior to Poland's. I bought a bottle at the store across the street for about $1.50 that was the equal of a good California Merlot at home. I'm not sure what the variety is—a young man told the clerk for me that I wanted "dry" and "red." and "local." My needs are simple.

Czech history eludes me. In my brain, it's all mixed up and part of the swirl of the Austro-Hungarian Empire. Because James Michener never wrote a novel about this country, I'm in the dark about Charles IV and only vaguely recall reading about Jan Hus and his reformation movement—or even the far more recent Masaryks.

I do remember the "Velvet Revolution" of 1989, though. Now it looks possible that the voters may return to the Big Brother days of pro Communist, or at least, Socialist rule.

The piercing cold has required layers and layers of clothing, from silk long underwear, to two outer jackets with four in between, plus two pair of socks, a woolen hat and gloves. The suitcases are nearly empty when we leave each morning.

Again Bob remembers the numbers. The #26 tram? I'm impressed.

Bob:
11/1 Prague
This was a day of leisure—no scheduled activities. We took the #26 tram into town for 10 K (30 cents) and wandered around with Clayton and Bea Stephens from Marblehead, Mass. At noon, we took them over to have lunch at the same place on the Market Square where we ate yesterday. Soup, goulash, beer, vegetables and wine, including tip: $7.

After lunch, we walked across Charles Bridge and took videos of the sidewalk entertainers, including a ragtime band and two puppeteers. We ate dinner tonight at an oriental restaurant near the hotel with the Stephens. Wonton soup, rice, chicken, beer for me. Susan had wine, soup, rice and vegetables. The whole thing was $20.

Tonight, Susan went to bed early and I watched "The Incredible Lightness of Being," a movie about Prague which we had seen at home years ago. It was in Czech. I watched it without sound.

Impressions of Prague:
Popular souvenir items—marionettes, miniature houses (modeled after the actual ones), glassware (this is expensive). Food is very reasonable and the beer is great. Both tram and subway are fast and cheap.

The Clock in Market Square was built in 1470; the entire square is over 500 years old. Just walking through Old Town is great recreation.

Susan:
Prague 11/3
We leave Prague today at 8 a.m. and drive 300 miles across Slovakia to Budapest, stopping for lunch in Brataslava, Slovakia's capital.

Yesterday our lecture (part of what Grand Circle calls "the Discovery Series") was terrific. The professor was a sweet-faced, white-haired gentleman who looked a lot like John Gielgud. His lecture was both informative and interesting.

From the moment he removed his wristwatch and laid it on the table in front of him, it was clear that he was a fine teacher. He introduced his talk with a brief outline and moved on to a 45-minute rendition of the complicated history of his country's economics, making it all clear and even compelling. I couldn't bring myself to ask how he taught open market economics (which he obviously believes in) during the forty years of Communist rule.

I should have asked this question. And why didn't I write down his name, for heaven's sake?

Afterward, he took us on a walking tour, which we all wish we'd had a couple of days ago. He pointed out buildings that we'd passed many times and gave us their history. "This is the Opera House where Mozart conducted the premiere of Don Giavonni." And "This was the home of the Smetana School of Music." It made Prague so much more interesting, gave it content and context. With his guidance, Prague changed from a crowded tourist attraction to a richly historic, charming city in which there is a story at every turn.

For example, he pointed out the pharmacy where I'd loaded up on Hall's cough drops the other day, and identified it as the one which sold herbs from King Charles IV's garden in the 14th Century. Wish I'd known that when I was in it. Yesterday (Sunday), it was closed. On a return visit, I'd like to hire the professor for a tour first, not last.

This will be hard without knowing his name...

Now that we've had the advantage of this excellent lecture and tour, I have decided that Prague is well-worth a return visit.

Bob and I left the professor on the Charles Bridge, following his directions to see "The Infant of Prague," which sits in a Catholic church in the area called "Lesser Town." For some reason, South American Indians come here in great numbers to worship this small bees-wax statue. It has a whole closet full of bejeweled outfits—more than 300 of them. (I picture the clergy changing it each day, like they're playing dolls.)

We found the place and, sure enough, a couple of South American folks were staring worshipfully up at the little figure when we walked in. To me, it isn't an impressive sight, just a small baby doll in fancy dress.

We ate dinner as part of an optional program last night that included a Mozart concert. Dinner was at Cafe Poet, where, according to our guide, President Vaclov Havel also dines. "But tonight he ees eel."

The guide (named Vlad) made sure to tell us that he had gained "Speshul permeeshuns" to drive us into the Prague Castle courtyard so we wouldn't have to walk. His "clout" had also enabled our bus to get closer to the boat dock a couple of nights ago. Sounds like tip-fattening stuff to me.

Again, only by repeating the exact dialogue could I convey this encounter accurately.

We were the only customers in the cafe and we were served by a waiter who would have preferred us to dine elsewhere. He smiled mirthlessly and looked bored when I said,

"I'd like some red wine, please."

"No."

"Excuse me?"

"Is not included. White wine is included."

"Okay. We'll pay extra. Dry red wine please."

"No."

"Excuse me?"

"White wine is dry. Red wine is halp-dry."

"I'd like some Frankovka red wine." This was the brand we'd bought at the grocery and it's very good and dry.

"Frankovka is not dry. Is halp-dry."

Through clenched teeth: "I'll take it. Please."

Bob said, "I'd like a large draft beer."

"No."

"No?"

"Is not included."

"They told us beer and wine are included."

"Not large. Small. Only small beer included. And not draft." What a twerp.

After dinner, we rode the bus out to Bertramka, the country estate of a couple who were friends and patrons of Mozart. After a brief wander through the rooms in which Mozart composed and slept (we saw manuscripts in his hand with ink blots and crossed-out notes), we were seated in an adjoining parlor.

Musicians and singers in 18th Century costumes and powdered wigs presented, in song, a playlet, which, frankly, I thought was a little dumb. These people are from the Czech National Theatre, possessed of enormous and impressive voices. Instead of devoting the brief evening to Mozart's music, a large part of the show was dialogue between "Mozart" and the woman who was playing Bertramska's hostess, a famous soprano of the day, concerning a song he was to have written for her.

It was silly and in German. We read the story from a poorly translated libretto. When the soprano confessed some small thing, the libretto explained, "She unbosoms herself." I suppose she was "getting it off her chest." However, in her

18th Century gown, there were a few enthusiastic turns in which she nearly did unbosom herself.

Yesterday morning I burned my hand. Too dumb. I accidentally tipped the cone of coffee grounds over and proceeded to pour the boiling water over my left hand instead. Now it's dark red, blistered, and ugly. Last night Bob put neosporin on it and I pinned a hanky around my hand. Now it's too swollen to get my watch on.

Ours is the kind of group whose members refer to themselves as "kids." "This way, kids," Nancy, who is a very nice lady, said yesterday.

Some of the men, like Nancy's husband, Ted, call us "girls," as in, "the girls are in the ladies' room." Or "the girls want to go shopping." Lots of jokes about women's shopping and driving that strike the men as hilarious. There's sort of a har-dee-har-har quality to their humor. I half-expect tacks on the bus seats and fake spiders in the food.

Thomas, our driver, left us in Budapest. We had no need for the bus there, so he'll return to his family in Krakow after dropping us off at the hotel. Both he and Halina had wedding anniversaries last week while on the road with us.

Thomas drives the bus with great skill. Last night at the entrance to Bertramka, which sits on top of a hill, cars lined both sides of the narrow street. Thomas maneuvered his huge vehicle around at its base, and shot straight up the road backwards. There being no room to turn around at the top, he had the choice of doing this on the way up or the way down. Good choice, Thomas.

Bob:
11/2 Prague

We left the hotel at 9 a.m. and headed for the subway, a five minute walk. It is easier to move our group by subway here instead of by bus since it takes only 5 minutes versus the half-hour or more in the heavy traffic. Arriving at the Musek stop, we walked to our meeting with a retired professor at the Institute of Economics.

Bob took notes and could thus remember the following details.

The professor started his talk by giving us some history of the room we were in. The building was built in 1790 by freemasons. Mozart had visited here on each of his five visits to Prague. It is on the site of a botanical garden of Charles IV (14th Century).

In 1872, it was remodeled to resemble Versailles. In 1918, it became the meeting room for the Board of Governors of the bank which then owned it. The bank closed in 1939. Since 1990, it has been used for economic research and education.

The lecture covered the Czech market system before, during, and after the forty years of Communist rule. The Professor then took us on a very informative walk through old town, new town, and across the Charles Bridge.

Susan and I had lunch of soup, bread, beer and wine in what is called Lesser Town. We walked around there, had tea at McDonalds, and then returned to the hotel.

At 5:30 p.m., our bus took us for dinner, which was followed by a Mozart performance in 18th Century costume at a house he frequented while in Prague.

Susan:
11/4 Budapest
Last night we arrived here after a ten hour bus ride and spilled into the elegant lobby of polished wood and glass in the Intercontinental Hotel, situated on the Danube near Budapest's Chain Bridge.

When we walked in, we must have looked like the barbarian hordes from the East next to the crowds of slim and tailored Japanese who were bowing and milling around the lobby. Shortly after arrival, we were served a "welcome drink" of champagne, in a snazzy dining room (white-lacquered baby grand, black-lacquered chairs and tables) just off the lobby.

Outside our window, the view is like a panoramic postcard. The Chain Bridge is lit at night and looks like a crystal necklace. All the important buildings on

Buda's slope are lit and reflect in the Danube below. Budapest is actually the combination of two cities: Buda on the hilly side of the river, Pest on the flat side.

The city is elegance itself, at least by night. A small Paris or Vienna of 19th Century buildings and "skwahrs," as Halina calls them. She walked us to a large square near here and down into a subway station. The 100-year-old train cars look like Tonka toys, yellow boxes that screech and squeal with age but are shiny clean, safe, and, we were told, run regularly.

We will be here for four more days with only a city tour, a lecture and the operetta on the schedule. And all those activities are today. The other days, we are free to explore Budapest on our own. Goody. I'm ready to lose these people (our travel companions) for a while. And there's a lot to see and do here.

Lunch yesterday was in Brataslava, capital of Slovakia, in another gleaming marble palace of a hotel. We were served more brown stuff in gravy with thick fries and apple strudel. After we ate, Bob and I walked to the town's center which is bustling but unlovely. A bus ride around town revealed lots of cement slabs darkened by pollution, but also lots of shoppers, lots of activity, and many late model cars.

On the way out of Brataslava, the highway is lined with miles of apartment buildings, "high-towers" Halina calls them, in the Soviet style of Early Project.

At the border, Bob reached 250 trucks before losing count. We were held up for about half an hour while the customs officers examined our passports and finally stamped them. (At other borders, we were told stamping was "inconvenient.")

The scene from our hotel window is noteworthy enough to have been added to UNESCO's World Heritage list in 1988. It's Easy to see why. Bob snapped many photos last night and more just now in the clear, sunny morning.

Bob:
11/3 Travel day—Prague to Budapest

We left Prague at 8 a.m. and stopped for lunch at Brataslava, capital of Slovakia. At every border crossing, trucks are lined up awaiting clearance to cross. They are searched for possible smuggled goods, but the real problem seems to be lack of personnel to do the inspections.

We arrived in Budapest a little after 5 p.m. and checked into the Intercontinental on the Pest side of the Danube. It is a beautiful hotel ideally located near the Chain Bridge and right on the Danube. Our room has a beautiful view of the bridge and the castle across the Danube on the Buda side.

After a brief orientation walk with Halina, Susan and I walked a few blocks and had a dinner on the "walking street." Soup, pizza, and beer for me; soup, salad, and wine for Susan. It cost about $16. There were two restaurants at the foot of the stairs going down from the street. Each had a hired guide to stand at the top and walk patrons down, making sure they got to the right place.

Susan:
Budapest 11/5
We have elected to go on the Danube Bend trip today because the guidebook recommended it highly. For the $138 price tag, it better be good.

Yesterday, we took an extensive city tour through both Buda and Pest (pronounced "Pesht") and it is a magnificent city. The building boom was during the 1890s, one of Hungary's prosperous decades. Ornate Nineteenth Century buildings stand alongside architecture of earlier vintage, some having escaped destruction, others lovingly restored.

One which escaped was the Synagogue, the world's second largest (the largest is in NYC). The Nazis of the Third Reich preserved it in order to have it as historical evidence of an "extinct race." The same was said of the Jewish Synagogue in Prague.

Our city tour took us through Pest to Heroes Square, which sits at the edge of a large park. As we de-bussed, vendors—men and women in heavy wool coats and scarves—materialized from behind the bronze statuary, with handmade sweaters and embroidered tablecloths draped over their arms. Each called out his/her price in florints, then added, "Take dollahs."

These weren't the in-your-face vendors who won't take no for an answer, but they were persistent, older folks, who looked to be in their late sixties and up. At one point, some silent signal passed through the whole bunch, although their numbers were spread widely on the huge open square. Mid-transaction, the old guy selling a tablecloth to Marie took to his heels and walked-ran off the Square and out of sight.

"What did I say?" asked Marie, holding her dollars in her hand. "I think I insulted him with my offer."

"I don't think so," said Bob. "There must be police somewhere."

"They've all gone," someone added. And sure enough, there wasn't a vendor anywhere. The whole group had practically vaporized, going from hovering and milling to total disappearance in not more than two minutes. We could see no police cars or authorities of any kind, but obviously, they could, and, we guessed, knew that they were street-vending without licenses.

We rode down the broad boulevards and over St. Margaret's Bridge into Buda. Winding slowly up its hills through narrow, cobblestoned streets, we reached the tile-topped St. Matthias Church built in the 14th Century.

Another scene which needed dialogue, and got it.

"Be back in the bus by 11:15, please," admonished our guide. "No shopping, please. We don't have time for that here."

We walked through the dark entryway into the church. Its interior is covered with frescoes of geometric design in deep blues, ochre, and gold. During their 150-year reign over Hungary, the Ottoman Turks used the church as a mosque, and the church still has a Moorish air to it.

Back outside, cameras at the ready, we moved to the oddly named Fisherman's Bastion in order to enjoy the view of Pest, then down the hill to the waiting bus. Once we were seated, the guide counted once, then again. Two of our number were missing.

"Who's not here?" she asked. Someone said, "That blonde woman and her friend."

Interesting that after nearly two weeks together, no one knew the women's names. Says something about the group's collegiality. (I should have used the guide's name here, but once again, I didn't write it down and forgot it as soon as we got off the bus.)

The guide looked exasperated about our two missing members. Her schedule called for returning us to the hotel at 11:45. It was 11:20 and there were still several more sights to see. "We saw them go into a store," someone offered. The guide scowled. Time passed and still the women didn't return. The guide paced back and forth outside the bus. She held a brief discussion with the bus driver. By now it was after 11:30.

Then one of the men said, "There they are" and the two appeared up the hill, progressing slowly toward the bus, chatting and laughing and holding shopping bags. They climbed on the bus unperturbed and smiled blankly at the applause they received.

We then rode to the pinnacle of Buda, got out, and rushed to take photographs of the gorgeous River Danube below and its flanking Buda and Pest.

The guide pointed out the mammoth "Liberation" statue of a girl holding out an olive branch. She noted that this behemoth was erected by the Soviets after they chased the Germans out of Budapest at the end of WWII. Say what you will about their form of "liberation," the statue is mighty impressive, at least in its skyscraper size.

What does this city remind me of? With its ornate and stately buildings, lemon-yellow, pale green, white, it looks a little like St. Petersburg, Russia. Or maybe Paris squished into a walkable, accessible space. Or an inexpensive Vienna. Easy transport via subway or trolley. Walking distance to just about everything, if you're in the mood and have on the right shoes.

This afternoon, a very tall, very thin, very young political science professor lectured us on Hungarian political and economic history. He moved from the early Celts to the Huns in 848 AD through the Hapsburgs and the Austro-Hungarian Empire. He talked about the country's right wing nationalism, which led to its joining Germany in the Second World War. "A vera beeg m'stake," he said.

He talked about the country's partitioning, its shrinkage to the present size.

Former citizens of Hungary now live under the political control of unfriendly or at least unsympathetic Slovakians, Romanians (Transylvania), and Croatians. It was no fault of theirs, said the professor. The borders just "moved over zere heads."

Clearly Bob is more interested in the day's events than I am. I failed to even mention the wonderful operetta concert.

Bob:
11/4 Budapest
This morning we took a city tour by bus and visited the Coronation Church (St. Matthias) on the Buda side of the Danube. We also drove around the Castle and a hilly residential area.

The view from our hotel window is spectacular. We are located right on the Danube on the Pest side. Looking across the river, we have a panoramic view of the Castle, the St. Matthias, and the Chain Bridge.

After lunch at the hotel, we walked to the "covered market" about a mile away. The large building has two floors with the second floor extending around the outside, the center being open. The first floor has many stalls of produce, meats, and spices. The second floor has stalls of fine linens, cotton tablecloths, other souvenirs.

We rode the tram back to the hotel and at 4 p.m. enjoyed a lecture by a young Ph.D. who discussed the history of Hungary, its former and current economic problems.

We had dinner at the hotel. Great salad bar.

At 8 p.m., we enjoyed a wonderful operetta performance by five women, four men, and a full symphony orchestra. They all had exceptional voices and the costumes were great. (Tickets cost $22 each.) This was the last performance of the year. Halina had wisely called ahead for tickets.

Susan:
Budapest 11/6

Yesterday's excursion up the Danube to its "bend" was okay. During the two-hour boat ride, we passed rows of small modern cottages close to the water's edge, many on cement stilts—getaways for Budapestians. The terminus was at Szentendre, a village first settled by Serbs escaping the Turks.

I missed the charm of this town, put off as I was by its tourist-y atmosphere. We are its only industry, it seemed. The townspeople stood in front of stalls and shops and beckoned us in. The prices were much higher than in town and talk about tchochkes! For the embroidery fan, there was much to choose from.

I'm tapped out when it comes to souvenirs, so while Bob tried to find something to photograph, I wandered aimlessly and, thus, missed everything of interest. Back in the hotel, I belatedly read about the "charming not-to-be-missed ceramic museum" and was upset that the guide had barely mentioned it, encouraging us instead to "look in the shops."

We also missed the Open Air Museum of Architecture and Ethnography. It may be closed for the winter, but it is located, according to the guidebook, only a few kilometers from Szentendre.

The bus drove us up up up a hill to a hunting lodge-turned-restaurant for another heavy meal, accompanied by gypsy music. I loved the music, and bought a tape. Then when the violinist came around with his blatant appeal for dollars (hand out, "help, please?"), Bob said something like, "We gave at the office," and pointed to the tape.

After lunch, we visited the remains of a fortification overlooking the Danube Bend. Although the day was cloudy, we had a spectacular view of many miles of river and valley.

We walked up a narrow path to the castle and then through its ruins, finding in them a small museum of wax figures depicting the favored tortures of the day (14th-16th Century): rack, stocks, etc. plus a room showing the daily life of a 14-16C peasant, fishing and farming.

The guide hadn't mentioned these things either and those who remained in the bus were annoyed that they missed them.

The climb helped tamp down some of the lunch's excesses but not enough. Too little exercise and the rich food here is absolutely unavoidable on tour. Even "clear" soups and salads are glistening with oil. The Hungarian diet is the unhealthiest I've ever encountered. When looking to improve their lower life expectancy, more attention should be given to diet.

I don't know how the populace remains so slim and generally attractive. The fattest people we've seen are in our own group. They clean their plates with gusto.

Dinner last night was at a charming, candle-lit, upscale (for us) restaurant, down a staircase and into a narrow room with heavy dark wooden table and chairs, white tablecloths, expert service. We ate well for about $23, including tip. It is the Cafe Soforforras, across from Pizza Jazz, our Monday night choice.

Today at last we are on our own. Much to see and do.

Bob manages to convey in far fewer words our lack of enthusiasm for the Danube Bend optional excursion.

Bob:
11/5 Budapest

Our breakfast buffets have been great in each hotel on this trip. However, here in Budapest, it is truly outstanding.

We left the hotel as a group at 9 a.m. and walked a short distance to our boat which took us to the "Danube Bend," so named because the river alters its course from an eastward direction at that point, to a southward one. There was little to see on the 1 1/2 hour ride and we were confined inside the boat. I would have preferred to be on the deck.

We left the boat and our bus took us to the village of Szentendre. It is picturesque with winding streets, but they are lined on both sides with outdoor displays of things to buy—mostly linens and such. We didn't find any bargains and even the paprika was expensive. I couldn't find much to photograph either.

The bus then drove us to a restaurant high in the mountains at Visegrad. We had a nice lunch accompanied by Gypsy music. Susan bought a tape of it.

After lunch, we drove to the Citadel, a fortress built in the 13th Century, following the Mongols' invasion. It became one of the strongest fortifications in the country. There were two impressive exhibits: one depicting various torture devices and the other showing scenes and tools of everyday life.

The drive back to the city took only forty minutes. Dinner at Sorforras Restaurant across from Pizza Jazz was very good.

Susan:
Budapest 11/7
A Budapest highlight for me: the Museum of Ethnography (which uses life-sized figures engaged in everyday activities to show the local culture). It is situated across the street from the massive and ornate Parliament Building. We did not go in— you have to save something for next time.

We spent hours wandering the Museum's halls, reading each explanation (thankfully, written in English, as well as Hungarian and German). Cultural morés from childhood to marriage to funeral practices are depicted in wax figures, with black and white photographs of the actual scenes enlarged on the walls behind.

In one room of painted furniture, a short video showed a young woman putting on an entire trunkful of clothes. She pulled up, wrapped around, and smoothed down layer after layer, going from slim to portly in about fifteen minutes when she was finally dressed for her big event.

There was much more, including a special exhibit photo essay of India and Far Eastern Mongolia, so richly technicolored that I wanted to add it to our destinations-list; and rooms of Turkestan, the Caucasus, Manchuria/Mongolia in yurts and carpets and coats and boots.

These kinds of museums are invaluable when trying to understand the people, culture, and geography of another country. And they work well even when there are no English explanations, as we found in the Museum of Ethnography in

St. Petersburg, Russia.

Next, we walked through St. Stephens, another enormous 19th Century basilica. In its sanctuary, a young dark-haired woman in a scarlet sweatshirt was patiently pulling her vacuum cleaner around the marble floor. Its battered canister slid along behind her like a squat red R2D2, dodging tourist feet and chasing dust under the rows of seats. These two were the most interesting sights in the place.

We wandered into an unimpressive display of "crown jewels," small cases of gifts to the Church, dusty crosses and things called "monostaces" (I think), and other religious articles, all decorated with the obligatory precious and semi-precious stones.

From there, we went to lunch at a place so congenial in atmosphere, so warmly Hungarian, that we reserved a window table for dinner. Again, it was cheap, about $11 for the two of us, including tip. The bowls of soup we ordered were huge, about 4" or 5" deep and about 4" across. That's a lot of soup. They came with a large basket of fresh brown and crusty white bread.

Naturally, we added beer and wine. Hungarian wine—dry red called "Bikavar"—is really good. Bob says the beer is, too. Although neither of us has figured out the words to ask, "Where is the bathroom?" we can now order dry red wine and draft beer in Polish, Czech, and Hungarian.

After lunch, we walked to the Covered Market and bought both sweet and strong paprika and other sundries. We returned to the shopping street (called Vaci Ut.) looking for the fat little stuffed clown I saw displayed in an unmarked case on the street. I wanted to buy it for my grandson Jack.

We stood staring at the case, trying to figure out which store it belonged to. There was no name, no address, just a display of dolls. Then a middle-aged woman appeared and gestured to us to follow her and we did, through a series of dark passages into a courtyard where a lighted door led into a toy store. Some stores are tucked so far into the bowels of the old buildings that they are impossible to find without these hired guides.

At 3:30 p.m., dusk settles in here and by 5, it was dark. Dinner, back at the lunch place (Cafe Muveszinas), was another gargantuan feast: two orders of chicken paprika and turkey breast in fruit would serve eight at home. Add the salads and the rice side dishes we each ordered and we had another of those plates that look undisturbed after twenty minutes under attack.

Today it is back to Heroes Square, the Synagogue, and the New York Cafe. Tomorrow, we leave long before dawn with a wake-up call at 4:00 a.m., and departure at 5:15 a.m. for the airport. Tonight is the farewell dinner at a restaurant in Buda called, I think, The Two Trumpeters.

I'm ready to go home. I won't miss any of our fellow travelers with the exception of the Stephens. (Yesterday I overhead the woman from New Jersey—I think of her as "Loretta"—ask our guide, "Just what are Muslims?" Halina was too dumbfounded to answer.)

In trying to puzzle out why the Stephens are so appealing and most of the others are not, I think it may be that we have matching senses of humor. We laugh at the same jokes: our own. I confess I really like people who laugh at my jokes. I interpret this as a sign that they like me. This may be shallow, but it's fact.

Also, I've learned that having done a lot of interesting things in life doesn't make a person interesting. One of our number has traveled and lived worldwide and has many (many, many, many) stories to tell. But he never asks other people questions, and seems to take for granted that they have nothing to say. I doubt he knows anything at all about any of his fellow travelers.

This man reminds me of the story comparing Gladstone to Disraeli. When you dined with Gladstone, it was said, you thought he was the most charming person on earth. When you dined with Disraeli, you thought _you_ were the most charming person on earth.

The point is, you can get real tired of the Gladstone-types real quickly.

Bob:
11/6 Budapest
After breakfast, we walked to the Ethnology Museum and spent two hours there. It is excellent. The building itself is beautiful, with high ceilings, broad staircases, different colors of marble.

We then searched for a pharmacy or some store that sold gauze bandages for Susan's hand, burned by coffee three days ago. We had lunch at a nice restaurant and made reservations to return for supper.

Later we walked back to the covered market. I completed my pin collection with one that says "Hungary." We finished the day by shopping along the walking street and having tea in a hotel tea-room.

Susan:
Budapest 11/8

It's 3:30 a.m., departure for the airport in an hour and a half. Yesterday, our last full day in Budapest, we packed in a lot. After walking to the Synagogue and checking out its impressive Holocaust Monument (a large silvery metal sculpture tree, names of the dead on its thousands of tiny "leaves"), we went to the recently restored New York Cafe.

This is not some Hard Rock Cafe or Planet Hollywood, as its name might imply, but a traditional, richly elegant "coffeehouse" where Budapest's artists, writers, composers, and political figures hung out in the last century under its ornately Baroque ceilings, flanked by fat pink and gray marble pillars.

It was nearly empty at 11 a.m. The hovering wait-crew was visibly irritated when we ordered only tea and took photos. But there was much to see and we were saving our stomachs for lunch in the park.

On our way, we stopped at the "Liszt Ferenc Museum." This is, in fact, the apartment in which lived Franz Liszt (Ferenc is "Franz" in Hungarian, last names first here). For this former piano student, a highlight of Budapest—indeed a mighty thrill— was to wander the three rooms, to see Liszt's bed and desk and piano, to read his notes and manuscripts, and to look at his family photos on the wall (explanations in Hungarian, German and English). Would that we had known earlier about the 5:30 piano concerts held there daily! Top of the list for the return visit...

Name of park? Name of architectural museum? Who was "Anonymous"? Susan—details, please.

We ate lunch at Robinson's Cafe at the edge of the large pond in the park behind Heroes Square. Lots of leaded glass windows, hanging greenery, wrought iron decor. A lovely interior with more good food: the usual soup, salad, bread, wine and beer. I ordered an extra dish of rice—dinner last night was awash in cream. Everything floated in its own gravy, except dessert, which was coated with schlag, cream-whipped and sweetened.

But back to our afternoon. After lunch, we walked to the museum, which sat over the pond's bridge, and is a collection of the nation's most notable architecture—Baroque, Gothic, and the like. We each took turns standing next to the hooded bronze figure of "Anonymous" for photographs and spent my last $5000 florints ($25) on a big handknit wool cardigan. "Bye bye, Sooozie," the vendor called as we walked away. "Bye bye, Bawb."

And bye bye, Budapest. It's time to zip the suitcases.

Bob:
11/7 Budapest
Today we had a late breakfast, then went off to visit the Jewish Synagogue. We didn't see the inside, but walked instead to the rear courtyard and saw the memorial tree. Each leaf has the name of a victim of the Holocaust. We looked for and found the plaque which Tony Curtis had dedicated to his father's memory. The guide had told us about this the first day.

Then we walked to the New York Cafe, located in a 100 year-old-former insurance building (New York Life?). We had tea in the very ornate restaurant.

More walking to the Franz Liszt Museum. This turned out to be his actual apartment where he had lived toward the end of his life. There were several pianos in the three rooms, including one willed to him by Beethoven.

Afterward, we walked to the Heroes Square and had lunch at Robinson's. We walked through an area nearby in which there were buildings of various types of architecture. Susan bought a hand-knit sweater for $25, or 5000 florints. Then we took the 100-year-old subway back to the hotel (70 fl or about 35 cents). An inspector asked to see our validated tickets at the exit.) We had our farewell dinner on the Buda side of the city.

11/8 Travel day—Budapest-Amsterdam-Virginia
Up at 4 a.m., bags out at 4:30. We were served continental breakfast in our room, thanks to Halina. Brown bread (as requested), orange juice, tea. We left for the airport at 5 a.m. There are two airports in Budapest. We departed from the older one (which I think is the smaller of the two) on KLM at 6 a.m.

We arrived in Amsterdam at 8 a.m. Left for Dulles at noon or 6 a.m. Baltimore time. We had good seats, aisle and window (2-5-2 configuration). I saw several armed guards at the airport. We landed 8 hours later at 2 p.m.

My general observations of Hungary:
People appear prosperous and happy. They have been free of Communism only since 1989. We noticed a number of very tall women. The people all look like us—there are no black people.

The retail stores have too many clerks. Inefficient and hurts profit margins.

The food in the restaurants is very good and reasonably priced. The most expensive dinner only cost $27 total. Usually, we spent less than $20 for huge portions. Beer and wine were also very good and inexpensive.

Most of the buildings date back 90 years or so, and are ornate with figures carved into the sides and other decorative sculpture. Some buildings still have bullet damage. The tallest are only five or six stories high. It's easy to recognize the Communist-era buildings: drab, rectangular blocks.

The toilets are clean. They usually have an attendant who collect 30fl or about 15 cents. I never mind paying when they are clean. But if you go to fast food places like McDonalds, the w.c.'s are free.

Susan:
11/22 Baltimore
For the past couple of weeks, we've been engaged in the normally confusing process of re-entry. Actually, things went more smoothly than usual upon landing, at both Passport Control and Customs. In fact, we were home by early afternoon on Saturday, Bob wheeling us over the highways from Washington to Baltimore like it wasn't 1 a.m. for him.

Now that re-entry is established, jet lag is behind us, clothes are put away and souvenirs are sorted, it's time to reflect on the journey we took. I always wonder, am I different because of this experience? What were its gifts? Did I gain more knowledge, or a clearer understanding of local issues?

Here are some of my thoughts:

There have been other Holocausts in history. Stalin murdered as many people as the Nazis, tribes in Africa destroy each other regularly, and the Serbs and Croatians "cleanse ethnically." In the name of God, people and their cultures have suffered torture and death nearly everywhere in the world.

But where and when did an entire "highly civilized" nation divert such energy, brains, and resources to destroy a whole culture of intelligent and loyal citizens while engaged in a major world war? The "final solution" was incredibly stupid as well as evil. To see the remnants of Germany's massive efforts brings this truth home.

The places we visited, regardless of physical beauty or proud histories in previous centuries, are haunted by the ghosts of WWII. The Communist era is recalled with derision, with snorts of cynicism, and relief at its demise. The Nazis are spoken of with shudders, in hard hesitant voices, or not at all.

As to Jews, lip service is paid, memorials are visited, but the sense remains: the ground is still fertile for active anti-semitism. And the people are white. We saw no more than two or three black people the entire trip. In these countries with their histories of violent prejudice, it probably doesn't do to stand out, ethnically-speaking.

So what was good? A lot. To the tourist, the citizens look industrious, and, in Hungary especially, prosperous. Transportation systems are impressive, and roads are good. As for food, there's a lot of artery-clogging going on, but people look fit, not at all blurred around the edges the way they did in parts of Russia.

Budapest is a city that works well. Traffic moves, subways run, crime is minimal, streets are clean. Prague is a fairy tale European city, but a little too Disneyland-ish for me, crammed as it is with visitors. It's a congested city that knows it's adorable—indeed, is overly aware of its charms.

Mark my words, though: Warsaw and Krakow are the Pragues of tomorrow. See them now while they are still visibly Polish.

[CHAPTER 6]

A Short Journal: The Treasures of Vietnam

This journal is from an entirely different travel experience: A luxury cruise aboard the Radisson Seven Seas ship, the "Song of Flower." Because there were only three ports of call, this Journey Journal is much shorter than my others.

The following pre-flight experience was harrowing. I include it as a cautionary tale—and because, at the time, I resisted the temptation to say, "I told you so."

12/30 Regent Hotel, Hong Kong

We had a pleasant, uneventful flight from San Francisco after an unpleasant beginning. We arrived at BWI (Baltimore's airport) early and sat around reading, snacking, and snoozing until our USAIR flight was called. Bob does not like to board a long flight early and gets annoyed with me for wanting to get on and get settled at the first opportunity. So I gave him his boarding pass and got on the plane alone.

When passengers were seated and attendants were walking down the aisle, closing overhead bins, I realized that Bob wasn't yet aboard. I tore up the aisle (in stockinged feet) and ran out of the plane and down the jetway, calling, "Bob! Bob!" as the doors ahead were closing. I pushed them open, now screaming, "Bob! Bob!" Near hysteria, I called, "Where is my husband?" to no one in particular. He was at the desk, having been refused entrance because he had tried to board too late.

Bob saw me and hurried over. A USAIR official let him through, saying, "You must board earlier, sir. We'll let you on this time, but don't do this again."

This next stuff isn't particularly interesting, but gets us from "here" to "there," and records the length of the flight for future reference.

As to the flight, it wasn't just a "flight." It became a way of life. We flew from

5 p.m. Sunday to 6:30 a.m. Tuesday. Okay, we crossed the International Date Line, but even so, it was six hours to San Francisco from Baltimore and a four hour layover in SF before the 14 hour flight to Hong Kong aboard Singapore Airlines.

But we had Singapore Air's good food, attentive service, individual TVs (watched "GI Jane," and "Conspiracy Theory," both of them pretty good), and clean bathrooms to get us through. I even managed a few hours of real sleep.

We arrived at 6:30 in the morning, the first plane into Hong Kong's airport. To comply with the landing law (no flights landing before 6:30 a.m.), we circled the airport for the final fifteen minutes. After a rapid turn through baggage pick-up and customs (the airport was nearly deserted), we were met by a woman named Polly, the local RSSC (Radisson Seven Seas Cruise) guide, who directed us to a minibus and several other folks booked on the Song of Flower cruise to Vietnam.

On the bus, we shook hands all around, introducing ourselves to the other exhausted, expectant travelers who had flown for the past 24 hours from San Francisco. There were Ellen and Robert from El Paso, Greg and Verna (with different last names) from Tucson, an elderly pair named Lee whose luggage didn't make it ("It's the bag that has all my formal gowns!" Mrs. Lee lamented), and ourselves.

We were at our hotel, the glamorous Regent, in less than 30 minutes and a bowing, scraping "assistant manager" named Eric led us to our room. He scurried in ahead of us, pointing out the temperature controls, the television controls, and checking windows and doors. This hotel can honestly support its claims to be first-class.

For starters, our rooms were ready for us even though check-in is normally much later in the day. (Bob says this is because tourism is way down here and the hotel has plenty of empty rooms.)

I probably should have pointed out that the bed would not have been turned down if we had flown from, say, Canton, or Singapore. That the Regent knew sleep-deprived people would be in the rooms is what impressed me.

Add to that these first-class facts—that the bed was turned down for napping, its thick spread folded in the corner, room-darkening curtains pulled closed, and bathrobes lying on the bed with slippers on the floor beside it.

The bathroom is a room, not a cubicle—a broad expanse of coral-colored marble with sunken tub, glass enclosed shower, separate closet for the toilet (a conference-capable phone on its wall) and a table which I can use as a writing desk in the mornings. A spray of orchids stood in a bud vase on the marble counter, another on the desk.

"Harbor" or "harbour." We are in lots of them this trip and I can't seem to figure out how to spell the word right. Is it still the "Harbour" after the British leave?

The wall opposite our bed is all window, and while the view isn't of Hong Kong Harbor, it is of the bustling street below, the adjacent park, and the world-famous Peninsula Hotel across the street from the park. We looked down on the rows of Rolls Royces parked in the circular drive. The hotel owns its own Daimler, which can be summoned by individual guests arriving by themselves at the airport.

Too excited to nap, we hurried down to the lobby after our luggage arrived to stroll around the neighborhood on an orientation walk with Polly. The only others who joined us were Larry and Harriet, a friendly couple who rose out of the cushy leather lobby chairs when we exited the elevators and introduced themselves.

I guess they knew us by our dazed, insomniac expressions. Both Larry and Harriet wore brown calfskin bomber jackets, and have lots of dark brown hair and quick smiles. They had arrived by Daimler, having flown from LA and somehow missed the welcoming Polly at the gates.

Obviously I was too tired to give the details of our visit to the tailor and pearl shops. Each was empty of customers, and full of clerks anticipating our arrival. Could Polly have a special interest here?

We followed Polly around the corner to Nathan Road, then up Nathan a few blocks, a quick stop into Polly's favorite tailor shop and pearl emporium, and back to the hotel. At that point, I needed the nap.

12/31 Hong Kong

Aren't we lucky, returning to this wonderful city in less than a year? Our hotel is on the Kowloon Peninsula, across from Hong Kong Island. It sits right on the Harbour and, standing in front of it on the wide walkway called The Esplanade, we have an unobstructed view of Hong Kong's jagged skyline of shining skyscrapers, topped with neon signs the size of giant billboards. Most of the luxury hotels and fancy shops are here in Kowloon. The Star Ferry to the Island (still just fifty cents) is a short walk down the Esplanade.

I had to use the actual dialogue here to convey the encounter with accuracy.

Scene on the Esplanade yesterday:

I was approached by seven young Chinese teenagers. "Hell-lew," said one. She was reading from a wrinkled sheet of three-ring notebook paper.

"Hello," I replied. The other six giggled softly. She continued.

"Hev yew a minute time to en-ser question?"

"Sure," I said. Now all seven giggled.

"Oh," said my interviewer. She read silently for a minute, fingering the paper and moving her lips. Then, "Ma num is Aim-ee. Dis," she pointed at a boy, "is Ennis. Un dat is Tone-EE, Will-Yum," she continued haltingly with her introductions. "What you num?"

Bob was snapping photos a few feet away. I called him over and introduced ourselves. Lots more giggles now. Bob pulled out his videocamera and began filming while Amy ran down her list of questions.

Clearly this was a school project because their teacher, a short forty-ish fellow wearing glasses, suddenly materialized, took Amy's paper, and smiled up at me. Without introducing himself, he began to check her answers, muttering inexplicable corrections to her grammar.

"Here," he said. "It's not 'where come from?' but 'when come you from?'" He crossed out her words and inserted his. "Ah!" he said, scratching out more of Amy's words. "Not 'what you choose to do' but 'what you like.'" He repeated this for emphasis. "'What you like choose to do?'"

With this, he pulled out his own camera, snapped my picture and, as he shepherded his little band away, called, "Thank!" then added, "Welcome you!"

No prices?

After this encounter, we walked up (down?) Nathan Road to the Wellcome Supermarket, which we had found on our last visit, and this time bought Bob's Chinese beer, a bottle of wine for me (anonymous cabernet), pretzels, and a bag of nuts.

I tried to describe the signs accurately here because they are a special feature of both Kowloon and Hong Kong.

It was getting dark by the time we returned to the hotel. Nathan Road still astounds at night: its signs look like frozen fireworks, huge squares of red, gold, and green neon. They are stretched, not across the stores' fronts, but perpendicular to them, reaching out so far that they meet signs from the other side of the street in its middle.

The streets don't seem as crowded as they were on our first visit a year ago—before the much-publicized hand-over to China—nor do they seem as prosperous as last time. I had been struck then by the people's sleek, sophisticated black-clad high fashion. Lots and lots of slim leather briefcases and cashmere coats. Pedestrians had exuded an air of financial success, of substance and gravity, of urgency and the need for speed as they wove through crowds. I had felt cloddishly suburban; large, pale, and tourist-y in my Easy Spirit shoes and white windbreaker.

This is an effort to notice things, to observe what's going on around us.

But today's crowd looks different. Not sleek, but squat. Not rushing, but sauntering. No Armani suits, no designer dresses, but plenty of plump, jeans-clad teens and people with bad teeth and skin. The clothing combinations—on women and girls at least—are appalling: tight black squares of black polyester miniskirts, or blue jeans, with heavy shoes that look like high-heeled chukka boots. Are they tourists from the Mainland? Such a dramatic difference in so short a time.

1/1/98 Hong Kong

Ordinarily, we avoid New Year's galas. They simply last too long. But last night's New Year's party was included in the cost of our cruise package. Still, like the flight over, it called for endurance. We left the hotel for the Hong Kong Jockey Club at 6 p.m. and didn't return until after 1 a.m.

Name of the suburb, please?

The Jockey Club which hosted us (there is another, smaller one in town) was about forty minutes away in a suburb of 40-story high rises, the most densely populated area on earth, according to Polly. We were herded into a ballroom with a balcony overlooking the enormous racetrack. Tomorrow is Opening Day for this sport, which is the most popular in Hong Kong.

The dinner was eight courses of ultra-elegant French (or maybe just Fancy) food. It was the kind of dinner that paused, mid-meal, for sherbet. We were served cream of pheasant soup—with deadly chicken flu rampant, most of us are eating nothing even associated with wings—and figs adorned the main veal-beef tenderloin combo. The dessert was gorgeous to look at, a mousse on checkerboard coulis made of chocolate with patches of fruit purée—strawberry, lemon, raspberry. The purée part was delicious, but I couldn't pry the chocolate portion off the plate. How impractical.

All courses were accompanied by free-flowing and fine Australian wine (French, too, but I stuck with the red) with the requisite champagne and brandy.

Here's an oddity: this gourmet repast was topped off by superbly smelling regular coffee, but when we asked for decaf, we got little envelopes of Sanka (yugh).

With thumping enthusiasm, the band played loud songs from the 60s and 70s. The girl singer was excellent and when we looked up from our plates to see her, we were stunned by her appearance. She was plump, sixty-ish, and looked more like the Filipino ladies' room attendant than a hip and swinging songstress. She wore shiny red rayon and stood with legs apart like a Sumo wrestler in big, square, red suede shoes with thick sensible soles. Between sets, she sat with the sound technicians, digging into the big black pocketbook on her lap for tissues and lipstick. She was so unlikely looking that, at first, Bob was certain she was lip-synching the songs. But no. We danced up close and it was all her. And she was good.

On re-reading this next passage, I see clearly that this was a no-last-name crowd. I also realize I could have added more physical descriptions—done more than merely

introduce the personalities.

The decibel level was too high to talk to the six other people at our table, so we just nodded and smiled at each other most of the evening, talking in quick spurts during the band's breaks. Names: Ron and Jerry (he's Ron, she's Jerry), Jeanine and Wally, all four from Seattle; Enid and Bob from Palos Verdes, CA. Nice, friendly people. During one conversation opportunity, a pretty, round-faced lady came over and walked around our table, shaking hands and saying, "Hi. I'm Trish from Kansas City." So far, this seems to be a most congenial group.

During the day yesterday, before the gala evening began, we took the included city tour. Even though we'd been to all the areas covered last year, we went along in order to meet more of our fellow passengers. And we were glad of it.

Because I described the city tour in last year's Journey Journal—you'll have to take my word for it—I omitted details here. But the sampan ride was new and I tried my best this time to recreate it in words.

A highlight of the tour was a sampan ride in Aberdeen's harbour. This is where the junks, which used to ply Hong Kong Harbour, now are moored. It's a watery village of old teakwood boats carrying on their decks nets of drying fish, clotheslines of hanging wash, cauldrons of cooking food, and squatting, smiling fisher-families.

Our sampan's captain was a snarling, smoking woman with curly bare feet and a sour expression. We rode around and between the rows of tied-up boats, waving at the friendly, smiling people and snapping photos.

It's always more interesting to read dialogue, I think. So I repeated this brief conversation instead of writing, "a man on the bus told us about Fanling."

On the bus ride back to the hotel, we were talking about what to do today when the man sitting in the seat behind us leaned forward and said, "I don't know if you like this sort of thing or not, but when I was here last, I rode the train to Fanling."

He introduced himself as Mike and the woman next to him as his wife Kathy. Mike has been a shipboard lecturer for Song of Flower in the past and so has traveled in this area a lot. "You ride the train for about thirty minutes north," he said. "It's just one or two stops from the Chinese border. There's a temple and a cemetery behind it, both worth seeing, I think, if you like that sort of thing."

We do like that sort of thing. Might take up his suggestion today.

Am I going on too long about the Regent? Clearly we're not used to such luxury.

When we returned to the room after the harbour tour, there was a magnum of (Moet & Chandon? I'm not a fan, but it looked good) champagne iced in a bucket with a discreet envelope addressed to "Mr. and Dr. Laubach" attached. Inside, the note read, "The Regent Hotel wishes you the best for the year to come."—Signed by the manager.

We were marveling over this touch of elegance when the doorbell rang and we opened it to a smiling man and woman carrying plates of sliced fruit and a pot of tea. "Your complimentary tea, Madame," the man said softly as he directed the woman to set her plate on the desk.

Even at The Greenbrier we've never had service like this. Other things that set the Regent apart: On the bathtub's wide rim stands a delicate porcelain jar of bath salts, refilled every day. The hangers in the closet are whole, not the breakaway kind that must be hooked onto their heads. The portable hairdryer is in its own leather case and not welded to the wall. The showerhead has multiple choices for spray pressure, and there is a European shower attachment in the tub, so I can wash my hair while I bathe. I've already mentioned the phone (with conference capability) in the water closet, the desk-table, and the bud vases of orchid sprays.

Oh, and the elevators are rapid-response. And the machinery in the Health and Fitness Center is the latest technology, each with its own television sets. Bowls of apples and fresh coffee sit on a sideboard near the check-in desk. An attendant is available to guide one through the new treadmills and stairmasters and weight machines.

Outside of the Fitness Center, there are two pools and one jacuzzi, which overlook Hong Kong Harbour. Coffee is served out there, too.

We are basking in this luxury and taking advantage of it all. Yesterday morning, I hopped from Fitness Center to pool to shower, drank the coffee and ate an apple. The night before, I lay in the tub, reading a book, for at least thirty minutes, then washed my hair. And this afternoon, we ate the fruit, drank the tea, and repeated over and over, "We are the luckiest people on earth."

It is 6 a.m. A heavy mist hovers over the Harbour and I can hear the mooing foghorns of the ships, plus the faint sounds of traffic on the street below our room. Sleeping has been a problem. Last night I worked to keep my eyelids open during the party and then, while in bed, I worked to keep them closed. I actually slept better on the plane ride over. But I feel pretty good. After all, it is 1998 and we are at the Regent Hotel in Hong Kong. What's not to like?

January 2 Hong Kong

Ah, the small triumphs of the independent traveler. Usually these experiences are missed by people on tour.

Yesterday, we managed not only to find the Hong Kong Kowloon Canton Railroad Station on foot, but we caught the right train to Fanling. It was as easy as looking at the large map near the ticket machine, finding "Fanling" above it, noting the ticket price (about $2 US each), and then putting that amount into the slots twice for two tickets. The HKC commuter trains use the same kind of fare-card system as Washington DC's metro.

The train was clean. Yet its wooden seats were nearly empty of riders. The calendar New Year is a holiday here for offices, but it's not important enough to close stores. People were packed into the trains coming into Hong Kong. We were among the very few leaving the city. The ride took about thirty minutes through suburbs of dense high-rises, followed by less populous towns to the small city of Fanling. Except for the ethnicity of the people, we might have been on Chicago's El or New York's Long Island Railroad.

At Fanling, we crossed the street, following signs to the Temple. On the sidewalk opposite the train station, a woman vendor squatted beside her wares, watching us without expression. The table next to her was piled with fruits, joss sticks, and huge white paper sacks the size of bedpillows.

So, you ask, what exactly are "joss sticks"? I knew you'd ask, and if I knew, I'd

tell you. They have something to do with memorializing the dead and are burned like candles.

At the top of a steep cement staircase stood the colorful temple, lacquered in red, yellow, and deep green. It was hazy with smoke from a large black pot, around which stood tiny, lined old women in gray pajamas. They held fistfuls of joss sticks and were lighting them in the fire.

Bob snapped some pictures while I walked around the Temple to its rear, in search of the cemetery. What I found was a set of walls, at least twelve feet high. Some were under roofs, others standing alone. In each wall were rows and rows of cubbyholes like Post Office boxes. Nearly all contained the ashes of people identified by black and white photos affixed to the cubby's opening. Under the pictures were dates of birth and death. Those few boxes without contents were marked with hand-lettered signs, "$30,000," presumably the price of urn space for the departed. Expensive, but efficient. It struck me as a fine way to both dispatch and memorialize the dead.

While I stood looking at the photographs, a solemn young man of about thirty, hugging two of the large pillow-like sacks, walked past me to an open furnace, which was blazing in the courtyard. He tore both bags open and began tossing the papers inside into the fire. This was the "money" sent to the hereafter to honor his relative. Soon he and I were blanketed with black smoke.

(We heard on CNN World News that the currency of some Southeast Asian countries has been so devalued that they stopped burning phony baht or ringats or rupyats at temples, and now are using fake US dollars in order to show the proper respect for the dead.)

Once again, I didn't get the correct name of this town. But I wanted to write my first impressions of modern city bustle and then contrast these with the old town experience.

Back at the train station, we continued north to the next town (Shian Shin?) just to see what it was like. At the top of the station stairs, a bald Buddhist monk in his saffron robe and bare feet held out his begging bowl. The blocks below were clogged with people, flowing in and out of modern stores and fast food restaurants (McDonald's was full; KFC was empty, with folks apparently fearful of contracting the deadly "chicken flu.")

We walked a few blocks, then turned left into an old section of town—onto narrow streets which looked interesting. Picking our way through the crowds, we couldn't help but notice the stares on the unsmiling faces. The shops were dark (most lit by a single bare bulb or none at all) and sold exotic things.

I wanted to convey here my feelings of foreign-ness, of being alien in this part of town.

In one medicine shop, large woven baskets of slimy, shiny gray things stood near the entrance. Evil-smelling stuff hung from twisted hangers overhead. Spice shops smelled better, but displayed products equally unrecognizable to us.

There were stores that sold more familiar goods, too: tires, bicycle parts, and vintage television sets. Everything looked battered and second-hand. And there was lots of rice for sale everywhere, in mattress-sized bags piled in corners and on the sidewalks.

It was much like Macao and equally unfriendly. My requests to photograph people, including children, were met with sour looks and heads shaking "no!" One guy gave Bob some kind of ugly sign with his hand when Bob asked if he could take his picture. We didn't recognize the gesture, but it created an eruption of nasty laughter among his pals. After a few blocks, we left.

Back in Kowloon, we ate dinner across the street from the Regent in the first-floor restaurant of the Sheraton Hotel. We'd had a good meal there the night we arrived, but in the mistaken belief that the 10% "service charge" on the bill referred to a tip, we'd left none. So we'd inadvertently stiffed the waitress.

The same woman was on duty last night. She remembered exactly what we had ordered (Thai curry for me, whole sole for Bob). No need to wonder why. This time, Bob overtipped extravagantly.

An odd scene: In this small restaurant of maybe twelve tables, three were occupied by young men and women who looked like they were on dates. Two of the women and one of the men carried on mobile phone conversations throughout much of the meal, leaving companions to eat in silence or to stare off in space.

People here are crazy for mobile phones. In crowds, at traffic lights, in the middle of intersections, on elevators, you can hear people talking away into teeny-tiny phones. At first, I thought the woman standing next to me in line at the train station was talking to herself, fist to ear. Then I came to my "senses."

What I wonder is, what's so important? Are all these people late for appointments or responding to emergencies? What did they do before this technology was developed?

1/3 "Song of Flower"

Yesterday we walked up Nathan Road to the Museum of History in Kowloon Park. What a charming, accessible, gem of a place. It is small with life-sized reproductions of a junk, a street of shops from old Hong Kong, a village home, lots of old black and white photos, and several short videos with good evocative background music.

We spent about two hours here, then walked back to the hotel, foraging through jewelry shops—gold is supposedly a good buy now with the dollar strong and gold prices down—and through clothing stores. Bob bought two pair of khakis, which were hemmed immediately, on the spot. By two o'clock, we were in the hotel's second-floor lounge, drinking tea and eating homemade pastries, waiting for the 3 p.m. departure for the ship.

Now I'm sitting in the ship's lounge, listening to a lecturer on Vietnam who is excruciatingly dull. For an hour and a half before that, we listened as the ship's travel director went through each day's itinerary, minute by minute, driving us verbally over each bump in the road. It was informative but WAY too long. No one should speak an hour and a half without a break.

Now this fellow, a professor with a large tummy and mustache, was droning on and on. Some voices are so flat that you can't pay attention to them even if you want to. He had one of those voices. He's scheduled to give four more talks onboard. I hope they are livelier than this one.

The worst part about this marathon of lectures is that I am to give my talk after lunch on journey-journaling. Who, in their right mind, would attend another talk today? This isn't University at Sea.

No description of our cabin? I can explain: We've had the same cabin three years in a row, so I described it in earlier Journey Journals, but I could have said something this time.

1/4 "Song of Flower" At Sea

My Journey Journal lecture yesterday went well. Even though it was scheduled for after lunch and after a full morning of being talked at, people showed up in the Main Lounge, some with notebooks in hand. Kevin (the Cruise Director) and I passed out paper and pencils, and Bob gave out the bound drafts of "Writing the Journey Journal." Everyone seemed pleased that there was a printed text to consult.

Some questions popped up that I ought to address when I modify the book for publication, like: How to keep at a Journey Journal when time to write is short? And how to pare down a wordy Journey Journal?

One lady came up afterward and said, "Here's another reason to keep a journal: it settles arguments. My husband and I are always disagreeing on little details, like where a certain restaurant was or when we did such and such. If I logged these things into a journey, I'd always win!" Good point. I'm going to add that to the book, too.

1/5 "Song of Flower" Haiphong Harbor, Vietnam

Our trip to and from Hanoi today was ten hours of sensory overload. On the bus out of Haiphong Harbor, our guide, Hua, told us that Haiphong Harbor has "two mee-yuns people" in population; Vietnam has seventy-seven "mee-yuns." The country runs 2200 kilometers north to south, "about two hundred tow-zun square mice." (I had a hard time understanding his thickly-accented English.)

Hua is a mass of nervous tics, foot-tapping, shoulder-shrugging, nose-snorting, and head-waving. He shakes his straight black hair like a horse swishes its tail, abrupt and jerky.

(In a whisper, Mike suggested that this mannerism might be the result of Agent Orange.)

The problem I had here was deciding what to describe. There were just too many new and exciting things. So I had to ask myself, what do I remember most vividly?

Then I divided my descriptions geographically and chronologically.

Highway 5 to Hanoi: Women were working everywhere—in conical hats, faces swathed against the sun and dust; bent over rice plants in the watery paddies; over shovels of dirt on the shoulders of highway construction sites; over roadside tables of green apples for sale; and moving through the crowded outdoor markets of kohlrabi, sprouts, and fruits.

Along the road, bicycles, mopeds, and the occasional pedaled sedan chairs crowded alongside our clean, new, air-conditioned mini-bus. Some bikes carried families of as many as four, with babies squashed between parents and children clutching their jackets from behind or balanced precariously on the handlebars in front.

In Hanoi: Men squatted on street corners. They encircled board games, smoking, laughing, and talking. There was a lot of eating going on, at low plastic tables on sidewalks, by the roadside, in doorways, and on benches. The hips-to-haunches, arms-akimbo squat was everywhere. People were perched like blackbirds on walls and curbs and even on grave markers in a cemetery.

To reach Hanoi's heart, our bus rode along broad avenues lined with mustard-colored buildings from the French colonial days. Ho Chi Minh's Mausoleum sits among green foliage near the Botanic Gardens. We trooped behind Hua for a closer look although we had been told that it was too late to go inside.

"It close now," said Hua. "Too bed. We too late."

As we watched, a prim line of schoolchildren, their teachers, and parents marched behind a uniformed guard, up the stairs and into the mausoleum.

"Why can't we join them?" asked Larry.

Hua looked nonplussed, then hurried over to one of the guards and spoke rapidly. Turning to us, he gestured for us to quickly fall in with the marchers. We did, walking silently into the cool dark building.

There lay a waxy Ho, arranged and glowing in his casket like a fine diamond on velvet. Uniformed honor guards, looking like teenagers in ill-fitting mufti, stood stiffly by, staring ahead. An occasional eye shifted to follow our slow shuffle around the spotlighted coffin.

We ate lunch at the Sofitel, formerly known as The Metropole. A fine French buffet was served by an army of waiters. Afterward, we waited for our bus under the hotel's portico, looking at the collection of vendors—young and old—standing on the grass, holding up goods and shouting, "T-shirt! Two dollah. Just two dollah." "Poss-card, one dollah!" "Stemps! Nice stemps! One dollah!" They were held at bay by two doormen who prevented them from crossing onto hotel property.

Before driving back to the ship, the bus dropped us off at Hoan Kiem Lake, where the small Tortoise Pagoda sits on an island in its center. Some of our group crossed the bridge to see it. We (Larry, Harriet, Bob and I) chose to walk around the old quarter nearby with its jumble of shops, vendors of pho (a clear rice noodle soup) and com (rice), produce, and flower markets.

On the city's narrow streets, the stores are, as Larry put it, "arranged like the Yellow Pages." Shoes, electronics, housepaint—each had its separate block or part of a block.

(Outside of Hanoi, we passed through an entire suburb devoted to the selling of homemade soy sauce. It was displayed on shelves in litre-sized containers, in front of every dwelling. Manhattan markets its goods in similar style, with its Garment District and Diamond District, etc.)

Once again, accurate description was difficult, so I just closed my eyes and tried to think, what do I remember most vividly about Halong Bay?

1/7 "Song of Flower" At Sea

At 8:30 yesterday morning, we walked down the gangplank and stepped onto a wooden excursion boat for a cruise around Halong Bay. In the Bay, hundreds of rocky islets jut high out of a calm sea into the cold, misty air. There are no beaches, no houses on these little islands, and very little vegetation. On the shore, a village of cement cottages hugs the steep mountainside. There is a walk constructed between the houses, above the water. More houses are being built and this Bay will soon hum with tourism. But not today. On this day, the Bay was eerily quiet.

Fishing junks appeared and then disappeared into the fog. Motorized junks with families perched on top slid by our small excursion boat, holding out white spiny coral for sale. Our boat was open to the cold air and I shivered in spite of the sweaters, windbreaker, and raincoat I wore.

For more than two hours, we rode between the rocks and snapped photos of these enormous lumps in the glassy sea. On-board, the small crew was jovial and allowed Larry to pose in the Captain's hat behind the wheel so that Harriet could take his picture.

In this mystical place, in a small wooden boat surrounded by fog and glass-smooth water, miles from shore and commerce (except for those coral sellers), you can imagine our surprise when a hard-eyed young woman appeared, carrying a small suitcase. Did she come from below? Above? We couldn't figure it out.

She dumped the contents of her bag onto the low table, which ran down the center of the cabin. There were dozens of hand-embroidered t-shirts and tablecloths to choose from, for those who came on-board with wallets.

When interest in this merchandise waned, the woman disappeared, tucking her money into her black slacks and clutching her nearly empty bag. We were still marveling at this oddity—of souvenir shopping in the middle of the Bay—when she reappeared with more goods. A whole new array of hand-embroidered things came out of the little suitcase: pillow covers, handkerchiefs, and scarves. Again, she did brisk business until we returned to the ship.

1/7 "Song of Flower" At Sea

Yesterday was a lovely day spent at sea. In the morning, before the enrichment lecture on Vietnam's early history (zzzzzzzz), I gave another workshop on journey-journaling. About twenty five people showed up in spite of its early start—9:15 a.m.—for a normally late-breakfast, sleep-in kind of crowd. I gave the same talk, but illustrated an entry by reading aloud what I wrote on Hanoi. Got nice applause at the end and several people told me they would start Journey Journals immediately.

In the afternoon, we ate a hearty lunch, lay in the jacuzzi, and sat around watching videos in our cabin.

We are due to dock at Da Nang within the hour.

1/8 Song of Flower

Yesterday morning we arrived at Da Nang around 7 a.m.. Disembarking the ship at 8:00 a.m., we rode three hours to Hue in another new, air-conditioned minibus, with our local guide, Hai.

And the driver's name is...?

The bus was driven by a former Viet Cong soldier, who, Hai told us, had driven the Ho Chi Minh Trail for years by night without benefit of headlights. Therefore, Hai concluded, we should feel quite safe with this driver on the narrow winding road through Cloudy Pass.

Hai has taught himself English—he became a high school principal after ten years in "re-education" camps following the "American War." The Vietnamese have the French habit of leaving off the final syllables of words and Hai's self-teaching did not include correct pronunciation, so it was often difficult to understand him.

For a long time, I puzzled over his statement, "We ee breh-fa on da walk-sighs," before realizing that he meant, "We eat breakfast on the sidewalks." In Vietnam, no one, according to Hai, eats at home. "My wy [wife] gi [gives] me mon [money] and I buy breh-fa on da walk-sigh."

He was right. In the mornings, people are gathered on sidewalks everywhere, stoking up on pho at low plastic tables.

When speaking of Tu Duc, the powerful prince in pre-Colonial times, Hai explained, "Becaw da prin was a ar-tik-el, he bil hees own tomb." We finally figured out that Tu Duc was an architect, not an "article," who built his own tomb. We visited this peaceful place. Tu Duc erected it while he was still young and healthy enough to cavort in its gardens and small pagoda by the lake.

Back on the bus, Hai gave us a brief talk on the religion and philosophy of "Confusim." It was very confusim.

Three people on the bus are writing in little notebooks. Jan sat across the aisle from us. "I'm glad to see you practice what you preach," she said when I wrote something in my on-the-road "reporter's notebook." Then she held up her own scrap of paper. "See what you've got me doing?"

The value of the trip was the journey itself, through the suburbs of Da Nang and into the countryside. The road wound north through Cloudy Pass on hairpin turns high above China Beach, where the sea delivered white, foamy waves.

We stopped at an overlook to photograph a small fishing village, Lang Lo, far below, and then we descended and drove through it. Its main street was lined with tiny, ramshackle restaurants and the ubiquitous plastic sidewalk tables.

"Here is mos' poplah seafoo' plays," Hai announced. It certainly looked inviting. I mentally added Lang Lo as a place to come back to...next time around.

For the few days we are here in Vietnam, there's just too much to see. Today we chose to drive to Hue, but others stayed in Da Nang, where they will visit the Cham Museum (Chams were early Vietnamese settlers) and the elegant resort at China Beach. If—no, when—we do this trip again, we'll take the other option.

But the Hue trip was well worth it—another day of sensory and cultural overload. Hue was the site of the 1968 Tet offensive where ten thousand civilians died during the twenty-five days of attack by the North on the ARVN/US forces.

The city is divided by the exotically named Perfume River (once it was lined with flowers). On one side, a cluster of hovels clings to the waterfront. Behind them, on the main avenue through Hue, stand blocks of French colonial buildings, some painted ochre, others white, still others a dusty rose. We passed Ho Chi Minh's high school. We also passed the alma mater of South Vietnam's one-time leader, Diem.

Across the river lie the ruins of the 19th Century Citadel. This is a walled enclave nearly destroyed during the "American War," which contains the Purple Palace and its pagodas, modeled after Beijing's Forbidden City. Today, restoration work is being funded by France and the U.N.

We passed through the restored Ngo Mon Gate in the wavy afternoon heat and walked around the Palace gardens. Not much more to see, except a big Buddha and a few dusty glass cases of souvenirs. This "museum shop" was manned by at least ten people, reminding us that this is a Communist country, with high, if bogus, employment.

Lunch was served at the Century Riverside Hotel across the river from the

Citadel. "Wash-up Rooms for Females" were designated by signs in front of the hotel's bedrooms on the second floor—apparently there are no public restrooms.

We lined up and sampled a wide variety of Vietnamese dishes, which immediately made me a fan. My favorite, pho, is a delicious concoction of gingery broth, thick rice noodles, kale and spinach into which the server plops a ladleful of chicken, or pork, or beef. I loved it.

Riding back to the ship, we saw hundreds of young women dressed alike in long white "au dais"—the tunic-topped wide pajamas that are popular here. These girls, Hai told us, are high school students. They sit straight-backed in their white clothes and pump through traffic and air pollution, looking like dark-haired Barbie dolls (without the jutting bosoms) and manage, somehow, to avoid the dust and grime.

In fact, the women commuters all looked like dolls, and so ladylike. They wore silks astride their bicycles and never seemed to catch a pantleg in the spokes or get ruffled by the converging mass of wheels.

This trip was notable for the congeniality of our fellow passengers.

1/9 Song of Flower—At Sea

We've found lots of compatible people on this trip. Luck of the draw, I guess. But I feel that we could sit with anyone at dinner and have fun talking with them. The only pair that we avoid is Bernie and Sheila, both nice people and interesting. But Bernie chews with his mouth open and spits little pieces of food when he gets excited about something. And his breath is bad. They're good on the bus, though, (sitting in front of us), enthusiastic and knowledgeable about Southeast Asia.

Another reason I liked Sheila: She raved about my workshop, said it was "fantastic." Told me, "I can't wait to buy the book." How could I not like this lovely woman?

We also stay away from the cigar-smoking fellow from New Jersey who has a thick brown mustache, tonsured hair and large sloping chest and tummy. Mike says he looks like a cookie jar. His cigars thicken the air, even on the open deck. And he smells like a cigar at all times. I caught myself in the ship's elevator with *him once and almost gagged.*

Thankfully, cigars are not allowed in the dining room, but cigarettes are. So we also avoid Karen and Jack at mealtimes. We like them a lot, but both are heavy smokers. Still, there are lots of other people with whom we can dine—Jan and Alan, Kathy and Mike, Anne (a young woman who owns a luggage store in San Antonio) and her friend Debra, and many others.

If we wind up at the dining room entrance alone, we just whisper to Mario, the headwaiter, "Find us somebody interesting," and he does. This is how we've met so many of our fellow passengers. And Mario does not disappoint us with his choices.

People have disappeared for days on this cruise, felled by seasickness or sore throats or bronchitis or worse. Deck 7 seems to be particularly vulnerable. We on 3 are of hearty peasant stock and our active numbers are undiminished.

This cruise has been an ideal mix of shore excursions and days at sea. Of course, we love the ship. If we were on one of those enormous impersonal ocean liners, we might not feel the same. But Song of Flower with its 178 passengers (and 120 in service crew), its relaxed dining schedule and un-assigned seating, its round-the-clock room service (at no extra charge), and its no-tipping policy is so congenial that we've enjoyed the days at sea hugely.

1/10 Saigon

Everybody will wonder, as did we, if there are visible reminders of the war. I wrote this next entry to answer that question:

Wow, we are here—in the famed Saigon, now known as Ho Chi Minh City (pronounced locally as "H'Ch'Mi Ci-tee"). No vestiges of the war are visible. For a Communist country, there's a swirl of entrepreneurial activity, at least at the street level. This city is noisier, more crowded, and has more street traffic than either Hanoi or Hue. In short, it's more Western.

The one disappointing destination was the CuChi Tunnels. I hope that is conveyed by this description, so other people won't waste their precious time.

We spent half of the day riding in a bus out to the CuChi Tunnels, a drive of about 75 km northeast of the city, via suburbs and rural roads. The ride was the most interesting part of the trip.

The tunnels themselves were a 250-kilometer, three-level, underground network of refuge and village access for the Viet Cong. They are interesting to hear about, fascinating to contemplate, horrific to imagine in use. Access to them was via disguised openings that looked no larger than, say, a large frying pan. These fierce little folk could pop up, mow down, and disappear without a trace, then show up in their villages without having to sneak through checkpoints or sentries. The tunnels had no living space, but were meant to enable troop movement without enemy detection.

That being said, the tunnels themselves are pretty boring—just a flock of narrow, dirt holes. We saw diagrams and heard a brief talk by a former Viet Cong soldier, explaining their use, pointing out the surgeries, the community rooms, the kitchens and designated openings for smoke exhaust—all on the diagrams. We are simply too big and most of us, too claustrophobic, to enter and see the real things.

I stepped down into one area that has been enlarged for tourists, looked around at the dirt walls, and climbed out. Bob stooped over and crawled through a long low tunnel to another area. Two guys from our group, showing their machismo, went down into the third level, and came out sweating, dirt-streaked, and red-faced.

My assessment of this optional excursion is that we could have learned as much by hearing a lecture and seeing the diagrams on-board. Seen one dirt hole, seen them all.

And CuChi shows clear signs of turning tacky. Near the parking lot is a dusty compound of caged monkeys, a soda stand, and a souvenir shop. Our guide proudly pointed out a tennis court, which looks incredibly incongruous in this setting. But, mark my words: It's only a matter of time before the CuChi Tunnel Resort appears and maybe the CuChi Tunnel Theme Park, as well.

The best way to write about this experience is just to take it (literally) one step at a time.

Between CuChi and Saigon, we stopped at a collection of thatched-roof huts, built around one small cement building. A young woman sat under a lean-to next to the house, rapidly spreading rice paste on a mold over a fire, holding down the mold's cover for thirty seconds, then scraping up the steamed circlet and laying it on a rattan panel for drying. Rice paper is made by the inhabitants of the little compound and hundreds of other people in this rural area. It is edible and used for wrapping spring rolls and making rice noodles.

Walking up to the building, I stepped inside the entry into a high-ceilinged room with plastic tiled floors, and a square wooden bed frame with only a mat on top of it—no mattress or pillow. Overhead hung a gauzy mass that must release as mosquito netting.

Next to the bed were a heavy rectangular wooden table and a dresser, on top of which sat a faded black and white photograph of a man in a goatee. A medal mounted on a card leaned against the picture. Next to this was a rice bowl of joss sticks. On the wall beside the bed was a diploma or certificate of some kind.

Several rattan panels covered with curling white circles of rice paper leaned against the opposite wall. I heard them cracking and creaking as they dried in the close hot air of the cottage. I stepped out of the entrance and nearly knocked over a wispy ancient (woman) standing there, smiling broadly. I had been inspecting her home. She gave her wordless, toothless welcoming smile to others, nodding for them all to come in, look around.

Back on the bus, our guide told us that anyone is welcome in a rural Vietnamese home at any time and without invitation. Giving the old lady money would have insulted her badly. "A fren-ly nod, a hello," are the only requirements, said the guide reprovingly. "They not beggars." He must have witnessed one of our number when she stuffed a dollar bill into a little boy's hand.

Only direct quotes can convey the guide's ineptitude.

This was about the only sensible information given us by our guide, Phong. He is, sad to say, pretty much a half-wit. In Saigon, he pointed out sights after we had passed them and only in response to questions (e.g., "Phong, what was that large impressive building back there?" "Dat bill-ing? Back dere?" "Yes. Way back there." "Dat Am-er-i-ca Em-bass-ee.").

Driving by stately mansions and official-looking buildings, he prattled on, unasked, about local drinking habits.

"Vietnamee dreen ice waht-uh," he said. "...Uh, meb-be tea wi ice...or no ice. Meb-be juh wah-tu..." I'm sorry. To me, the citizens' favorite drink is rarely interesting, unless it's something unusual, like bat blood.

Again, the actual words of the woman bring the scene to life.

Vendors in Saigon are persistent. As we rode along one wide street, a motorcycle pulled up alongside. Its driver kept pace with us in the bus, and a woman clutching the cyclist's waist waved at us tourists from behind. We all waved back.

With one hand, the woman reached into her shoulder bag and pulled out a t-shirt. Showing an impressive entrepreneurial spirit as well as good balance, she held up the shirt in her right hand and two fingers with the left. Two dollars. We laughed in surprise. Encouraged, she smiled brightly and called out, "You buy?"

The bus moved on through traffic. "You buy?" she called again. We turned a corner and waved at her through the back window.

"You come back?" she hollered hopefully as our bus picked up speed and we disappeared from her sight.

We passed the Opera House (now under renovation) and the Continental Hotel from which Walter Cronkite and other television journalists regularly reported on the war. (Phong didn't tell us this. We figured it out ourselves when we returned to the city in the afternoon.)

In the city and suburbs, there is much construction of those little cement dwellings like the one we invaded in the countryside. We can see that the ground floor is one open room, about 10' by 10'. Inside are shiny tiled floors and, sometimes, tiled walls, too. A verandah usually runs across the front, and long door-length shutters hang on either side of the single large window and entrance. The roofs are flat.

The size of these homes depends upon the size of the family living there—more kids, more floors. Some are four, five single rooms, stacked on top of each other. The whole effect is cute. I loved these houses.

Barbara, the woman who came to both my Journey Journal talks aboard ship, told me that she finds herself noticing much more about each day's excursion. "This is forcing me to pay attention," she said. "I really appreciate that." And I appreciate her saying so.

These next encounters show the Vietnamese, rather than tell about them. Once again, dialogue helps the reader "hear" what's happening.

In the afternoon, Bob and I took the shuttle bus from the ship to Saigon's center and walked through the crowded sidewalks to the Ben Thanh Market. This enormous building of tightly-packed stalls is manned by sales people who vie valiantly for the potential customer's attention, shrieking into whichever ear is closest, "Come buy this, lady!" Or "You like t-shirt, gennaman?" The noise level was stratospheric and the temperature inside the market was even hotter than outside, which was a blistering 98 degrees. Sweat dribbled down Bob's face and off his nose. "Let's get out of here," he shouted.

Just then, a rat crossed our paths near the meat stalls. "Okay," I agreed and we left through the nearest door.

Out on the street, Bob said, "I'd like to find a pin for my hat." So we started the search, ducking in and out of stores all along Le Loi Boulevard, stepping over a legless beggar, and threading our way through the sidewalk pho stands.

No luck. Nobody even knew what Bob meant, until we came to a slender little fellow who overheard Bob asking a merchant, "Do you have any pins? Like this?" (pointing to pins from Hanoi and Hue on his hat).

The man sidled up to Bob and asked, "You want pin?"

"Yes!" said Bob.

"I get you," he said and disappeared into the crowd. He returned minutes later with a fistful of old Army medals.

"No, no," said Bob in disappointment. He took off his hat and pointed to the pins again. "Like this. Not medals but pins."

The man studied the pins, nodded somberly, and again disappeared. We turned and began to walk down Le Loi, resigned to a pin-less visit to Saigon. Waiting for the traffic light to change, I sensed a commotion on the sidewalk *behind us and turned to see a whole neighborhood of people running our way, led by the thin would-be salesman. He called out, "Wait! I have!" "WAIT," chorused his companions.*

We waited and when he reached our sides, panting slightly, he opened his fist in triumph to reveal three small enameled pins, just what Bob wanted, each imprinted with a different scene and the name, "Saigon."

"Perfect!" we said.

The man smiled in pure joy. His friends nodded and smiled, too. Everyone looked pleased with their friend's success.

"How much?" asked Bob.

"One dollar!" the man said with enthusiasm. Bob gave him three dollars and we left the little band standing on the corner, waving goodbye.

Last night, a small troop of local Saigonese entertained us. Three men and three women—all dainty and graceful, with smooth skin and beautiful smiles—arrived at a theater to play odd stringed instruments and dance for us. One dance was accompanied by the clicking of tiny china teacups in the dancers' fingers. It sounded like castanets. The pleasant tuneless twang of the instruments was sort of New Age and soothing—nothing you could hum as you exited the theatre, but pleasant nonetheless.

In Saigon Harbor at night, a soft breeze cooled the temperate air. Dinner cruises glided by in boats outlined with little white lights. Motorized junks moved back and forth across the Harbor ferrying commuters to their homes on the other side of the river. They looked like wind-up toys against the colonial-era buildings along the waterfront, the tankers in the harbor, and the "Song of Flower." We stood with Kathy and Mike, Jerry and Ron, speculating as to which quaint buildings will disappear into steel and glass first. It is our great good fortune to see Saigon "Before."

The band set up their instruments on the deck for this last night in Saigon. Kevin, the Cruise Director (he's also a professional singer), sang songs from the Fifties and people danced. Bernie and Sheila are such good dancers that we stopped our conversation to watch them.

Today we sail at 10 a.m., down the Saigon River into the South China Sea. We have two more days at sea before landing in Singapore. Tonight, we've been invited to sit at the Captain's table for dinner.

1/12 Singapore Harbor (Harbour?)
Our last two days passed quickly. Dinner with the Captain was fine, if a little too long.

Last night we ate with two men (and their wives) who had fought in Vietnam with the same company and were returning to the country for the first time.

Both are earnest, handsome. and as close-cropped as in their Army days. One of the men, Todd, runs the Richmond Home for Boys. Pat, the other Vietnam vet, grew up in the Home, and became a hugely successful businessman (he won the Horatio Alger award this year). He took several boys from the Home with him to the White House for the Award Ceremony. "He wanted to show them that they could do well, too," said Todd. Pat was too modest to talk much about himself.

The men referred to "'Nam" and "Way" (Hue), and spoke of being "incountry." (It is hard to imagine these cheerful guys calling people "gooks" and spraying them with bullets. I couldn't.) All four were great company. I hope our paths cross again sometime.

We feel that way about many of our fellow passengers. In the back of my Journey Journal, I've noted their names and addresses and plan to keep in touch. A lot are traveling on the Song of Flower for the third, fourth, or fifth time. So it's possible that we will meet again. We like this ship and keep coming back for more.

Now we're packed and ready for Singapore. Bye bye, Song of Flower.

Available writing time was brief in Singapore, too short for long descriptions. I left out a couple of places entirely—like the Hawkers' Market and Little India—for lack of time and just wrote down the highlights.

1/13 The Singapore Regent Hotel, Singapore
Last night we went with Allen and Jan McLean (friends from the ship) to the Night Safari at the Singapore Zoo. This is our sixth visit to this city and we've always

been asked by people who've also been here, "You mean you didn't go to the Night Safari?" It really is an unusual, interesting jaunt.

We took a cab out there (about $7 US), arriving at 7:30 p.m. and hopped onto the little train for the forty-five minute trip around the zoo. Of course, it was dark by then. But spotlights are situated so that the lairs of the animals are adequately (but not brightly) lit. The tram stopped twice for us to walk around and look more closely at the leopards, tigers, giraffes, and other wild animals, all in open areas with only natural barriers like shrubbery and streams to separate us from them. We were home by 9:30. It was well worth the visit.

In the afternoon, Bob and I walked at a sensible saunter through the steamy heat, down Orchard Street to Tang's Department Store. We bought souvenirs for Bob's office assistants—some porcelain rice dishes—and stainless steel flatware for ourselves. The dollar is so strong that prices seem cheap, unlike our previous trips.

1/14

Yesterday, all reason aside, I bought a 22K gold necklace, a long heavy chain of tiny, hand-stamped butterflies, a portion of which detaches to become a bracelet. As the deal was closing, I impetuously added two pair of gold earrings. Gold is cheap now, the dollar is strong. I think that at $656, I made a good bargain.

Having since checked out local U.S. prices, I realize that the deal was not only good, it was laughably terrific. I'd never bought real gold before and didn't know.

And I liked the salesman, Robin Ngin. He was soft-spoken and spent lots of time handing me various sizes and designs of necklaces. After an hour of hooking and unhooking, I said to him, "Well...I need to think it over..."

Instead of looking crestfallen or turning sour, he said, "Yes. Okay. I unnahstand. Is lot of money." He directed us to a Nepalese tea shop a few doors down. There we sat, drinking Darjeeling tea, while I rationalized the buy. I was as sold on the salesman as I was the necklace. He was so pleased when we returned.

We asked Robin about Singapore politics. He, like other Chinatown merchants, is angry at the high cost of rents and the glitzing-up of the neighborhood. The rampant removal of old buildings has halted for now, so there is hope that this wonderful enclave will survive. He muttered a few harsh (thickly-accented) words about the political system. Neither of us could understand very well what he said.

Bob took his picture for our album and we said goodbye. I like visiting a foreign city for the second, third, sixth time. We used to say, "There are so many places to go, we don't want to revisit any." But now I see the worth in having worked out the mysteries of the mass transit systems, found a few good eateries and anchor points, and packing adequately for the weather.

Also, it seems that so many primary tourist attractions have become too commercial and corny. It's the secondary sights and the neighborhoods of local citizens that we like to visit now. An ordinary ride on a public bus through the center of town is fun (especially when it's double-deckered) and even more so when we've already seen the local Empire State Building or Niagara Falls. In other words, the sightseeing pressure is off on return trips, and we can just enjoy ourselves.

This Regent Hotel is as lovely as Hong Kong's. The doorman told us that the regional finance ministers (from the Malacca Straits countries of Malaysia, Singapore, and Thailand) are meeting here today to discuss the financial crisis that has melted down their currencies and stock markets. Lots of limos and security-types in dark glasses are milling around the front entrance.

It is close to Lunar New Year, so tonight we spent our final hours here walking around Chinatown again, looking at the gaudy red and gold ornaments and geegaws with tassels either hanging in stalls, or displayed on folding tables in the streets. Overhead, colored lights were strung across the streets, smoky from the food being cooked in open stalls.

We passed a tiny elderly man, sawing away at a one-stringed musical instrument, singing some tuneless Oriental number that sounded like "Heeenie Hawng Hangee Hawng." So ethnic, so exotic. So Singapore Chinese. At this obvious photo-op, Bob aimed his video and told me to put a few coins in the can at the old man's feet.

I did so. The sawing stopped. He stared first at me, then at Bob's camera, leaned over and said to me in perfect English, "Help me out on this one," and abandoned his "Heenie Hawngs" for an ordinary "Happy New Year to You," to *the tune of "Happy Birthday." We have it all on tape.*

We have checked out; our bags are in the hall. In spite of the heat, I'm wearing the travel vest and jacket with all on-plane necessities tucked into my many pockets. I find myself less anxious about these transitions these days and am actually looking forward to the plane trip with its many movies and many hours in which to read. It's been a fine, fine journey. I'd come back in a heartbeat. But now it's time to go home.

1/31 Baltimore

Reflections on Vietnam: I keep thinking about the way in which the Vietnamese people cooperated with each other in the streets. Bicycle traffic was heavy but it moved like schools of fish—smoothly, without interruption, around us pedestrians and oncoming mopeds, cycfopeds, and cars.

On the road to Hue through Cloudy Pass, a narrow mountain passage of hairpin turns, we encountered several trucks while passing on curves. Ordinarily this would have terrified me. But somehow, in Vietnam, you got the feeling that no one would drive too fast, or would be too hostile or boiling over with road-rage and so, there was no danger. People here, it seems, trust each other. It was so refreshing.

I also thought about the futility of war. Especially "That War." Former Viet Cong and ARVN soldiers work closely together now. The current regime endorses a modified kind of Communism that encourages entrepreneurial activity. "We never lost a battle," said the former U.S. Army soldier on our trip, "but we lost the war." A point to ponder: If we had never entered the conflict, wouldn't the country be much the same as it is today?

[CHAPTER SEVEN]

An Even Shorter (and domestic) Journey Journal: A Chautauqua Reunion

The Journey Journal isn't just for lengthy international treks, but also for domestic journeys, however brief. I use a recent winter-time trip to my summer haunt, the Chautauqua Institution in upstate New York, to demonstrate the Journey Journal's versatility.

I know I should have put some history and background in about Chautauqua itself, but instead I jumped right in.

Sunday—Chautauqua Institution, Chautauqua, NY
Yesterday at 6:a.m., I waved goodbye to Bob and our dog Broker and rolled out of the driveway, headed for Chautauqua, New York and the annual reunion of the Motet Choir, which sings together each morning during the Chautauqua summer season. Midway through winter, with the old season fading from memory and the new one still several months off, the group feels the strong need for some off-season singing and shmoozing. Therefore, the Motet Choir holds this annual reunion in January and has done so for decades.

My car was packed with a thermos of strong Starbucks coffee, a pile of music- and book-audiotapes, an apple, and my overnight bag. And, because my destination was Chautauqua with its frequent winter "lake effect" snowstorms, I had also stashed a pair of boots, some mittens, earmuffs and an icescraper in the back seat. These things looked unimaginable and ridiculous in the 60 degree Baltimore morning.

The drive was two books (Elizabeth George and Richard Patterson, both abridged) and one music tape long: about seven hours. Somewhere around Ridgeway, PA, the air turned cold and snow lay between the remnants of cornstalks like white dust. Outside of Warren, the road to Sugar Grove was edged with glassy ice and I could now easily imagine the boots and mittens on my feet and hands.

I use the shard metaphor to help the reader visualize this scene.

The first view of the 22-mile long Lake Chautauqua always lifts my spirits. At 1 p.m., it lay before me at the foot of the long hill on Rt. 69 north of Sugar Grove. With a Palestrina Mass in loud accompaniment to the panorama, I nearly bubbled over. In the summertime, from this vantage point, the lake looks like a shard of fallen sky. Yesterday it was gray and the shoreline was lacy with icy froth. But it was no less majestic.

A little background on this trip:

I've never been to this winter gathering of summer singers, never seen Chautauqua in the grip of winter. Lake effect storms of damaging proportions have kept me at home in the past. But this year, I was ready and determined to get here. My sturdy little 4-wheel drive Subaru is sleek and recently well-serviced (at a cost of $982). I had my canteen of water and a new package of Hall's Throat Lozenges to oil up my unused, off-season vocal cords for the rigors of long rehearsal sessions.

I am a day late, having missed the first big gathering on Friday night—we had theatre tickets in Baltimore. On Thursday, we returned from our three-week trip to Vietnam. So, I'm not only a day late, and but also sodden with jet lag. Still, the air and the atmosphere invigorate me here.

Here is the most important part of the Journey Journal—bringing the place to life through description.

The gate house was, of course, deserted. Snow coated the tennis courts and the small brown hut that serves as a tennis clubhouse in-season looked inappropriate and useless in the cold, almost like lawn furniture.

But the streets, the tall Victorian houses, the bare trees and pines, all thickly frosted with white—these looked not forlorn and out of place but seasonal, Christmas-y without ornaments.

Some unwinterized homes, so easily identified in the summer ("You're at the Penn Arms? That's the dark brown frame, right? or "I'm staying at the Spencer, the big yellow building near the Amphitheater") are now zipped into huge snowsuits, canvas-covered roof to ground, and are completely unrecognizable.

I use dialogue to make this scene more interesting.

Rolling into the single remaining parking place in front of Bellinger Hall, I marveled at the liveliness of the place. It bustled with red-cheeked, frosty-nosed folks, tricked-out in ski gear, stamping around the parking lot. One fellow walked over and said, "Hi, Susan. You don't remember me." (I guess my face was blank.) "I'm Gordon Jones. I took your class a couple of summers ago."

"Gordon. Hi. Who are all these people?" I asked. Nobody looked familiar.

"This is the Skytop Ski Club," he said. "We're here for the weekend."

"I'm here for the Motet reunion," I told him. "Do you know where those folks are?"

He held open the door to Bellinger for me and I pulled my roll-aboard luggage over the snow and up the stairs inside. In the main dining room, groups of men and women sat at long trestle tables, eating from tupperware bowls and platters, and drinking from pitchers of juice and milk. The cheer level was high.

Gordon directed me through the hilarity to a door. "I think they're in there. They've been rehearsing all morning."

But I could find no one. Oh, my. Lunch break. Then Elizabeth Curtis, a soprano from Buffalo, appeared. "Susan!" she cried. "You got here!" We hugged and Debbie Caldwell came around the corner, wiping food from her mouth. "Susan! Hi! Have you eaten?"

Five or six Motet members leaned against the counter of a small kitchen, dipping into a container of cookies, passing bags of chips and pretzels. "Everyone's gone to Jim's Diner, but there's lots of food here," said Elizabeth.

I recognized Steve Crosby, David Caldwell, and a fellow named John. The other two, a gray-haired couple, were strangers to me. This reunion brings together people who haven't sung or even attended Chautauqua for years. They come for the camaraderie. Debbie introduced me to Edna and Joe, a pair from somewhere in Pennsylvania. "Welcome! We heard you might not make it," Edna said.

What a pleasure to be greeted in such a friendly welcoming way. It was worth the seven hour drive.

Bellinger Hall, home during the summer season to students, looks like a college dormitory with long narrow halls and featureless white-walled rooms. Mine holds a twin bed, a wooden closet, a small dresser and a single chair. A door opens to the bathroom, which I'm sharing with Steve and his wife, provided they remember to unlock my side when they're finished and I do the same.

With no rehearsing to do, I walked to the car, found the big winter boots, earmuffs and gloves and suited up for a trek around Chautauqua's perimeter. The snow was falling hard now and covered a layer of ice, so this would be a challenge. I ended up looking down instead of up and around at winter in Chautauqua.

The North-End condominiums were the same hive of activity as Bellinger Hall. Cars filled the parking lots; lights were on on every porch. Stepping cautiously through the snowy ridges of the road down the hills to the Packard Mansion, I could see that the lake was frozen black.

Explaining the "Chautauqua Experience" always leaves one babbling.

Two people came tramping toward me, talking and laughing. They called out, "Hello! Isn't this gorgeous?!" The Chautauqua mood of shared bounty and simple gratitude is alive and well, even in the depths of winter. What is it about this place? What inspires this joy? Since it isn't summer, we can't claim that it is the stimulation of the lectures or the symphony orchestra or the ballet. It's as if some kind of spirit-lifting, time-release drug that works during the nine-week summer session, known as "The Season," also works during the winter.

I think it may be that people find their better selves here. It is so often said of Chautauqua, "But this isn't the real world."

I say, "Yes, it is. This is the real world." Out there, events conspire to mess us up and throw us off course. But here, things and people work as they should. And that makes us joyful.

I walked on, along the lake to Miller Park. The clock on the Bell Tower was outlined in tiny white lights. A low fog hung over the water, clouding the other shore. The Baker Hotel, for over a hundred years a crumbling mass of open pipes, *sloping floors, and water stained ceilings, lies in pieces on its little front lawn and along Miller Street. Workmen haul and hammer, though it's a wintry Saturday. The Hole appears to have been gutted. (I'm glad that this is being done on purpose rather than by the fire it has invited for years.)*

Bob says, "I don't want to see Chautauqua off-season. It would be too lonely." Hah. The bookstore, I see through its windows, is filled with customers, thumbing through books, fingering the merchandise, standing in line to pay for their newspapers. I feel a warm burst of air, fragrant with baking muffins and brewing coffee, at the corner door of Sadie J's eatery. Even the Amphitheater seems not to be deserted but merely resting, taking an off-season nap.

Susan, it would have been nice to get the names of your host and hostess—Richard and Anna Antemann.

At 5 p.m., we gathered at a home overlooking the lake in the Chautauqua Shores neighborhood, which is just outside the gates of the Institution. Inside the large contemporary A-frame, people were discarding boots and hats and shrugging out of storm coats, laughing and hugging each other. "So good to see you!" was the most commonly heard greeting. The host and hostess (whose names escape me—they haven't sung in Motet since I've been a member) leave for Florida tomorrow, but managed a long counterful of casseroles, dips, vegetables, homemade bread, sodas, and wine.

I didn't know any of the faces, although I was hugged and greeted as if I were kin. Who are these people? I wondered. Then Jeremy, the surgeon from Ohio, appeared with his wife. Steve, Sara Bradford from Buffalo, Debbie and David, Shirley Slater (all the way from Ft. Wayne, Indiana), Carl and Jean Badger, Carolyn the Presbyterian minister—well, it was suddenly a roomful of friends, old and new.

We ate, laughed, caught up on each other's news until 6:30. Then we pulled on the outer layers and drove over to Jim's Diner, the little restaurant adjacent to the Main Gate. Jim opened his diner just for Motet—something he does every year for the reunion. It's an old silver-sided dining-car with a counter and round stools covered in cracked red plastic inside the door. We sat in the ply-paneled back room at long tables arranged in a U-shape and were served plates of beef, mashed potatoes, gravy and green beans—good diner fodder.

Badger (he prefers to drop the "Carl") led us in a full-throated, four-part Doxology before we sat to eat. Jim and his whole crew of cooks and wait-persons came out of the kitchen and stood, smiling broadly while we sang.

"Beautiful!" Jim said when we'd finished.

Badger leaned over and said in a low voice, "Jim told me he does this dinner just to hear our Doxology each year."

After dinner, we reconvened in the large rehearsal hall on Bellinger's ground floor and sang until after 10 p.m. I found myself falling forward at around 9:30 and rather than pitch out of the chair, I left early. We rehearse again before the "concert" at Hurlbut Church today at 10 a.m. This is the weekend's finale.

Well, not quite. After the church service, Francesca Rappole's family traditionally hosts a luncheon for us all, at which we repeat the church program. I'll check out of the room and leave from the lunch by 2 p.m.

Monday—Baltimore

This is just a "what happens next" kind of entry.

Sunday began with another trudge around Chautauqua's perimeter. The snow had stopped and the sun was out. On this blue and white postcard of a day, I wasn't the least bit startled to meet up with a horse-drawn sleighful of people at Bestor Plaza. I mean, *of course* a Currier and Ives team of four large draft horses is plodding along Roberts Avenue, packed with folks, both large and small. Caught up in the spirit of the thing, each of them waved at me.

We rehearsed at Hurlbut Church for an hour and a half. Two small boys raced around the sanctuary, rounding corners at high tilt. Ross MacKenzie, the Director of Chautauqua's Department of Religion, came stomping in the front doors, calling hello as he walked up the aisle during a brief break. "I received this on my e-mail this morning," he said. In his faint Scottish brogue, he read us a greeting from Jack Grigsby in Florida.

After Ross left, we returned to rehearsing the six songs Badger had chosen. By *mutual agreement, one long Latin thing was dropped as too challenging for only two rehearsals.*

Parishioners began to file into the pews around 10:45 a.m., a broad mix of ages from babies to elderly. Most were dressed for the weather in heavy slacks and puffy jackets; very few wore the standard Sunday-go-to-meeting clothes. I recognized several worshippers—Denny from the School's Office and her husband sat rocking their new baby in an infant seat on a back pew. Linda Krueger from the Maple Inn gave me a big hug just before the service began.

The minister spoke briefly, walking up and down the aisle in folksy fashion. "The Motet Choir will be our sermon today," he said.

We sounded fine. To be embedded within this crowd of trained singers sensitive to fortes and pianissimos, ears cocked to the blend of each other's voices, is a midwinter treat to be savored.

And we sounded fine again at lunch which was served fireside in one of those over-sized Victorian mansions on Lake Drive. The interior was drop-dead gorgeous with high ceilings, vast rooms, fireplaces, floor-to-ceiling bookshelves, grand piano, and Chautauqua tchochkes everywhere.

I left promptly at 2 PM. While still on the Chautauqua grounds, my car slid gently—into a curb. Bonk! I had no problem backing up and starting off again, but the Subaru pulled hard to the right all the way home. So…it's into the garage for the little fellow this morning. I'm sure his wheels were freakishly knocked out of alignment.

[CHAPTER 8]

TROUBLESHOOTING

By now, I hope I've persuaded you that you, too, can and should do Journey Journals. But I know that even the most motivated of Journey-Journalers run into trouble. Here are some of the pitfalls most frequently encountered, and how to avoid and deal with them.

1. "Okay, I started out my Journey Journal with a bang. Then I missed a day, then another. And now I'm so far behind I can't remember enough to write about my trip."

What a testament to the need for journey-journaling. If you can't remember what happened in two day's time, how will you remember anything about your trip in a month or a year? You won't. So don't be discouraged because you missed a day. It's like sticking to a nutrition plan rather than going on a starvation diet. It's okay to indulge yourself a little bit every now and again.

But get back to the task as soon as you can. If you end up with a day or two missing from your Journey Journal, you'll still have plenty of memories from the other days. It's worth the effort. Believe me.

2. "My Journal sounds so long-winded. I write too much, and it's not very interesting to read."

Try cutting out all adverbs, the words that end in "-ly." Get rid of the "very"s and the meaningless word groups, such as "by and large," "each and every," "time and again," and the like. If a sentence doesn't add information, cut it. If you're sincere about self-editing, I recommend reading William Zinsser's *On Writing Well* and Strunk & White's *The Elements of Style*. Both are classics—deservedly—and both are brief.

That being said, I want to assure you that it is far better to write too much than not at all. You can cut out the windy parts when you type up your Journey Journal.

3. "I have the best of intentions—I take along notebooks and pens—but I just never seem to get started."

Indulge yourself with a clean new Journey Journal in which to write and with the pens that you like best. Get the Journal cracked, primed for the days ahead. Start your journal at home with a packing list for the trip, with important phone numbers or addresses, with the serial numbers from your travelers checks. Write yourself a note the morning of your departure, or write a description of people in the airport or on the train. Make notes about the meals you're served in transit or the children running up and down the aisle. Warm yourself up by forcing words out of your head and onto the page. Think of these as stretching exercises.

Find someone who can be a journaling buddy—your spouse or a fellow passenger who will listen to your daily entries. It can be fun to hear another person's thoughts about the previous day's experiences. And it's a powerful motivator if someone else is waiting to hear yours.

4. *"Is it worthwhile to read your Journey Journal aloud while on the trip?"*

Not only is it worth reading aloud, consider your Journey Journal as written *to be read aloud*. Bob loves to hear what I've written about our days on the road, so I read my daily entries to him at breakfast or while we're sitting in the airport or any other available time. He doesn't like to read his own entries out loud, so I read his, too.

It is motivational to know that someone wants to hear what you have recorded. You are far less likely to skip a day's entry and run the risk of disappointing your journal buddy. But it's also a way to see if the sentences say what you want them to say, if you left out—or left in—too much. Reading aloud is a form of self-editing that will make your Journey Journal far more interesting in the long run.

5. *"Is it dangerous to be seen taking notes in some foreign countries?"*

Well, if you are on a high-level Middle Eastern tour of top-secret defense sites, you probably are already smart enough to know that relying on memory is more prudent that writing out what you see. Most leisure travelers, however, won't be touring places so dangerous that they can't record the experience. But if you sense any danger, wait until you're back on the bus to write your notes.

6. *"Do you take any special precautions with your Journey Journal?"*

I have occasionally wrapped my on-the-road notebook in a zip-lock plastic bag along with my pen to protect it from rain. And I never pack my journal in luggage that we plan to check. Never. The journal rides in coach with me.

7. *"I have arthritis in my hands and can't write comfortably or legibly. How do I do a Journey Journal?"*
For those who find writing impossible because of injury or arthritis (and only for those), I suggest using a tape recorder. It's awkward because you must get over the embarrassment of talking aloud to yourself on tour and back in your room. But at least you have a record of your trip's on-site insights and impressions.

Upon returning home, hire a secretarial service to transcribe your tapes into hard copy. Don't avoid this step. An audiotape is not a Journey Journal, just a collection of its ingredients. Not transcribing your spoken words is like pointing to the kitchen cupboard and saying, "Yes, I've made dinner. It's in there."

[CHAPTER 9]

Final Reflections

Not enough time is given these days to the value of thinking. Imagine the distress that can be avoided with forethought—and the value that can be added to experience with sufficient reflection. This is especially true when it comes to travel.

Instead of simply collecting countries or destinations—"Yes, I've been [to fill in the blank]. Great place"—I want to extract their effects on me. "How much larger is my mind now that I've seen Gololand or Fuji or Detroit?" I ask myself. "How do I see the destination differently now that we've been there?" Compare it. Contrast it. "Work that brain," I say to myself with exasperation. "It needs the exercise."

Again, the early hours of the morning are best for me. But you may prefer late night. Or mid-afternoon. What is required is a block of time without undue distraction. In our neighborhood, there are many walkers wearing earphones and expressions of concentration. Would you interrupt their listening? Would you divert them from the music or the lecture or the book on-tape that they are concentrating on? Of course not.

So here, in connection with the Journey Journal, is a means of escape—one which allows for concentration and reflection and discourages conversation any time of day. *My suggestion:* Walk with earphones, tape player in hand, but without playing a tape. You may have to stop occasionally and write down your best random thoughts. Observers will think that you are taking notes on the informative lecture to which you are listening. All the more reason for them not to interrupt the flow of your valuable thought.

Start your reflections by mentally reviewing each day of the trip, as far as you are able without your Journey Journal in hand. Here is a test on what stuck, on what your most vivid recollections are. What happened? And what happened next? And after that? And what do you think about it?

Sometimes you just don't know what you think. It might take weeks, even a month, until you have a viewpoint truly sharpened by your travel experience.

To be sure that you take this invaluable step in your Journey Journal, mark your calendar and re-read the events of your trip at this future date. Then add your reflections when they've had a chance to bubble to the surface of your mind.

To me, reflecting on your trip marks the difference between the accidental and the intentional tourist. In Anne Tyler's book of the same name, the accidental tourist was not an enthusiastic one. He found himself in foreign countries and strove to blunt their foreign-ness by locating those places which made him feel that he was still at home.

Intentional tourists seek out and notice the odd, the new, the peculiar. They revel in it. They compare and contrast it with life at home. They expand their scope. And to be certain that their thoughts and their memories are clear, they write them down. In fact, they are not tourists at all. They are travelers.

Whatever your recollections and reflections are, write them in your Journey Journal. Link them to real life. Have your opinions changed? Have you learned new things? Do you want to learn more? What should non-travelers know about the place you visited? Do you want to go back, and why?

Fresh from the travel experience, undimmed by time, your perceptions are of value. Capture them—for your own fun, your family and friends, and even posterity.

In the end, side your Journey Journals are your trips' finest souvenirs.

[ABOUT THE AUTHOR]

An avid traveler, SUSAN LAUBACH has Journey-Journaled in over 50 countries, and has lectured professionally on travel writing techniques for many audiences, including passengers on Radisson Seven Seas Cruises, and students at the world-famous Chautauqua Institute in upstate New York. From Provence, to Uglich, to Lombok and beyond, Laubach has expertly honed her travelogue formula.

Laubach is also author of *The Whole Kitt & Caboodle: A Painless Journey to Investment Enlightenment*, called the best basic book on investing available by the National Association of Investment Clubs. Before writing the book, she worked from 1978 to 1992 in one of the country's premier brokerage houses, Alex. Brown & Sons, where she rose to become one of the firm's consistently outstanding revenue earners.

Prior to her career in investing, Laubach worked in theater. During this time, she wrote nine plays for young people that have been produced professionally. She is also the author of four children's books, and holds a master's degree and Ph.D. from the University of Virginia.

The mother of five grown children, Susan Laubach resides in Baltimore, Maryland, with her husband—and frequent travel companion—Bob.